SCIENCE AND RELIGION

From Conflict to Conversation

John F. Haught

PAULIST PRESS
New York • Mahwah, N.J.

also by John F. Haught
published by Paulist Press

THE PROMISE OF NATURE
WHAT IS GOD?
WHAT IS RELIGION?

Library of Congress Cataloging-in-Publication Data

Haught, John F.
    Science and religion : from conflict to conversation / John F. Haught.
        p. cm.
    Includes bibliographical references and index.
    ISBN 0-8091-3606-6 (alk. paper); 0478-4 (cloth)
    1. Religion and science. 2. Religion and science—History.
    I. Title.
BL240.2.H385   1995
291.1′75—dc20

95-32124
CIP

Published by Paulist Press
997 Macarthur Boulevard
Mahwah, New Jersey 07430

Printed and bound in the
United States of America

Contents

Preface

For almost twenty-five years I have been teaching a course on science and religion to undergraduates at Georgetown University. During just this one quarter of a century the cosmic landscape has dramatically shifted, and so has my whole approach to the subject. These years have witnessed, for example, fascinating debates and finally a virtual consensus about the big bang origins of the universe. During this period science has gained a fuller grasp of the chemical basis of life and the physiological aspects of mind. Sociobiology has made its debut during this period, inviting us to acknowledge more explicitly the genetic constraints on human culture, ethics and even religion. And the debates about God and evolution have heated up.

In addition, since the decade of the seventies we have become more aware of the intimate connection between our own existence and the physics of the early universe. Recently we have observed the emergence of chaos theory and the new scientific interest in patterned complexity. And by now we have gained a more palpable impression than ever before that the entire universe is a still unfolding and unfinished story. Finally, during these twenty-five years we have been alerted more compellingly than ever before to the global ecological crisis.

Do these developments have any significant religious or theological implications? I have written this book in order to set forth some responses to this question. I have tried to draft it in a way that would be accessible to scientists, theologians, students and any others who may be interested. And I have employed a style of presentation that I hope will challenge readers to think more clearly about an issue surrounding which there is still an enormous amount of public confusion.

1

A sufficiently serious and extensive public exchange on this book's topic has not yet taken place. There are, of course, important scholarly books, journals, and programs dealing with science and religion, and these are extremely valuable to the relatively few who can become involved with them. But by and large the complexity of current discussions by experts forbids serious engagement by most non-specialists. This is unfortunate, since what Alfred North Whitehead stated in 1925 is still germane to our own situation:

> When we consider what religion is for mankind, and what science is, it is no exaggeration to say that the future course of history depends upon the decision of this generation as to the relations between them. We have here the two strongest general forces...which influence men, and they seem to be set one against the other—the force of our religious institutions, and the force of our impulse to accurate observation and logical deduction.[1]

I have written this book, then, as an introduction for non-experts to the central issues in science and religion today. My hope is that the general reader, the scientist, the student, and the theologian can all easily follow along. I am convinced that until we attain at least some initial clarity on the available ways to approach the topic, genuine and widespread dialogue cannot begin. So although the ultimate objective of this work is conversation, I think we can begin to arrive at it only by first examining what the various parties are bringing to the table. This is what I have set out to do in the following pages.

I would like to thank Arthur Peacocke and Charles O'Connor for reading the manuscript and for their many helpful suggestions. In addition I thank the many students I have had over the past twenty-five years, for it is only through their generous cooperation and encouragement that I have been able to develop the approach presented here.

Introduction

Has science made religion intellectually implausible? Does it rule out the existence of a personal God? Doesn't evolution, for instance, make the whole idea of divine providence incredible? And hasn't recent biology shown that life and mind are reducible to chemistry, thus rendering illusory the notions of soul and spirit? Need we any longer hold that the world is created by God? Or that we are really intended by Something or Someone to be here? Isn't it possible that all the complex patterning in nature is simply a product of blind chance? In an age of science can we honestly believe that there is any direction or purpose to the universe? Moreover, isn't religion responsible for the ecological crisis?

These questions make up the so-called "problem" of science and religion. Today they may seem no closer to resolution than ever; yet they remain very much alive and continue to evoke an interesting range of responses. My intention in this book is to set forth the most important of these, and in doing so to provide a kind of "guide" to one of the most fascinating, important, and challenging controversies of our time.

I see four principal ways in which those who have thought about the problem express their understanding of the relationship of religion to science. (1) Some hold that religion is utterly opposed to science or that science invalidates religion. I shall call this the *conflict* position. (2) Others insist that religion and science are so clearly different from each other that conflict between them is logically impossible. Religion and science are both valid, but we should rigorously separate one from the other. This is the *contrast* approach. (3) A third type argues that although religion and science are distinct, science always has implications for religion and vice versa. Science and religion inevitably interact, and so religion and theology must not ignore new developments in science. For the sake of simplicity I shall call this the *contact* approach. (4) Finally, a fourth way of looking at the relationship—akin to but logically distinct from the third—emphasizes the subtle but significant ways in which religion positively supports the scientific adventure of discovery. It looks for those ways in which religion, without in any way interfering with science, paves the way for some of its ideas, and even gives a special kind of blessing, or what I shall call *confirmation*, to the scientific quest for truth.

In the nine chapters that follow, I will describe how each of these (conflict, contrast, contact, and confirmation) deals with the more specific questions in science and religion listed in the opening paragraph. But while laying out each approach as directly as I can, I shall not disguise my own preference for the third and fourth. I think that the "contact" approach, supplemented by that of "confirmation," provides the most fruitful and reasonable response to the unfortunate tension that has held so many scientists away from an appreciation of religion, and an even larger number of religious people from enjoying the discoveries of science.

The sense of "conflict," as we shall see in detail, is generally the unfortunate first response to an earlier and uncritical "conflation" of science and religion. The idea that science is locked in eternal combat with religion is, I think, an understandable reaction to the common practice of mixing and confusing their respective roles. On the other hand, the "contrast" approach, while perhaps a necessary first step away from both conflation and conflict, is also unsatisfying. Even though the line it draws in the sand appeals to many theologians and religious scientists, it leaves too many relevant questions untouched and too many opportunities for intellectual and theological growth untapped.

And so the following chapters will put special emphasis on the "contact" and "confirmation" approaches. In the end, any adequate treatment of science and religion requires that, without giving in to temptations to conflate them anew, we focus on those ways in which they concretely affect each other.

What Do We Mean by Religion?

When I speak of "religion" in this book, I am thinking primarily of *theistic* belief in the "personal" God associated with the so-called "prophetic" faiths: Judaism, Christianity, and Islam. Also, under the category of "religion" I mean to include the kind of reflection on religious faith commonly known as "theology."

I shall be asking specifically whether science really does rule out, or perhaps render less credible than before, the existence of the transcendent, loving, creative, personal, and redemptive deity spoken of in the "God-religions" and their theologies. Although my own orientation is that of a Roman Catholic Christian, I shall be presenting our topic from the much wider perspective of what the God-religions have in common, and I shall not dwell on the specific theological emphases of each tradition. Another kind of treatment of science and religion could profitably address specific differences, but here my concern is more sweeping. For although there are obvious differences among the Abrahamic faiths, today they all have to face the same question together: is modern science compatible with what they call "God"? Put otherwise, can the concerned, creative, salvific deity depicted in their scriptures and theologies survive the challenges of modern science?

In conversations involving scientists and theologians we could conceivably work with a much broader understanding of religion. Yet the more general our definition, the less pointed these discussions would be. For example, we might define religion as a "way of orienting ourselves in life,"[1] or as "ultimate concern."[2] But since even scientific skeptics are probably "religious" in these vague senses, new developments in sciences like biology or physics will offer no significant challenge to their "faith." Most scientists hold at least something to be of ultimate significance, even if it is only the pursuit of truth, honesty, or scientific method itself; such sweeping understandings of religion are scientifically incontestable. But for many scientifically educated people today biology, physics, and other sciences do raise questions about the idea and the existence of *God*. Hence it is especially appropriate for us to inquire here about the relationship of science to *theism*—that is, to the theological affirmation of God shared by Judaism, Christianity, and (wherever it pertains) Islam—than to the more non-specific religiosity which nearly everyone has in some measure.

Likewise we could conceivably define religion as a "sense of mystery." But this notion of religion also provokes little significant protest from many of the scientific elite. Even Albert Einstein, who was an "atheist" (that is, someone who denies the existence of the God of theism), confessed to being a "religious" man—in the sense that he revered the "mystery" of the universe. In his mind there could be no conflict of science with religion as long as we understand the latter as implying a feeling of incomprehensible mystery and not belief in God.

It would not be completely pointless, of course, to think of religion as "ultimate concern" or as a "sense of mystery." Many scientists are able to reconcile themselves to "religion" by understanding it in a non-theistic fashion. A few of them have turned to the East and elsewhere for a kind of mystical setting within which to connect their science to a larger vision of things, especially one that would not require their taking into account the troublesome idea of a personal God. Some of these quests have produced very interesting results, and in no way would I discourage them. I think, though, that it is more pertinent to the concerns of most readers of a book like this to ask directly about the compatibility of science with the God-religions. Perhaps, in another kind of work, we might move outward and eastward. But rather than turning to Taoism, Buddhism, Hinduism, and elsewhere for ways of contextualizing our scientific perspectives, we shall be asking here about science's relationship to the kind of religion that most of us were taught to believe in, or at least that has significantly shaped the history of Western thought. So "religion" in this book will mean theistic belief, unless otherwise noted.

The imposition of such a restriction in definition, however, may already be too much for some readers. Perhaps you are so "turned off" by what you take to be theistic religion that there is little hope for my arousing any interest in it on your part, let alone in trying to connect it with science. Perhaps, too, it was your own scientific learning that turned you away from this kind of religion in the first place. Maybe, like the many skeptics we shall meet in the pages ahead, you would have been willing to settle for a cosmos that is cared for by God, but your scientific education made it impossible for you in all honesty to embrace such a universe. Perhaps you see no place for talk about God at all, especially after the way theology has treated Galileo and Darwin.

Some readers may feel akin to a friend of mine who teaches at an Ivy League university and who exemplifies what I shall be calling "scientific skepticism." Several years ago I asked him to address my class on science and religion, and here is how he justified his own scientific journey away from the religion of his childhood:

> There is not a shred of evidence that the universe is purposeful or that it
> is influenced by any kind of deity who cares for me. As I look out into
> the stars and galaxies I see only the cold indifference of the cosmos

which accentuates the isolation and precariousness of my existence on this insignificant planet. For warmth and comfort I turn to my family, friends and society. These are sufficient for me. As for why we are here, there is no other explanation than sheer chance, and it is really a question that doesn't bother me much anymore. After becoming familiar with neo-Darwinian theories of evolution it is hard to imagine how any intelligent person can adhere to the idea of a purposeful universe. When I was in college I struggled to hold onto the religious faith I had received from my parents. However, the scientific and especially the evolutionary picture of the cosmos seemed more and more contradictory to my religious faith. I was converted to the scientific outlook as the most honest and exciting, even if not the most comforting approach to the world. It's not that I look down upon religious people, since I number some of them among my best friends. But I cannot intellectually reconcile my scientific outlook with any theistic vision of things.

If you have similar sentiments, I hope this book will help you understand better why such opinions arose in the first place. On the other hand, you may have found, as I have, that recent scientific developments have made the idea of God no less religiously intriguing and intellectually compelling than it was before the age of science.

In any case, the encounter of religion with science has generated a considerable amount of confusion. I intend this work then to be a kind of introductory guide for those who wish to see their way through to some degree of clarity on a very complex subject. The price of any attempt at clarity, of course, is that important items will inevitably have to be left out. But since I envision this work as no more than an introduction I assume that certain omissions will be tolerated.

Before we can begin exploring the ways in which theology might interact with ideas about evolution, the physics of the early universe, molecular biology, neuroscience, chaos theory, ecology, etc., we need to look more closely at our four main "approaches" to the general topic of science and religion. In the first chapter I shall examine these in some detail, and then apply them to specific issues in the subsequent pages.

1

Is Religion Opposed to Science?

When we hear the words "science" and "religion" we immediately think of the stormy history of their relationship. But the chronicle of religion's encounter with science is by no means one of warfare only. Throughout these pages we shall observe that there are at least four distinct ways in which science and religion can be related to each other:[1]

1) *Conflict*—the conviction that science and religion are fundamentally irreconcilable;

2) *Contrast*—the claim that there can be no genuine conflict since religion and science are each responding to radically different questions;

3) *Contact*—an approach that looks for dialogue, interaction, and possible "consonance" between science and religion, and especially for ways in which science shapes religious and theological understanding.

4) *Confirmation*—a somewhat quieter, but extremely important perspective that highlights the ways in which, at a very deep level, religion supports and nourishes the entire scientific enterprise.

A grasp of these four approaches should help us wend our way through the thicket of issues that make up the subject matter of this book. Let us now examine each of them more closely.

I. Conflict

Many scientific thinkers are quite certain that religion can never be reconciled with science. If you are a scientist, they say, it is hard to imagine how you could honestly also be religious, at least in the sense of believing in God. Their main reason for drawing this conclusion is that religion apparently cannot demonstrate the truth of its ideas in a straightforward way, whereas science can. Religion tries to sneak by without providing any concrete evidence of God's existence. Science, on the other hand, is willing to test all of its hypotheses and theories against "experience." Religion cannot do this in a way that is satisfying to an impartial witness, skeptics claim, so there must be a "conflict" between the scientific and the religious ways of understanding.

Both historical and philosophical considerations seem to substantiate such a grim verdict. Historically, we need only recall the obvious examples: the church's persecution of Galileo in the seventeenth century, and the widespread religious and theological aversion to Darwin's evolutionary theory in the nineteenth and twentieth. The slow pace by which religious thought comes to terms with such scientific ideas, and the fact that many theists still have a distaste for them, suggest that religion will never get along with science. Since so many believers in God have resisted the findings of astronomy, physics, and biology, is it any wonder that religion comes across as inherently hostile to science?

More important than these historical considerations, however, are the imposing philosophical (specifically epistemological) obstacles that religion and theology present to scientific skeptics. The main problem here is that religious ideas seem to be experientially untestable. That is, they apparently exempt themselves from the rigors of public examination, whereas science always submits its ideas to open experimentation. If empirical scrutiny shows a scientific hypothesis to be mistaken, then science willingly discards it and tries out alternatives, subjecting these also to the same rigorous process of inspection.

But can you do the same with religious teachings? Don't they dodge all attempts to demonstrate their truth observationally? Don't theists, for example, go on believing in God no matter what they observe in the world, including enormous suffering and evil? Doesn't Judaism, for example, say of its Lord: "Even though He slay me, yet shall I trust in Him"? And aren't all religious interpretations of the world, for that matter, fundamentally unaffected by the contradictions to them that we actually experience?

Putting this another way, it seems to skeptics that religious teachings are "unfalsifiable." Karl Popper, one of the most renowned philosophers of this century, argued that genuine science must strive to come up with evidence that will show its ideas to be mistaken. That is, science has to risk the "falsification" of its various claims.[2] For example, since relativity theory predicts that light waves will always bend in the presence of gravitational fields, scientists should look for possible instances in which this prediction might not be true. Then if they cannot find any evidence to the contrary, this means that relativity is a pretty strong theory for weathering all attempts at falsification. Falsifiability is the mark of a theory's scientific status. A willingness to allow its ideas to be falsified purifies science and shows it to be a truly open and honest way of learning about the nature of things.

But can religion display a comparable openness? Scientific skeptics (i.e. those who reject religion in the name of science) declare that religion lacks the robust probity of science. The God-hypothesis, for example, seems to be completely beyond falsification, so it cannot pass muster before the courts of science. Can you imagine any situations and experiences that might lead you to deny God's existence? If you cannot, then the idea of God must be unfalsifiable—and therefore is not to be taken seriously.[3]

Religion is based, skeptics often claim, on *a priori* assumptions, or "faith," whereas science takes nothing for granted. In addition, religion relies heavily on untamed imagination, whereas science sticks to observable facts. And religion is highly emotional, passionate and subjective, whereas science strives to remain disinterested, dispassionate and objective. These antitheses seem to add up to nothing less than an insuperable mutual hostility between science and religion.

In the remaining chapters of this book we shall have occasion to examine numerous expressions of scientific skepticism and its conviction that religion is opposed to science. But we should note here, at least in passing, that the skeptics are not the only ones to insist that religion clashes with science. Biblical literalists (people who think the words of the Bible are literally true) also often see a conflict between their faith and some well established scientific theories. Whenever scientific ideas do not correspond with the letter of the Bible (which is quite often), biblical literalists argue that science must be wrong and religion right. This is especially the case with regard to evolution, but also with miracles, the creation of the universe, the origin of life, and other issues. Many Christians in the United States and elsewhere maintain that the Bible teaches the "true" science and that secular science should be rejected if it does not correspond with the letter of scripture.

In addition to biblical literalists, there are still other critics who think that science is the enemy of religion. They argue that it was the coming of science that caused most of the emptiness and meaninglessness in modern life and culture. When science separated the experience of "facts" from our human need for eternal "values," they argue, it emptied the cosmos of any real meaning. And since the main business of religion is to teach us the meaning of things, it cannot be reconciled with science. We would be better off if the scientific revolution had never occurred.

In a controversial new book, for example, the British journalist Bryan Appleyard passionately argues that science is "spiritually corrosive, burning away ancient authorities and traditions," thus leaving modern experience devoid of the traditional sense of meaning. Science, therefore, is inherently incapable of coexisting with religion. It is not a neutral way of knowing at all, but a subversive and even demonic force that has evacuated our culture of its spiritual substance. It is impossible, Appleyard goes on to say, for anyone to be both religious and scientific in any honest, straightforward way.[4]

Appleyard's contention that science is "absolutely not compatible with religion" is confirmed from the other side by scientific skeptics, although for them science brings about the liberation rather than the emptying of culture. While they are certainly aware that today many religious believers see no conflict between religion and science, and that many theists are admittedly good scientists, skeptics still claim that both the logic and the spirit of science are fundamentally incompatible with any form of theistic religion. As the Cornell historian of science William Provine puts it, we have to "check our brains at the church house door" if we are to be both scientist and believer.[5] More specific reasons for this judgment will be offered in each succeeding chapter.

II. Contrast

Many scientists and theologians, on the other hand, find no such opposition between religion and science. Each is valid, they argue, though only in its own clearly defined sphere of inquiry. We should not judge religion by the standards of science, nor vice versa, because the questions each asks are so completely disparate, and the content of their answers so distinct, that it makes no sense to compare them with each other. If religion and science were both trying to do the same job, then they might be incompatible. But they have radically dissimilar tasks, and if we just keep them in their separate jurisdictions, preventing them from invading each other's territory, there can never be any real "problem" of science and religion.

According to this "contrast" approach, the impression that religion conflicts with science is almost always rooted in a previous confusion, or "conflation," of science with either a religious or a secular belief system. ("Conflation," a term that appears often in the pages ahead, simply means the collapsing of distinct items in such a way that their differences are apparently lost.) To avoid conflict, then, the contrast approach insists that we must first avoid conflating science and belief into an undifferentiated smudge. It was, after all, the inability of medieval theology to distinguish religion clearly from science that made Galileo's ideas seem so hostile to believers in the seventeenth century. The church's failure to acknowledge the separate domains of science and religion led its officials to condemn Galileo's novel ideas as though they were an invasion of their own territory. This, of course, was a most unfortunate misunderstanding, leading as it did to much of the hostility that many scientists still feel toward religion.

However, we should now know better: religion and science have no business meddling in each other's affairs in the first place. To avoid possible combat, our second approach claims, we should carefully *contrast* science with religion. Science and religion are such completely independent ways of understanding reality that it is meaningless to place them in opposition to each other.[6]

Conflation, in this view, is an unsatisfactory attempt to avoid conflict by carelessly commingling science with belief. Instead of respecting the sharp differences between science and religion, conflation weaves them into a single fabric where they fade into each other, almost to the point of becoming indistinguishable. Today, for instance, many conservative Christians argue that since the Bible is divinely inspired and inerrant, it gives us the most reliable *scientific* information about the beginnings of the universe and life. Some of them call their fusion of science and belief "creation science," and they renounce the Darwinian theory of evolution in favor of a literalist interpretation of the biblical accounts of the world's creation. They insist that since the biblical stories are "scientific" they should be taught in public schools as the best alternative to evolutionary biology.

Another common brand of conflation is "concordism." Rather than rejecting science outright, concordism forces the biblical text to correspond, at least in a loose way, with the contours of modern cosmology. In order to salvage the literal truth of the biblical book of Genesis, for example, some religious scientists match the six days of creation with what they consider to be six corresponding epochs in the scientific account of cosmic evolution. Religion, in this interpretation, must be made to look scientific at all costs if it is to be intellectually respectable today. In his book *Genesis and the Big Bang* the physicist Gerald Schroeder, for example, argues that relativity theory, with its challenge to the common sense notion of absolute simultaneity, once again allows us to take literally the six-day sequence of creation as depicted in the Bible. He attempts to show that what appears as a single day from one frame of reference may, from another, be billions of years. So the Bible agrees with science after all, and physicists can now embrace religion![7]

The conflation of science and religion is born out of a very human craving for unity in our understanding of the world. Because it seems to harmonize science and religion so neatly, it appeals to millions of people. At first sight its blending of religion with science would seem to be a credible way of avoiding conflict. However, history shows that eventually the incommensurate strands of science and religion will begin to unravel, and a sense of conflict may then take the place of superficial agreement. New developments in science, such as in evolutionary biology, geology or astronomy, put an end to easy alliances of a literalist biblicism with scientific interpretations of nature. Avoiding conflict by ignoring the vast differences between scientific and religious ways of understanding leads inevitably to fruitless confrontations. Unfortunately, these are what the mass media focus on, giving many people the impression that science and religion are perpetual enemies.

In the pages ahead we shall be speaking a great deal about "conflation." But because its fusion of science and religion obscures any real relationship between them, conflation cannot qualify as a valid fifth entry into our typology. Our quest, after all, is for an appropriate way of understanding the relationship of science and religion. But in order to relate any two items we must first be allowed to distinguish them, and this is precisely what conflation forbids us to do. Nevertheless, conflation is the point of departure for so much of the controversy surrounding this book's topics that it will constantly be lurking in the background of our reflections. We might even describe the objective of this book as that of clearing a passage out of the tangled muddle of conflation and toward the free and clear space of genuine "conversation," a journey that will require our passing through a consideration of the four types I am designating as conflict, contrast, contact, and confirmation.

The "contrast" approach, therefore, is a significant episode in this clearing of the way, since it proposes an enticingly simple way of heading off the conflict that arises out of conflation. In order to avoid the mutual hostility to which conflation inevitably leads, advocates of this second approach often ingeniously argue that we must uncompromisingly seal science and religion into separate containers. To deflect the impression of contradiction between them we must never allow them to leak out into a common stream of meaning. By thus insulating them we can suppress any prospect of mutual opposition.

In any case, two things can be opposed to each other only if they are playing the same game. For example, it makes no sense to compare a move in chess, either favorably or unfavorably, with a play in baseball. A completely disparate set of rules governs each game, and so it is senseless to say that one is better than the other. Likewise, since science and religion do not belong on the same playing field together, there is no point in comparing one with the other. We should not place them in competition or conflict with each other. So goes the contrast proposal.

To be more specific, advocates of this approach typically emphasize that the "game" science plays is one of examining the natural world empirically, while religion's is that of expressing the ultimate meaning that transcends (lies beyond) the empirically known world. Science is concerned with *how* things happen in nature, religion with *why* there is anything at all rather than nothing. Science is about *causes*, religion about *meaning*. Science deals with solvable *problems*, religion with unsolvable *mystery*. Science answers specific questions about the *workings* of nature, whereas religion expresses concern about the ultimate *ground* of nature. Science is concerned with particular truths; religion is interested in explaining why we should seek truth at all.

Where many theologians allow for clear logical distinctions between the tasks of science and religion, the contrast approach sees such differences as a reason for sharply *segregating* the two. Only by drawing an unbroken line between them can we avoid the conflation that leads to conflict. Contrast envisages science and religion as independent, autonomous ways of knowing. Only by putting them in separate camps, it insists, can we prevent eventual warfare between them. And so it holds that the whole ugly affair between Galileo and the church could have been avoided if theology had not intruded into an area that today we would cede to science alone.

So perhaps the *safest* approach to take to this book's subject is that of contrast. Many theologians and scientists are understandably attracted to it because it seems to keep everything so clean, allowing us to embrace both the discoveries of science and the beliefs of religion without any fear of possible antagonism.[8] Perhaps it is even almost essential for us to pass through the discipline of contrast as we make our way out of the confusions of conflation and move toward a more nuanced discussion of science and religion.

Another reason for its appeal, however, is that the contrast approach also allows us to distinguish science from the assumptions that underlie scientific skepticism. For it is not just creationists and benighted religious believers who practice the questionable art of conflation. Scientific skeptics typically also conflate science with a belief system of their own. Their belief system is not theism, of course, but rather "scientism."[9]

Scientism may be defined as "the *belief* that science is the only reliable guide to truth." Scientism, it must be emphasized, is by no means the same thing as science. For while science is a modest, reliable, and fruitful method of learning some important things about the universe, *scientism* is the assumption that science is the *only* appropriate way to arrive at the totality of truth. Scientism is a philosophical *belief* (strictly speaking an "epistemological" one) that enshrines science as the only completely trustworthy method of putting the human mind in touch with "objective" reality.

According to our "contrasters" such a doctrinaire conviction is itself by no means the product of any detached, objective, or neutral process of scientific knowing. Rather, it is a kind of faith-commitment not entirely unlike the kind we find in religion. Devotees of scientism place their trust in scientific method itself, but no more than religious believers can they scientifically demonstrate the truth of this faith. They trust deeply in the power of science to clear up all confusion about the world, but they cannot scientifically justify this trust without logical circularity.

Skeptics often trust in science almost as though, like the gods of religion, it were our savior from the original sin of prescientific ignorance. As the contrasters are quick to point out, however, there is no possible way you could set up a scientific experiment to demonstrate that science is the only reliable guide to truth. For such an experiment would already presuppose belief in the effectiveness of science to lead us to the right conclusions. Thus scientism is in fact no less a conflation of science with belief than is "scientific creationism."

Hence, if theism is flawed because the God-hypothesis is unfalsifiable, then it seems only fair to ask whether scientism can itself meet the falsification test. To do so its advocates must be able to state under what conditions it could be falsified. They must actively look for ways to show that science is inadequate. Instead of doing so, however, they steadfastly *assume* it to be true, no matter what. At least in this respect their faith in science looks suspiciously like the religion they reject for being unfalsifiable.

Thus, the contrast approach helpfully reminds us that it may not be science but *scientism* that is the enemy of religion. The implicit conflation of science with scientism, they will argue, is what lies at the root of most modern opposition by scientists to religion. Without usually being aware of it, scientific skeptics have uncritically fused the scientific method with scientism, a belief system that assumes, without any scientific demonstration, that science is the *only* appropriate way of looking at things. And so it is little wonder that they quite ingenuously conclude that science opposes religion. The method of contrast, however, prohibits the conflation of scientific method with *any* belief system, be it religious or secular, since sooner or later such a facile sort of union leads to unnecessary conflict.

For this reason also the contrasters cannot join forces with Bryan Appleyard's defense of traditional religious culture against the evils of "science." For, as far as they are concerned, it is not really science, as Appleyard argues, but *scientism* that emptied modern culture of its religious depth. We must clearly and consistently distinguish science from scientism, and this is exactly what Appleyard fails to do. Implicitly he acquiesces in the conflation of science and scientism that skeptics call by the innocuous name "science," and this failure to be clear about the distinction is what causes his misdirected rage.

III. Contact

The method of contrast may be an important step toward clarity, but it still fails to satisfy those who seek a more unified picture of reality. As Ian Barbour would say, it is a helpful first approximation, but contrast leaves things at a frustrating impasse.[10] The urge to discover the coherence of all our ways of knowing is too powerful for us to suppress indefinitely, and so I suggest here that we consider a third approach, one that I shall simply call *contact*.

This way of relating religion to science is not willing to leave the world divided into the two realms defined by the contrast position. Yet it does not wish to revert to the superficial harmony of conflation either. It agrees that science and religion are logically and linguistically distinct, but it knows that in the real world they cannot be as easily compartmentalized as the contrast position supposes. After all, religion in the West has helped shape the history of science, and scientific cos-

mology has in turn influenced theology. It is impossible to separate
them completely, even though we can try to make clear logical distinctions in our definitions of them.

In addition, it seems unlikely that just any old cosmology will be
compatible with just any old theology, as the contrast position would
seem to allow. The kind of world described by evolutionary biology
and big bang physics, for example, cannot peacefully coexist with the
picture of God that Newton, Descartes, and perhaps even Thomas
Aquinas idealized. Whether they are aware of it or not, theologians
always bring at least implicit cosmological assumptions to their
talk about God, and it is only honest that they acknowledge this fact.
It often happens, however, that their cosmological assumptions are scientifically out of date. The contact approach, therefore, is concerned
that theology always remain positively "consonant" with cosmology.[11]
Theology cannot rely too heavily on science, but it must pay attention
to what is going on in the world of scientists. It must seek to express its
ideas in terms that take the best of science into account lest it become
intellectually irrelevant.

For this reason, the contact approach looks for an open-ended conversation between scientists and theologians. The term "contact"
implies coming together without necessarily fusing. It allows for interaction, dialogue, and mutual impact but forbids both conflation and
segregation. It insists on preserving differences, but it also cherishes relationship.

Contact proposes that scientific knowledge can broaden the horizon
of religious faith and that the perspective of religious faith can deepen
our understanding of the universe. It does not strive to prove God's
existence from science but is content simply to interpret scientific
discoveries within the framework of religious meaning. It does not seek
to shore up religious doctrines by appealing to scientific concepts that
may on the surface seem to point directly to a divine designer. The days
in which scientific ideas could be used to seal arguments for God's
existence are over. Still, it is convinced that, without in any way interfering with scientists' own proper methods, religious faith can flourish
alongside of science in such a way as to co-produce with it a joint
meaning that is more illuminating than either can provide on its own.

The kind of religion we are discussing in this book, for example,
characteristically strives to instill in its followers a special way of looking at things, and this perspective, as it turns out, is ideally suited to
frame recent developments in biology and physics. Rooted in the story

of Abraham, the prophetic faith traditions invite their followers to look for the *promise* that lies in all things. Judaism, Christianity, and Islam think of genuine "faith" as a confidence that new life and undreamed of possibilities are latent even in the most desperate of situations. The authentic religious attitude, then, is a steadfast conviction that the future is open and that an incalculable fulfillment awaits the entire cosmos.

At first sight such a hopeful orientation of consciousness would seem to be anything but compatible with the "realism" that science demands of us. And yet, as we shall note often in the following chapters, many religious thinkers have found what they consider to be a remarkable accord between a faith-perspective shaped by a sense of reality's promise, and the universe now coming to light as a consequence of new developments in science.

It is probably in "contact" of this sort that the most interesting conversations between scientists and theologians are occurring today. Admittedly, these conversations sometimes resemble high-wire acts, and the participants occasionally plunge back down into either conflation or contrast. Contact is much more difficult to stabilize than are the other approaches. To avoid burning up in the fire of conflation or being frozen in the ice of contrast it assumes at times a rather fluid and even turbulent character. Its efforts to find coherence are interesting and promising but seldom completely conclusive.

There are many ways in which such contact is occurring today, and in each chapter to follow we shall see specific examples. The "contacters" will insist that what science has to say about the world does indeed make a difference in our religious understanding. And they will propose ways in which a religious consciousness attuned to science may, without any altering of the empirical data, provide a coherent setting in which to situate the results of scientific exploration.

Finally, we should mention here that in recent philosophical discussions of the nature of science, the ways of science and theology do not appear nearly so divergent as either the conflict or the contrast position insinuates. Science no longer appears quite so pure and objective as we used to think, nor theology so impure and subjective. Both science and theology generate imaginative metaphors and theories to interpret certain kinds of "data," but in neither case is it always clear just where metaphor or theory leaves off and "fact" begins. Indeed the consensus of philosophers today is that there are no uninterpreted facts. And so we are now more aware than ever before that in both science and theology there is an aspect of human "construction" which we previously failed to notice. This does not mean that our ideas are therefore inevitably unobjective, but it does mean that we cannot enshrine as absolutely unrevisable any particular forms of expression that we employ in our quest for truth.

Recent examinations of the culturally and historically conditioned nature of scientific understanding, for example, make us question whether we can simply assume that science is the pure model of objectivity that scientific textbooks make it out to be. Scientific textbooks, as Thomas Kuhn has pointed out, tend to "mask" or cover up the squabbles and conflicts that underlie the evolution of scientific understanding. They give students the impression that scientific method is a straight-arrow way to the truth, whereas the actual history of science indicates that growth in knowledge is not nearly that direct.[12] It may be harder now to draw as sharp a line between science and other ways of thinking as we used to.

Nevertheless, though scientific "facts" are always in some sense our own constructs, and are inevitably theory-laden, they are not simply wild guesses that have no reference to a real world existing independently of our preferences. In some way, though chastened by our new understanding of the social nature of knowing, we may still trust that both scientific and religious ideas refer to a real world, one that transcends mere wishing. This appreciation of the mind's capacity to put us in touch—in an always provisional way—with the real world is known as "critical realism." Critical realism, as distinct from naive realism, maintains that our understanding, both scientific and religious, may be oriented toward a real world, whether the universe or God, but that precisely because the universe and God are always too colossal for the human mind to encompass, our thoughts in both science and religion are also always open to correction.[13]

Science and religion make meaningful contact with each other, therefore, only when they agree to play by the rules of what we are calling critical realism. Good science, in this covenant, hopes to approximate, more or less, the way things are in nature, but it is always willing to be critical of its ways of representing the world. And a theological method committed to the same principles of critical realism allows that our religious symbols and ideas are also always in need of constant correction, but that in a finite way they too may point toward a Transcendent Reality, one that is infinitely elusive but also always truly "there."

Scientific theories and religious metaphors, in this epistemological contract, are not just imaginative concoctions, as much modern and postmodern thought asserts. Rather, they bear an always tentative relationship to a *real* world and its ultimate ground. This world beyond our representations is always only incompletely grasped, and its presence constantly "judges" our hypotheses, inviting us continually to deepen our understanding both in science and religion. So it is their mutual sharing in this critical openness to the real that provides the basis for genuine "contact" between science and religion.

IV. Confirmation

While it would be quite fruitful to leave our discussions in science and religion at the stage of contact, I would personally prefer to go even further. I appreciate all the efforts to discover consonance between science and religion, but I envisage an even more intimate relationship of religion to science than any of the first three approaches has yet explicitly acknowledged. I shall propose here, and throughout this book, that religion is in a very deep way supportive of the entire scientific enterprise.[14]

Religion, of course, should not be solicited to reinforce the dangerous ways in which scientific knowledge has often been applied in practice. My proposal is simply that religion essentially fortifies the humble desire to know. That is, it confirms the very drive that gives rise to science in the first place.[15] I call this fourth approach "confirmation," a term equivalent to "strengthening" or "supporting," because it holds that religion, when carefully purged of idolatrous implications, fully endorses and even undergirds the scientific effort to make sense of the universe.

I am aware that science has come under heavy criticism today. Many critics even think that it is responsible for most of the ills of the modern world. Were it not for science, they say, we would have no nuclear threat, no global pollution of the air, soil and water. We and our planet would probably be better off without it. Science, they claim, is at root an assault upon nature, a crushing exercise in control. It is a Faustian effort to wrest all mystery from the cosmos so that we can be the masters of it.[16] Some even argue that science is inherently patriarchal, an exploitation of nature closely tied to our culture's oppression of women.[17]

Obviously theology would not wish to endorse science if it were inherently connected to these evils. But I suspect that much criticism of science mistakenly identifies it with trends and motives that can, at least in principle, be clearly distinguished from science itself. *Essentially* speaking, I consider science to be a modest but fruitful attempt to grasp empirically, and as much as possible with mathematical clarity, some small part of the totality of reality. Any pretensions to omniscience such as we find in scientism are not a part of science at all—a point that Appleyard cannot accept, but one that the contrast position rightly clarifies in its protest against conflation.

Most criticisms of science fail to acknowledge that at root science flows out of a simple, humble desire to know. We must distinguish this fundamental longing for truth from other human desires—such as the will to pleasure, power, or security—that place science in servitude to impulses that have nothing to do with truth-seeking. When I say that religion supports science, therefore, I am not arguing that it favors all the twisted ways in which science is exploited and conflated. I am simply saying that the disinterested desire to know, out of which science grows and flourishes, finds its deepest confirmation in a religious interpretation of the universe.[18]

Such an approach does not look for or expect in return any scientific endorsement of religion. Rather it simply maintains that a religious vision of reality inherently fosters the scientific exploration of the cosmos. The contrast approach wisely points out how dangerous it is for religion to seek support for its teachings in any particular scientific theories, since currently accepted scientific ideas may easily be discarded by the next generation of explorers. But science has nothing to lose and everything to gain by rooting itself in religion's fundamental vision of reality as an intelligible whole grounded in the ultimately trustworthy Being that followers of Moses, Jesus, and Muhammad call by the name "God."[19]

This, again, is not to argue that religion provides scientists with any information about the universe of the sort that science can gather all by itself. Religion has no special insights to dish out about particle physics or the genetic code. Its confirmation of science in no way involves any conflation or fusion with particular scientific hypotheses and theories. Rather, its support of science goes much deeper, though it is seldom appreciated by either scientists or theologians.

The *confirmation* approach may be stated as follows: religion's claim that the universe is a finite, coherent, rational, ordered totality, grounded in an ultimate love and promise, provides a general vision of things that consistently nurtures the scientific quest for knowledge and liberates science from association with imprisoning ideologies.

Science, to be more specific, cannot even get off the ground without rooting itself in a kind of *a priori* "faith" that the universe is a rationally ordered totality of things. Scientists always rely on a tacit faith (which they seldom reflect on in an explicitly conscious way) that there is a real world "out there," that this real world hangs together intelligibly, that the human mind has the capacity to comprehend at least some of the world's intelligibility, and that no matter how far we probe there will still be further intelligibility to uncover. Without this kind of trust there could be no incentive to look for the order present in nature or to keep looking deeper into the specifics of this order.

Even in the mind's spontaneous quest for insight, coherence, and truth there is a dynamism not far removed from what we may call "faith." As we see plainly in modern physics, but also in other fields, a fundamental objective of the scientific quest is to find whatever it is that unifies or holds together the universe that we are exploring. Science, no less than religion, is borne along by this quest for a unifying knowledge. But at the roots of a scientist's irrepressible desire to make coherent sense of things there lies a basic confidence, nothing less than a "faith," that reality will eventually yield to our desire to find in it the unity of some kind of order.

Thus faith, in the sense of a basic trust in the limitless rationality of the real, is not opposed to science but is its very wellspring. Science, like all human knowing, has what Michael Polanyi calls a "fiduciary" aspect (from the Latin *fideo*, to trust).[20] Without this element of trust there would be no incentive to pursue the truth through science in the first place.

What then is the precise connection of religion to this prerequisite trust? We must be careful not to let religion intrude into the actual work of science, but it is my conviction that religion does provide *confirmation* of the trusting that inevitably underlies science. Religion, I repeat, cannot add anything to the list of scientific discoveries. It is not in the business of disclosing things about nature that science can arrive at on its own. Rather, religion by its very nature is concerned that we put our trust in reality's over-all rationality. And in this sense religion is much more intimately connected to the epistemological *roots* of scientific inquiry than the other approaches have enunciated. Religion, taken as a confirmation of the faith assumptions out of which science springs, and not as an alternative source of scientific hypotheses, will not obstruct, but only promote, the work of science.

Religion comes about in human culture because of our awareness of the fact that trust can fail, and its central mission is continually to revive this trust. It does not initiate our trust, since a capacity to trust in reality seems native to us, but instead functions to revive our trust when it fails. Religion, Schubert Ogden correctly notes, is best understood as "re-assurance," a re-plenishing of the basic confidence we may have lost in the course of living. Religion exists because our reliance on reality is subject to constant erosion by the pain, tragedy, hostility, absurdity, and death with which the world confronts us.[21] There are any number of experiences that can lead us to doubt the intelligibility of the universe. The point of religion, though, is to encourage us to trust anyway. It seeks to restore our hope in the face of despair, to help us cling to the conviction that there is a final meaning and promise to things, a meaning and promise that can light up even those experiences that seem to make the universe absurd. The word "God" points us toward this mysterious meaning and promise, toward that which guarantees the world's ultimate coherence and trustworthiness.[22]

Religious symbols, stories, and teachings persuade us that there is an infinitely wider perspective than our own, and that our own minds are not encompassing enough to take in the whole horizon of being at any given moment, but that nonetheless things do make sense in terms of an ultimate frame of reference. Religion implies therefore that we need continually to press onward, beyond the narrowness of current understanding, and go in search of this transcending breadth and depth. Such an impetus, I am saying, can also quietly energize the enterprise of scientific discovery. Scientists can be theists, in other words, because their discipline thrives on the conviction that the world does finally make sense.

Religion, I have said, invites us to assume a posture of trust in the ultimate intelligibility of things. Abandoning ourselves to such trust, I would then argue, does not lead us into conflict with science but instead prepares our consciousness for the journey of scientific discovery. "Confirmation" goes further than the "contact" approach by attaching itself directly onto the faith that scientists have to possess as they embark on their forays into the world's endless intelligibility. The place to locate religion in relation to scientific discourse, therefore, is not as the answer to specific scientific questions (since this would be conflation), but as a response to the root question concerning why we should go forth on the adventure of truth-seeking in the first place. The business of religion is not to place itself alongside of science as a competing set of "answers" to scientific questions, but to confirm the scientist's trust in reality's coherence.[23]

Skepticism has rightly exposed the naiveté of associating religion with the solving of problems that are more suitably left to science. Whenever we submit religious teachings as the answers to specific scientific puzzles, skeptics quite rightly chastise us. For example, when the scientific creationist offers a biblical story of creation as a better scientific account of origins than evolutionary theory, the skeptic rightly reacts by pointing out that religion is trying here to subvert honest scientific inquiry. However, if we read the biblical accounts of creation not as an alternative and competing body of scientific information, but as an invitation to experience the ultimate trustworthiness of reality, then there need be no conflict.

In our attempts to clarify the relationship of religion to science we can avoid both unnecessary conflation and dualism if we keep to the view that religious expression is most appropriately concerned with grounding our trust, not with solving scientific questions. For when we situate religion in this way we see how it functions as the confirmation rather than the contradiction of science. Religion then is deeply related to science without being conflated with it. Religion's implications for science are much more radical, intimate, and nourishing than the other three approaches have allowed us to see.

Conclusion

The four approaches I have just outlined set the pattern for the following chapters. Under the headings of conflict, contrast, contact, and confirmation I will present the positions of each approach as it responds to the fascinating questions that science is raising for religion today. These positions will be presented as though representatives of each were present here, appealing to you in the first person plural. I invite you to go along with this somewhat "polemical" style of presentation in order that we might arrive at a vividness and clarity that would not emerge in a purely third person condensation.

I shall employ this deliberately provocative and repetitive format not in order to heighten tensions, but simply to provide a kind of prologue to meaningful conversation in science and religion. And although my own leanings will become visible in the contact and confirmation sections of each chapter, I shall allow each of the four "voices" to present as convincing an argument as possible. Obviously, no single chapter can provide more than a sampling on the topics under dispute, but as we proceed I hope that the fragments of each approach will come together into a fuller and more coherent picture.

Finally, as we shall see more clearly in Chapter 8, all of the issues to be investigated in the pages ahead converge on the large, obviously too large, question of whether in the light of modern science we can any longer plausibly maintain, as did most of our ancestors, that there is some "point" to the universe. It is out of an implicit preoccupation with cosmic purpose, and this larger concern's bearing on the always related question of the meaning of our own individual lives, that we are compelled to ask about such things as evolution and God, Einstein and God, chaos and God, the universe and God. The question of cosmic purpose will never be far from us as we move forward, and we shall return more explicitly to it when we draw near to the end of our expedition.

2

Does Science Rule Out a Personal God?

As I noted earlier, it is quite easy even in an age of science to be "religious" in a very general sense. Atheists and agnostics themselves can usually point to something of such importance in their lives that it calls forth from them an "ultimate concern" that they may be willing to call "religion." But what about belief in a "personal" God? Hasn't the advance of scientific knowledge now rendered this kind of religion quite obsolete? Under the four headings below I shall set forth what I take to be characteristic answers to this question by advocates of each of the four positions just outlined.

In order to highlight the distinct features of the separate voices we shall be listening to in this book, *imagine that you have in front of you representative spokespersons for each of the four ways of relating science to religion.* **Allow each of the four groups to present its case directly to you here without interruption, and in subsequent chapters permit them to extend their respective points of view into other issues. (I ask the reader to envisage large quotation marks around each presentation, both in this and subsequent chapters.)**

I. Conflict

Scientific skeptics[1] would likely reply to the question of whether science is compatible with belief in a personal God in words similar to these:

It is hard for us to imagine how anyone who takes science seriously can come to any other conclusion than that the idea of a personal God is now utterly unbelievable. Science offers no evidence whatsoever that any divine personality underlies the universe or has ever had any interest in it. Physicist Steven Weinberg, to name one prominent representative of scientific skepticism, expresses our position very clearly in his recent book, *Dreams of a Final Theory*. The deeper science looks into the nature of things, he says, the less the universe seems to bear any imprint of an "interested" God.[2]

Before the advent of science, we concede, it was easy enough to attribute natural occurrences either to many personal deities or, later on, to a single God. The good things of the earth seemed like gifts flowing forth from a divine beneficence, and even the bad things—storms and floods, earthquakes, droughts, and famines—appeared to be the workings of divinity. To religiously devout people, the whole cosmos was an expression of some immense Intelligence and Will lurking beneath, above, or behind phenomena.

However, the situation has now changed dramatically—largely because of science. Little by little science has "demystified" the world, probing into one phenomenon after another and finding only mindless matter beneath the surface. The deeper science has dug, the more impersonal the universe has appeared. Formerly the predictable laws of nature hinted at a divine intelligence, but since the time of Newton the notion of inertia and other impersonal ideas of physics have increasingly made the idea of God superfluous, and the cosmos more and more self-explanatory.

For a while some of our fellow scientists, nostalgic for mysticism, conjectured that the emergence of life from dead matter was such a miraculous occurrence that only a living God could have breathed it into the cosmos. But now science has shown that the secret of life lies in lifeless molecules and atoms. Vitalism, the view that a special, non-material force is necessary to bring life into the universe, is now defunct. From the point of view of chemistry and physics there is nothing extraordinary about life at all.

But, you might object, doesn't the wondrous fact of human consciousness make this a miraculously personal universe? How could a cosmic process completely unconnected to a transcending Intelligence bring about thinking and "personal" beings like ourselves? To this we reply that neuroscience has by now advanced to the point where it looks as though even the phenomena of human mentality and personal selfhood are eventually going to be fully explained also in purely material terms. In his book *Consciousness Explained*, for example, Daniel Dennett has recently written that we are now in a position to give a complete elucidation of consciousness in terms of the principles of basic science.[3] Given enough time—and we have had billions of years—dead matter and a completely impersonal set of natural processes are quite capable of producing beings with minds. The universe does not have to be grounded in a personal God for this to happen.

New developments in cosmology and physics convince us skeptics that scientists like Weinberg are correct to suspect that the universe is utterly devoid of any underlying personal principle of providential care. Weinberg surmises that physics may be on the brink of discovering some "final theory" that will explain the "fundamental" laws of the universe. And when it does, will we detect a divine Friend lurking beneath or behind the final laws of nature? Weinberg convinces us that we will not.[4]

Obviously, then, science clashes sharply with religion on this point. The "personality" of God, after all, is indispensable to Jewish, Christian, and Islamic faiths. Without belief in a God who has features analogous to, though infinitely more exalted than, those we associate with human personality, these faiths would collapse completely. That God is in some sense intelligent, rational, free, loving, faithful, etc. is essential to their kind of religion. But now, as Weinberg reminds us, physics, the science that leads us down to the most fundamental levels of reality, has found not the slightest hint of any such "interested" deity.

It is not as though Weinberg is alone in his conviction that the universe is fundamentally impersonal. A good number of his fellow scientists agree with him, and by no means least among his allies is the most celebrated scientist of our century, Albert Einstein. Einstein talked a lot about God, it is true, and he even spoke of himself as a "religious" man.[5] But he was religious only to the extent that he believed that there is something permanently mysterious about the universe, or in the sense that we should be committed to "superpersonal" ethical values that can give meaning to our lives. Like Weinberg he clearly denied the existence of a personal God.

Ironically, Einstein's most oft-quoted words are that "God does not play at dice with the universe," and perhaps this precept has misled many to think of Einstein as a theist of a sort. Yet it is clear from the wider context of his writings that by this declaration he intended only to proclaim his belief that the universe is lawful and intelligible. He did not actually embrace the transcendent God of theism. To him there is no personal deity who exists independently of the universe, as theistic religion claims. The notion of a personal God, he wrote, is not only unnecessary for science; it is a primitive superstition that even religion can now do without. Belief in a personal God, said Einstein, is the main cause of conflicts between science and religion.[6] Many of us agree with this judgment.

Weinberg, however, observes that Einstein's reference to himself as a religious man is still somewhat misleading. Having eliminated a personal God from his understanding of religion, Einstein could easily declare that "science without religion is lame and religion without science is blind." But, as Weinberg goes on to say, Einstein's atheistic definition is hardly compatible with what most people understand by the term "religion." For at least in our own cultural context religion usually entails belief in an "interested" God, One who makes promises, shows love and concern, and acts to save the world.

In discussions of science and religion, Weinberg persuasively argues, we must take "religion" as it is actually understood by religious people. Most of them, in the West at least, believe that the universe is grounded in a divine *Person*, a Being endowed with intelligence, will, affectivity, purposiveness, responsiveness, etc. So we are not doing justice to these people, Weinberg implies, if we take the term "religion" or "God" and wring it so dry of personalist features that believers themselves would not recognize it. We need to be more candid in discussions of science and religion, and avoid twisting language to make ourselves seem less opposed to religion than we really are.[7]

Consequently, if we adhere to Weinberg's sound advice, and conduct our conversation with theists on their own terms, we can only conclude that science cannot be reconciled with religion. Of course, it would be nice to believe that the world rests securely in the hands of an interested, personal God. But as we look through all the complex layers of nature with the penetrating devices of physics, we see nothing at the bottom of it all except the blank neutrality of an obviously impersonal cosmos. Listen to Weinberg's own words:

> About a century and a half ago Matthew Arnold found in the withdrawing ocean tide a metaphor for the retreat of religious faith, and heard in the water's sound "the note of sadness." It would be wonderful to find in the laws of nature a plan prepared by a concerned creator in which human beings played some special role. I find sadness in doubting that we will. There are some among my scientific colleagues who

say that the contemplation of nature gives them all the spiritual satisfaction that others have traditionally found in a belief in an interested God.
Some of them may even really feel that way. I do not. And it does not
seem to me to be helpful to identify the laws of nature as Einstein did
with some sort of remote and disinterested God. The more we refine our
understanding of God to make the concept plausible, the more it seems
pointless.[8]

Religious people take God to be a personal Being passionately concerned about the world. This is the kind of religion at issue in the present book, not some vague devotion to ethical values, or sensitivity to
the mystery that enshrouds the universe. An atheist can easily claim to
be "religious" in the sense of being committed to ethical values or
being awed by the mystery of the cosmos. Einstein, as we have seen,
considered himself "religious" in both of these ways. But, as Weinberg
emphasizes, the controversy about science and religion has real
piquancy only when we ask whether science is compatible with the
interested, personal God of theism. Can science accommodate the
divine Intelligence and Will that Jews, Christians or Muslims believe
in? We think that it cannot, and we shall have the opportunity to give
many more reasons for our verdict as this book progresses.

II. Contrast

*To this skeptical position the "contrast" theologians would typically
respond in words similar to these:*

In light of the distinctions laid out in the previous chapter, we "contrasters" have to ask Weinberg whether perhaps it is not *scientism*
rather than science that rules out the existence of a personal God. Is
pure physics itself adequately equipped, as Weinberg clearly supposes,
to give us any information at all that might help us settle the issue of the
existence of a personal God? It seems only fair to ask this question
because by definition the science of physics leaves out of its field of
inquiry anything that has to do with "personality." Indeed, the amazing
success of physics is due in great measure to the fact that it deliberately
abstracts from any discussion of things so complex as personality.
From the very start physics modestly subjects itself to severe methodological constraints. It realizes that it cannot deal with all the complexity in a universe that includes living and thinking beings. And so it set-
tles for a stark mathematical simplicity, confining itself to a

quantitative description of matter alone. Particle physics as such has no stake in making sense of human history, the struggle for freedom, the problem of evil, or the nuances of personality. These all lie beyond its chosen sphere of inquiry, and it would become completely paralyzed if it got tangled up in them.[9] Therefore, why should we expect physics to shed any light at all on something so remote from its field of inquiry as the question of the existence of a personal God?

Physics leaves out anything that has to do with personality (features like intelligence, will, feeling, love, care, freedom, creativity, etc.); so we should indeed be very surprised, and even disappointed, if a "final theory" in physics would uncover anything other than an "impersonal" universe. If physics is not inherently wired to receive any personalist signals, should we wonder that none show up on its display screen?

The existence of a "personal" God is not an issue that science, including physics, can ever resolve. Science and religion are so radically independent that we should not expect one to shed very much light on the other. Science works at a high level of mathematical abstraction, and so its equations are not a suitable medium through which to express any conceivable divine love and concern in which the universe may perhaps be embedded. Moreover, contrary to Weinberg's assumption that physics puts us in touch with the "fundamental" levels of reality, physics actually works with ideas and abstractions already considerably removed from the concrete complexity of the real world. We sharply contest the idea that physics, or any other branch of science for that matter, ever puts us in touch with *fundamental* reality.

Hence the impersonality of the universe to which Weinberg alludes is not a discovery of science so much as it is a *belief* rooted in his implicit scientism and naturalism. If one holds to the belief that science alone can give us the fullness of reality, then the inevitably impersonal results of science, and especially physics, will be enshrined as absolute, foundational, and final truth. But in our view the putative impersonality of the universe is not so much a conclusion of physics as it is the consequence of the scientistic *belief* that physics alone can put us in touch with fundamental reality, as Weinberg implicitly claims it can. It seems clear to us that it is not science but only a conflation of science with scientism that leads skeptics to the impression that there is a conflict between science and religion on the issue of the existence of a divine personality.

Such conflict is the consequence of a failure to sort out carefully just which questions are proper to science and which to belief systems like scientism or religion. Ever since the unfortunate Galileo affair, most alleged instances of conflict between science and religion have followed almost inevitably from conflations of science with belief systems. Either theologians have carelessly crossed over into the realm of science, or scientists, usually without being aware of it, have couched their ideas in the clothing of scientism.

The alliance of science with the belief system known as scientism will inevitably clash with theistic religion. And scientism, we should note here, is closely associated with a correlative set of beliefs known as "scientific materialism."[10] Scientific materialism is a belief system built on the assumption that all of reality, including life and mind, is reducible to and completely explainable in terms of lifeless matter.

But in what sense, you might be wondering, is scientific materialism just another belief system? Our answer to this question is that, like religion or myth, scientific materialism holds out an ideal for its followers to strive toward. It provides a goal that energizes all of their scientific efforts and even their very lives. The sacred dream of scientific materialists is that sooner or later all of reality, even human consciousness, will be completely understood in terms of basic sciences like chemistry and physics. Exhaustive materialist explanation is the holy grail that gives many scientists something momentous for which to struggle every day of their lives. It even gives them a reason for living. And to that extent it is just as much an idealistic belief system as what we are calling religion.

The materialist belief, however, has become so intimately intertwined with modern science that today many scientists hardly even notice the entanglement. And so they often present as "science" what is in fact a set of unproved metaphysical assumptions carelessly conflated with scientific method.

Scientific materialism, we must re-emphasize, is nothing less than a system of beliefs or assumptions alloyed uncritically with a valid and neutral method of knowing, namely, science. In philosophical jargon, scientism is the epistemological component, and materialism the metaphysical ingredient of an influential modern creed that functions for many scientists in very much the same way that religion functions for its devotees. Scientific materialism resembles religion, and can be called a belief system, because it systematically answers many of the same ultimate questions that religion responds to: Where do we come from? Where are we going? What is the deepest nature of reality? What is our true identity? Is there anything permanent and imperishable?,

etc. The answer to all of these questions, according to scientific materialism, centers around the concept of "matter." The clarity and simplicity—the hard-rock "realism"—of the idea of "matter" has enormous appeal to many scientists and philosophers. It satisfies a deeply
religious longing for a solid and comprehensible ground upon which
to base their knowing and being.

However, we have to be consistent. Our *contrast* approach emphasizes that we must sharply distinguish science or scientific method
from *all* belief systems, not just from theistic religion. And scientific
materialism is no less distinguishable from science than is religion. Yet,
making this distinction clear today is often quite difficult. In fact, in the
writings of scientists like Weinberg and philosophers like Dennett, scientific materialism is so intimately folded into their "scientific" presentations that it is only with great difficulty that they can be persuaded to
distinguish between them. Often it is impossible.[11]

Nonetheless, we are convinced that it is the naive merging of science
with a materialist or naturalist belief system that misleads many modern
intellectuals into thinking of science as irreconcilable with religion. For
it has yet to be shown that any *purely* scientific discovery contradicts the
idea of a personal God, though it is not hard to show that scientism and
scientific materialism do so. What we have here, then, is not a conflict
between *science* and belief in a personal God, but a conflict between
two irreconcilable belief systems.

The illusion that physics puts us in touch with fundamental reality
goes back to a way of thinking about nature initiated by Galileo and
subsequently endorsed by modern philosophers, especially John Locke.
They made a fateful, and now somewhat questionable, distinction between "primary" and "secondary" qualities. Primary qualities are those
aspects of phenomena that do not seem to depend for their existence on
the presence of a perceiving subject. They are the measurable or quan-
tifiable aspects of things, for example, the position, momentum and
mass of a physical body. It is with these allegedly "objective" qualities
that physics traditionally dealt.

Secondary qualities, on the other hand, are those sensible features of
things that require for their existence the presence of a perceiving subject. These are the qualities we associate with the five senses (taste,
touch, sound, smell, and sight), so they are apparently more "subjective" than primary qualities. A body would lack any taste, for instance,
if there were no tongue to interact with it, or it would have no color
without eyes to see it. So the qualities of taste and sight must be less

real than the primary qualities which remain the same whether a perceiving subject interacts with them or not. Secondary qualities seem to derive their fragile existence, at least to a considerable degree, from the presence of perceiving human subjects.

Once modern thought got used to this distinction it began to assume that the universe was "fundamentally" made up of impersonal primary qualities, and that it is only our human presence here that turns the cosmos into a colorful or "personal" one. The sphere that physics is concerned with is taken to be the flatly impersonal substrate that allegedly lies, permanently the same, beneath the color and beauty that our senses project upon it. The world of art, poetry, and especially religion, on the other hand, is assimilated to that of secondary qualities, and thus taken to be highly subjective and therefore "unreal." And since no personal God shows up in the "really real" arena of colorless, odorless, and soundless primary qualities, modern thought has arrived at the conclusion that the "objective" universe, when taken independently of any human presence, could not plausibly be called personal.

We would argue, however, that the so-called primary qualities are really mathematical abstractions. They themselves are not concrete or "fundamental" at all. It is only a materialist belief system that confuses impersonal, abstract primary qualities with concrete reality. Whitehead insightfully referred to this confusion as "the fallacy of misplaced concreteness."[12]

Identifying the mathematical abstractions of physics with concrete reality is equivalent to what we are calling the conflation of useful scientific ideas with a materialistic belief system. This (con)fusion, as Whitehead also lamented decades ago, has so thoroughly infiltrated the minds of most modern scientists and philosophers that our suggestions here will probably fall on deaf ears. But we are convinced that the amalgamation that religious fundamentalists make between the Bible and natural science is no more problematic than the unfortunate compound concocted out of modern science and materialist ideology.

Therefore, forgive us if we incessantly reiterate this exhortation to you, the reader: in order to head off the conflict that inevitably follows conflation, please make a clear distinction between scientific method on the one hand and *all* belief systems, whether religious or secularist, on the other. To employ science in pursuit of a fragmentary and always revisable understanding of nature is one thing. But to make science out to be the privileged and even exclusive arbiter of what is real is to range far beyond science itself and enter deeply into the murky interior of a belief system (scientism). We should all have learned from the case of Galileo that belief systems have no business tampering with the results of empirical science, and that science can say nothing about the ultimate nature of the cosmos—for example, whether it is related to a personal God or not. Only a strict segregation of science from creeds will ever let us think unconfusedly about religion's relation to science.

How then can we talk plausibly about a "personal" God in a scientific age? Our answer quite simply is that the idea of a personal God comes to us through God's self-revelation. And we become convinced of the reality of this revelation not through science but through a totally different kind of experience, one involving religious faith. Scientism insists that we should accept as realistic or meaningful only those experiences, ideas, and theories that can be scientifically tested. But we find this requirement too narrowly dogmatic and arbitrary. In the first place, as was made clear in the previous chapter, the claims of scientism are themselves untestable and unfalsifiable. But in the second place, who is to say that religious claims are not as firmly rooted in experience as scientific ones?

When we talk about religious experience, after all, we are not referring to illusory ideas that our psyches have invented and left floating around in our heads. We are thinking of genuinely concrete experience, very much like that of the encounter of one human person with another. In religious experience a divine "selfhood" has taken the initiative and grasped hold of us, sometimes as solitary individuals, but more often in the context of a community of faith. Of this we are certain in a way that completely eludes any scientific attempts at verification. Nor do we seek the support of science to corroborate the fact of our encounter with a personal God. This would be as absurd as one person's trying to prove scientifically that another has fallen in love with her.

We do not need the help of science to settle our doubts about whether or not there exists a personal God who cares for us. Science, after all, can only put us in touch with "objects," whereas in our religious experience we have been addressed by a divine "Subject." We did not wish for this encounter, and in fact we have usually tried to run away from it, afraid that it might challenge us to live our lives in a deeper way. But in the end we were not able to escape its overpowering invitation. We eventually allowed ourselves to be embraced by it, and discovered to our joy that the transformation it wrought has been deeply liberating and, we think, truthful in the deepest sense. What it has accomplished in our lives has made us certain that our faith is rooted in the experience of something quite Real, even though this kind of "experience" differs radically from the shallow empirical method that scientism wants to make the criterion for *every* brand of certainty.

Our view, following the wisdom of our traditions, is that we each have a special capacity to experience God, or, better, a capacity to recognize that we have already been lovingly embraced by God. But the "faculty" through which we come to this awareness of a divine self-revelation needs to be awakened in us. And we cannot accomplish this awakening all by ourselves. In the modern world, the religious sense has gone into a deep slumber, at times anesthetized by the assumptions of scientism and scientific materialism. But though it is asleep, especially in those who think the world has been demystified, it can still be stirred to life by a power beyond our own plane. In order for this arousal to take place, however, our consciousness must be disentangled from the clutches of scientism. And this is why we always begin and end by insisting so vehemently on the need to make a sharp contrast between science and belief systems. As we move into other topics, you will see how efficient our approach is in settling the central issues in science and religion.

III. Contact

However, a third voice will arise at this point:

But can things be so simple? Others of us who are concerned about the relationship of science to religion have serious difficulties with the contrast approach. Even though we agree that we should keep science logically distinct from religious and naturalistic belief systems, are there no implications in science, including physics, for our understanding the character of ultimate reality? Isn't it a bit naive to expect that science would have no metaphysical or theological implications? Can we completely separate our understanding of a "personal" God from what science is telling us about the universe? Should we even try to do so?

For example, if there is a personal God who creates and sustains the natural world, is it too much to expect that physics might uncover at least some hints about the nature of this alleged divine presence? Or, if religion advises us to trust that God is forever faithful to the divine promises, can't we expect science to provide at least some signals that this vision of things is not completely out of touch with the nature of the universe?

Likewise, doesn't theology have to take into account, and try to make some sense of, those scientific discoveries that make the universe seem so apparently indifferent and even hostile to us at times? Isn't the contrast approach simply trying to avoid the messiness of a conversation that could lead us to a deeper appreciation of the intricate relationship of science with the idea of God? There is something puritanical about a theology that seeks to remain so completely untouched by the fascinating ideas now being generated by physics and other sciences.

Recent astrophysics, for example, tells us that the universe has taken around ten to fifteen billion years to evolve to the stage when human beings came into existence. Is theology out of bounds if it asks why an allegedly interested God would allow the universe to get so old and so large before producing persons? Why couldn't we, in the light of science, easily see our species as just an accidental afterthought in the cosmic production? Doesn't the new cosmology rightly challenge our theology, and especially ideas of a "personal" God that arose long before we knew what we know now about the enormous age and size of the universe?

Along with the seventeenth century philosopher Blaise Pascal, it seems appropriate for us to ask whether we humans have any significance within all the immensity of time and space that science has uncovered in this century. Never in all of human history have we felt the temporal and spatial magnitude of the cosmos bearing down so imposingly upon us. Our religious traditions arose, we must always remember, long before we had any sense of such cosmic enormity and human smallness. We cannot suppress the suspicion, therefore, that current cosmology requires some modification of the picture of God that religion has given us. As the astronomer Harlow Shapely once put it, can we any longer get by with the anthropomorphic, one-planet deity that religion has bequeathed to us? Doesn't current cosmology have at least *some* implications for our theology?

Many theologians and scientists today are looking for a much closer engagement of science with the idea of God than the contrasters permit. Without falling back into conflation, which the contrast approach rightly refutes, we are seeking more "contact" between the idea of a creative, faithful, personal God and the new picture of the universe that science is laying out before our eyes. But what kind of personal God could we possibly correlate with the physical and astrophysical findings of modern science?

We cannot answer this question all at once. However, we think that contemporary science does challenge us to begin asking anew whether an "interested God," to use Weinberg's expression, is any longer plausible, and to state in fresh terms what this God might be like. Scientists have every right to request that our God-talk be intelligible to them. Theology must be publicly responsible, not the private preserve of those who insist on protecting revelation from exposure to scientific reason. This means that the theology of today has to talk about God's personality, if it talks about it at all, in terms that fit contemporary scientific cosmology. At the same time our ideas of a personal God cannot be smaller than the universe science has shown to us.

Therefore, we have no desire to retreat, as the second approach often seems to do, into a safe theological haven where in order to protect ourselves from any possible conflicts we immunize our theology completely to new developments in science. We think that theology should actively strive for harmony with the latest developments in cosmology, although it should do so in a tentative way and without becoming too closely interlocked with any particular theories.

It is useful to recall here that ever since the time of their earliest expressions, religions have always been tied up with some cosmology or other. Biblical talk about God, for instance, presupposed a three-tiered cosmos, with the earth sandwiched between the firmament of God's dwelling place above, and the underworld controlled by evil powers below. Generations of believers have accepted this ancient cosmology; it has been inseparable from their faith in the redeeming, personal God of the Bible. But what happens to this faith when modern science demolishes the primitive pictures of the universe in which theism first came to expression? The conflict position argues that science has now finished off religious faith once and for all. The contrast approach, on the other hand, wants to protect the baby of faith from being thrown out with the bath water of cosmology, and so it insists that faith should always be carefully protected from close intermingling with *any* mythic or scientific pictures of the universe. Rudolf Bultmann, for example, one of the most important Protestant theologians of this century, tried in this manner to salvage the core of Christian faith from any potential erosion by developments in scientific cosmology. His rescue operation involved connecting the idea of God primarily to human subjectivity or freedom, and leaving the objective world of nature to the secular interpretation of science. The inner world of the human subject or of historical existence, he implied, is the domain of faith, and the impersonal realm of nature belongs to science. Numerous theologians, as well as many religious scientists, have been quite satisfied with this kind of split between science and theology, hoping thereby to avoid any contradictions between them.

Our approach, however, is not so willing to seal off theology from contact with new developments in science. We want to avoid conflation as well as conflict, of course, but we think that theology risks becoming irrelevant to many scientifically enlightened people unless we hazard some conjectures as to how the idea of a personal God connects with current conceptions of the physical universe.[13] After all, we humans are a part of the universe, living on a continuum with non-human nature. We belong to the universe much more than it belongs to us. Thus there can be no purely divine-human encounter. If there exists a personal God, this God would be "interested" in the whole cosmos and not just human subjects.

So we would like to relate the idea of God to the universe of evolutionary biology, relativity and quantum physics, and to the latest findings of astronomy. We shall do so in more detail in subsequent chapters. Our conclusions will be tentative, and they will have to undergo the constant stress of revision. Moreover, we expect our efforts to meet with considerable opposition. Religious conservatives, who cannot separate an antiquated biblical cosmology from their ideas of God, will be troubled by our attempts at contact with modern science, physics, evolution, and chaos theory. They may even reject our ideas as "heretical." Skeptics, on the other hand, will see our search for dialogue with science as the desperate last-ditch defense of a religious faith which "science" has already purged from intellectual culture. And the defenders of contrast will detect in our approach a dangerous compromise with conflation.

But we envisage our search for contact as the most appropriate direction for theology to take today as it seeks to converse with people whose thinking has been shaped by big bang theory, quantum mechanics, chaos theory, and molecular biology. In each chapter to follow we shall be setting forth a little bit more of what our search has discovered, so that by the end of this book you will have a more rounded picture of our proposal. But for now we must limit ourselves to providing a brief and undeveloped example of how one might find a sort of consonance between the idea of a personal God and the universe of modern physics.

Understandably many theologians and scientists are wary of attempts to find theological significance in current physics. The story is told, for example, of how in 1921 Einstein visited the Archbishop of Canterbury who asked him what possible implications relativity theory might have for theology. Einstein bluntly replied that there were absolutely none, that relativity is a purely scientific matter having nothing whatsoever to do with religion. Many scientists and theologians would probably agree with Einstein, but the astronomer Arthur Eddington, a Quaker, did not. He was convinced that there are indeed implications in relativity for our understanding of God.

Which of the two should we listen to, Einstein or Eddington? Certainly Einstein, if we mean that relativity theory may have very little to contribute *directly* to religious thought. However, Eddington's point may also be well taken if he means that relativity has considerably altered the cosmological landscape and that religious thinkers cannot avoid thinking of God in terms of what we now take to be the general shape of the physical world after Einstein. Theology always presupposes some cosmology or another, and cosmology does make a difference to our theology's conceptualization of any God who possibly transcends and grounds this universe. Theology should not be based directly on physics, of course, but physical cosmology does place constraints on what may plausibly be said about God and God's relation to the world.[14]

Without in any way deriving our thinking about a personal God from physics alone (since "physico-theology" has long proven questionable) we have discovered that the new physics meshes quite nicely with the religious conviction that the universe flows out of a transcendent divine love. We shall see this more clearly when we examine the possible theological implications of big bang theory, whose foundations are already laid out in Einstein's general theory of relativity. But even aside from the big bang we might argue that modern physics shows much more congruity with the idea of an "interested" God than does the "classical" physics of Newton and Laplace, which identified fundamental reality with primary qualities. For the God of classical physics was a remote, impersonal divine mechanic, eventually edged out of the world-picture altogether by modern rationalism and scientism. If "God" made an appearance in classical cosmology at all it was usually as a kind of distant first cause who became dispensable after initially setting in motion the cosmic bodies comprised of primary qualities. This was hardly an "interested" God. There could be little intimacy between God and a physics so utterly opaque to spirit or mind. After Einstein, though, the physical universe looks different, and so would any idea of God we might want to relate to it.

Relativity physics may not have anything directly to say about God, but it does construe the cosmos in a way that allows for a more intimate indwelling of both mind and God in nature. It implies, for example, that the primary qualities of Newtonian physics are not so objective or fundamental as materialism used to think. In fact Einstein showed that our measurements of position, momentum, time, space, and mass (so-called primary qualities) are not invariant, but depend in some way upon the situation of the observing subject. This means that the physical universe is not easily separable from the observer's *mind*, a feature we locate at the heart of personality.

Quantum mechanics, the other major development in the physics of the twentieth century, also implies that the mind of the observing subject (or the instrument of observation) is much more mysteriously mixed up with matter than classical mechanics allowed. The so-called "measurement problem" implies that if we know the position of a physical particle we lose track of its velocity, and if we can measure its velocity we do not know its position. Perhaps the reason for this baffling barrier to intellectual control is that the human mind is so deeply interior to physical reality that a purely objective grasp of nature from some outside vantage point is impossible.

If, therefore, the universe of modern physics is so suffused with our own mentality, it is not so great a stretch of the theological mind as it formerly may have been to allow also that the cosmos is inherently more open to the presence of what religion calls "Spirit" than an older physics allowed. In religious experience it is especially the sense of spiritual presence that allows us to think of God as interested or personal rather than remote and indifferent. Our point here then is that theology today has every reason to be excited about the way in which scientific thought has, at least by implication, made the natural world once again a fitting habitat for mind and Spirit.

Moreover, with its notion of a world comprised of interrelated *fields* of force and not just isolated chunks of matter, contemporary physics gives us a much "softer" picture of physical reality than an older materialist mechanism allowed. As theologian Wolfhart Pannenberg has written, it is now possible for theology to use the scientific idea of a "field" of force as a new metaphor for expressing the religious sense of divine spiritual presence in the universe.[15] We must be cautious, and not take the notion of "field" too literally here, since it functions as an inadequate model even in science. But our theological language is always tentative and metaphorical, and so new shifts in cosmology may provide us with fresh language to express God's relation to the world. Moreover, since we acknowledge that no particular model is ever adequate to express the depth and richness of this relationship, we encourage experimentation with a multiplicity of cosmological concepts in our theology. This in fact is what theology has always done, though usually unconsciously. Here we suggest that the idea of a "field" of force, though certainly not an adequate metaphor by any means, may be helpful in leading us away from older and cruder mechanistic ways of thinking about how a divine Spirit might influence the world.

This is intended to be no more than a small sampling of how new developments in science may allow us to conceive of matter in a way that allows it to be much more open to the caring presence of a personal God than the now obsolete materialism permitted. Our argument is that theology cannot afford to ignore the opportunities for fertile reformulation that may be provided by new discoveries and theories in physics and other fields. It is our view, as stated here, that some of the new ideas in physics, for example, mesh quite nicely with the idea of a personal divine presence. We see a new harmony between science and theistic religion today that previously eluded us. We do not go so far as to argue that we can prove God's existence on the basis of the new cosmology, but we do think that scientific cosmology is providing fertile new images for a revitalized theological reflection. In the chapters that follow, we shall give further examples.

IV. Confirmation

Finally, a fourth approach argues that the idea of a personal God, far from being opposed to science, positively supports it:

We agree that religion cannot add to or subtract anything from the plausibility of any particular scientific theory. But this does not mean that religion has no connection with science. Our proposal, perhaps appearing a bit audacious in tone but actually quite modest in motivation, is that religion, properly understood, confirms the entire scientific enterprise. It does so by justifying the fundamental trust that nourishes all scientific inquiry. Our conviction is that we can go beyond conflict, contrast, and even contact in formulating religion's relationship to science. Here we are claiming specifically that faith in a personal God has a unique capacity to confirm our trust in reality's endless intelligibility, a trust without which scientific inquiry is hopelessly crippled.

Einstein himself acknowledged that science has to reach outside of itself for the energy to pursue the truth consistently. It is quietly dependent, he said, upon something like faith:

> ...science can only be created by those who are thoroughly imbued with the aspiration toward truth and understanding. This source of feeling, however, springs from the sphere of religion. To this there also belongs the faith in the possibility that the regulations valid for the world of existence are rational, that is, comprehensible to reason. I cannot conceive of a genuine scientist without that profound faith.[16]

Our view is that faith in a personal God nourishes the trust that science silently draws upon as it makes its excursions into the unknown. Science needs to take for granted, since it cannot prove conclusively in advance, that there is a certain reliability or consistency to the physical activity in our universe. Although scientists expect it always to be surprising, they do not anticipate that the universe will ever be capricious. The confident expectation of coherence and predictability is essential for the very launching of the scientific adventure. If we discover a law that applies in some instances we trust that it will apply in all. For example, we anticipate confidently that carbon will bond with oxygen, hydrogen, and nitrogen in the same way always when conditions are the same. We have no right to expect that nature will be so predictable and reliable, but we *believe* that it is and that it always will be.[17]

However, human trust is vulnerable to all sorts of threats that could easily make us despair, and it is for this reason that religion has become such an important part of human life. Our religious faith points us toward what it takes to be a permanent and always reliable ground on which to base our trust. It tells us that nature's reliability is rooted in a transcending fidelity. In the teachings of Jews, Christians, and Muslims the basis of this fidelity can be nothing less than a "personal" God.

But why do these faiths insist on a "personal" God? The main reason is that trust requires a sense of reality's underlying *fidelity*, and nothing in our experience brings home to us the fact of fidelity more intensely than another person's faithfulness in keeping promises. Nothing less than personal could fully evoke our own personal trust. Theistic religion maintains that if there is to be any firm foundation for our trust it has to have *at the very least* the qualities of a person capable of making and keeping promises. It is hard for us to imagine how an allegedly impersonal "ultimate" could ever conceivably arouse fully the capacity for trust that lies buried in the depths of our own personal existence.

Obviously when we speak of a "personal" God we do not mean to be too literal. "Person" is a symbol of God, one of many available pointers to the absolute. But we wish to avoid any notion that God is less than personal either. Theistic religion cannot settle for a purely impersonal absolute since this would not be a sufficient reason for our own personal trust in reality. An impersonal ultimate, such as Einstein seems to prefer, could not make or keep promises, and so it could not be an adequate grounding for a fully *human* kind of trusting.

In the absence of a promising and faithful God, the cosmic reliability that science needs to lean on in order to make accurate predictions about the future could be adequately provided only by the supposed eternity and necessity of the cosmos itself. The laws of nature could be fully trusted, in other words, only if they have existed unchangingly forever. It is for this reason that even today some scientific skeptics look for every possible way they can to eternalize matter. For apparently only in this way can they free the universe from any semblance of caprice. However, as later chapters will show, the project of eternalizing matter has recently come upon hard times. Science itself no longer looks kindly upon the idea of a universe of infinite duration. And if the universe has not existed forever, it would quite possibly lack the internal necessity that has justified so much scientific trust in the inviolability of natural laws.

How then, if the universe is not eternal, could we possibly ground the reliability of nature in such a way as to give authority any longer to scientific prediction? Our own proposal is that science can quite plausibly find confirmation in a view of reality that locates the foundations of the universe in the eternal fidelity of a promising personal God.[18] We are not presenting here any argument for God's existence. Rather we are saying nothing more than that a consciousness steeped in the sense that at the deepest level of reality there lies a divine fidelity is a consciousness already primed to do science. Obviously, this does not mean that a scientist has to be a religious believer. This is not at all what we are saying, for we know that many excellent scientists are agnostics or atheists. We are only voicing our opposition to those like Einstein and Weinberg who think that belief in an interested, personal, promising God is incompatible with science. Futher, we are maintaining that faith in this personal God is much more than just compatible with science. It is powerfully supportive of science as well.

Weinberg is right, of course, to argue that *science* does not discover a personal God hidden in, beneath, or behind the cosmos. People arrive at the idea of a personal God, if they do so at all, through religious experience and not through scientific observation. But having arrived at faith in such a ground of trust, they have even more reason than before to venture forth on the journey of scientific discovery, anticipating that the world will always meet them not only with a faithful consistency but also with the surprise that keeps science alive.

While unconditional faith *in* science (scientism) leads to conflict with religion, religion is not opposed to the faith that *underlies* science. On the contrary, religion can vitalize the faith or trust in reality that science needs in order to persist in its exploration of the world. If we place religion in the role of fortifying this trust, it confirms rather than contradicts science. In no way does it stand between the scientist and truth. Religious trust in a personal God cannot be verified or falsified by science, but when a person's consciousness is already shaped by the trust that such religious faith can bestow, it has the capacity to fuel rather than frustrate the adventure of scientific discovery.

Finally, a strong case can be made for the view that the radical monotheism of the God-religions has provided a most favorable historical context for the emergence and flourishing of science. By grounding the natural order in the rationality of a personal God, theism conditioned the Western mind over the course of centuries for the kind of faith in natural order and cosmic coherence that scientists have to take with them into their work. Whitehead has argued, for instance, that it was especially the theology of the Middle Ages that prepared Western consciousness to anticipate that the universe would be rationally comprehensible. "Faith in reason," he writes, "is the trust that the ultimate natures of things lie together in a harmony which excludes mere arbitrariness....The faith in the order of nature which made possible the growth of science is a particular example of a deeper faith."[19] For us this "deeper faith" has been most fully brought to expression in those religious traditions that affirm the reality of a promising and faithful "personal" God.

3

Does Evolution Rule Out God's Existence?

In 1859 Charles Darwin published *On the Origin of Species*, his famous treatise on what we now call "evolution." It is one of the most important books of science ever written, and even today experts consider it to be a generally accurate account of the story of life. Theologically speaking, however, it caused a fierce storm of controversy, and we are still wrestling with the question of what to make of it. Does Darwin's theory perhaps put the final nail in religion's coffin? Or can there perhaps be a fruitful encounter of religion with evolutionary thought?

For many scientists evolution means that the universe is fundamentally impersonal and Godless. In fact, Steven Weinberg, whose position we reviewed in the preceding chapter, asserts that evolution refutes the idea of an "interested" God much more decisively than physics does.[1] Only a brief look at Darwin's theory will show why it disturbs the traditional religious belief in a loving and powerful Deity.

Darwin observed that all living species produce more offspring than ever reach maturity. Nevertheless, the number of individuals in any given species remains fairly constant. This means that there must be a very high rate of mortality, since more young are produced than ever reach maturity. To explain why some survive and others do not, Darwin noted that the individuals of any species are not all identical: some are better "adapted" to their environment than others. It appears that the most "fit" are the ones that survive to produce offspring. The vast majority of individuals and species lose out in the struggle for existence, but during the long voyage of evolution there emerge a staggering diversity of life, millions of new species, and eventually the human race.

What, then, is so theologically disturbing about the theory? What is it about evolution that places in question even the very existence of God? It can be summarized in three propositions:

1. The variations that lead to differentiation of species are purely *random*, thus suggesting that the workings of nature are "accidental" and irrational. Today the source of these variations has been identified as genetic mutations, and most biologists still follow Darwin in attributing these to "chance."

2. The fact that individuals have to *struggle* for survival, and that most of them suffer and lose out in this contest, points to the basic cruelty of the universe, particularly toward the weak.

3. The mindless process of *natural selection* by which only the better adapted organisms survive points to a universe that is essentially blind and indifferent to life and humanity.

These three inseparable ingredients—randomness, struggle, and blind natural selection—all seem to suggest that the universe is impersonal, utterly unrelated to any "interested" God. Darwin himself, after reflecting on the "cruelty," randomness, and impersonality in evolution, could never again return to the benign theism of his ancestral Anglicanism. Though he did not completely lose his religious faith, many of his scientific heirs have been much less hesitant to equate evolution with atheism.

From the middle of the last century up until today prominent thinkers have welcomed Darwinian ideas as the final victory of skepticism over religion. T. H. Huxley, Darwin's "bulldog" as he was known, thought evolution was antithetical to traditional theism. Ernst Haeckel, Karl Marx, Friedrich Nietzsche, and Sigmund Freud all found Darwin's thought congenial to their atheism. And numerous others in our own time closely associate evolution with unbelief. Given this coalition of evolution and hostility to theism it is hardly surprising that the idea has encountered so much resistance from some religious groups.

Darwin himself, however, did not envisage so unambiguous a union between evolution and skepticism. If he moved toward unbelief at all it was not without undergoing a great deal of personal anguish and mental reservation. In 1860, a year after the publication of *The Origins*, he wrote:

There seems to me too much misery in the world. I cannot persuade myself that a beneficent and omnipotent God would have designedly created the Ichneumonidae with the express intention of their feeding within the living bodies of caterpillars, or that cats should play with mice. Not believing this, I see no necessity that the eye was expressly designed. On the other hand I cannot anyhow be contented to view this wonderful universe, and especially the nature of man, and to conclude that everything is the result of brute force. I am inclined to look at everything as resulting from designed laws, with the details, whether good or bad, left to the working out of what we may call chance.[2]

And while some modern authors have tried to turn Darwin into a propagandist for scientific atheism, he is perhaps best described as a reluctant agnostic. He did not casually jettison his religious heritage. Even while on his famous sea-voyage he had entertained the prospect of becoming a country parson, and the fact that he is buried not far from Isaac Newton in Westminster Abbey is testimony that he did not ruffle the feathers of the religious establishment to the degree that has sometimes been imagined.

Yet we must ask here whether the Darwinian (or now the neo-Darwinian) picture of nature in evolution is after all compatible with religion, and, if it is, in what sense? Answers to this question generally fall into the four categories we are following throughout this book. Here is a brief summary of what each has to say on the topic of evolution and religion.

I. Conflict

Is it any wonder that we skeptics find in evolution the most compelling scientific reasons for rejecting theistic religion? The three features of chance, struggle, and blind natural selection are so antithetical to any conceivable notion of divine providence or design, that we find it hard to understand how any scientifically educated person could still believe in God.

Richard Dawkins, a British biologist, presents our position handily in his book *The Blind Watchmaker*.[3] His thesis is that chance and natural selection, aided by immensely long periods of time, are enough to account for all the diverse species of life, including ourselves. Why would we need to invoke the idea of God if chance and natural selection alone can account for all the creativity in the story of life? Before Darwin, we concede, it may have been difficult to find definitive reasons for atheism. The order or patterning in nature seemed to beg for a supernatural explanation, and so the design argument for God's existence may have made some sense in those days. But no longer. Evolutionary theory, brought up to date by the discoveries of molecular biology, has demolished the divine designer that most educated people believed in before the middle of the last century. Evolution has once and for all purged any remaining intellectual respectability from the idea of God.[4]

In his book *Natural Theology* which set forth the standard academic and theological wisdom of the early nineteenth century, William Paley had compared nature to a watch. If you chanced upon a watch lying alone on the ground, he wrote, and then examined its intricate structure, you could not help concluding that it had been made by an intelligent designer. It couldn't possibly be the product of mere chance. And yet, the natural world exhibits much more complex order than any watch. Thus, Paley concluded, there has to be an intelligent designer responsible for nature's fine arrangement. This designer, of course, could be none other than the Creator God of biblical religion.

But Dawkins demonstrates to our satisfaction that the divine designer is no longer needed:

> Paley's argument is made with passionate sincerity and is informed by the best biological scholarship of his day, but it is wrong, gloriously and utterly wrong. The analogy between…watch and living organism, is false. All appearances to the contrary, the only watchmaker in nature is the blind forces of physics, albeit deployed in a very special way. A true watchmaker has foresight: he designs his cogs and springs, and plans their interconnections, with a future purpose in the mind's eye. Natural selection, the blind, unconscious, automatic process which Darwin discovered, and which we now know is the explanation for the existence and apparent purposeful form of all life, has no purpose in mind. It has no mind and no mind's eye. It does not plan for the future. It has no vision, no foresight, no sight at all. If it can be said to play the role of watchmaker in nature, it is the *blind* watchmaker.[5]

Even though David Hume and other philosophers had already severely battered the design argument for God's existence, Dawkins thinks that only Darwin's theory of natural selection provided a fully convincing refutation of natural theology. "Darwin made it possible to be an intellectually fulfilled atheist."[6]

The order and design in the universe may seem on the surface to point to a divine "watchmaker" who devised its intricate parts. But evolution has allowed us to look beneath the deceptive surface of nature's orderly arrangements. The pattern and design that seem so remarkably miraculous to the scientifically illiterate can now be fully accounted for by Darwin's impersonal theory of evolution. The theory rules out any proper appeal to the God-hypothesis. For if there is a watchmaker at all, it is not a divine intelligence but the process of blind natural selection that has put the parts of nature so wonderfully together over the course of billions of years of trial and error. The aimless forces of evolution are sufficient to explain all the marvels of life and mind.

Dawkins, we should add, is not alone in this conviction. Most evolutionary biologists today have difficulty with the religious position. It is scarcely an exaggeration to say that the Neo-Darwinian theory of evolution has become the main modern challenge to theistic religion. So, if religion is to survive as an intellectually plausible interpretation of the universe today, it will have to pass through the fires of evolutionary theory. Our opinion is that it will burn up in the process.

Clearly it is fear of this possibility that leads so many of our opponents to adopt the "creationist" position. They are aware that creation stories in the Bible contradict the evolutionary interpretation of the cosmos and its origins. But, deeper than that, they rightly sense evolution's fundamental incompatibility with *any* religious vision. We are not surprised then that they share our conviction that evolution and God are incompatible.

One version of creationism is particularly annoying to us. "Scientific creationism" or "creation science," as it is sometimes called, rejects evolutionary theory as *scientifically* unsound, and it offers the Bible as the source of an alternative "scientific" theory of the creation of life.[7] It argues, for example, that the paucity of intermediary forms in the fossil record implies that the book of Genesis, according to which God created living beings in their present forms in the beginning (10,000 or so years ago), is a better "scientific" hypothesis than evolution. It claims that the biblical text is more suited to the actual data of geology, biology and paleontology than is Darwinian science.

"Creation science," however, is really not science at all. It does not seriously accept the self-revising method required by true science, nor does it allow the view that the gaps in the fossil record might be compatible with other, revised versions of evolutionary theory, such as that of "punctuated equilibrium" now being proposed by Stephen Jay Gould and Niles Eldredge.[8] Creation science would not even be worth

discussing were it not for the fact that its devotees stir up so much public controversy in their attempts to keep evolutionary theory out of
schools and textbooks.

Our position, though, is that evolution is incompatible with *any and
all* religious interpretations of the cosmos, not just with Christian fun-
damentalism. The prevalence of chance variations, which today are
called genetic "mutations," definitively refutes the idea of any ordering
deity. The fact of struggle and waste in evolution decisively demonstrates that the cosmos is really not cared for by a loving God. And the
fact of natural selection is a clear signal of the loveless impersonality of
the universe. Theology after Darwin will have to look these facts
squarely in the face, and we don't think it can survive the encounter.

II. Contrast

Our position, you will recall, is that science and religion are such
disparate ways of looking at the world that they cannot meaningfully
compete with each other. This means that evolution, which may be
quite accurate as a scientific theory, bears not the slightest threat
toward religion. "Conflict" arises not from the science of evolution
itself, but from two different kinds of conflation. On the one hand, "scientific creationists" try to merge biblical accounts of creation with
modern "science," and on the other hand, scientific skeptics generally
collapse evolutionary theory into an ideology of their own, "scientific
materialism."

Here we shall first examine "scientific creationism" and then follow
that up with a critique of materialist evolutionism. We would like to
emphasize, though, that we are in no way attacking *scientific* theories
of evolution, and at the end of our presentation we shall even show how
our theology is logically consistent with the three items that our adver-
saries find antithetical to religion, namely, chance, struggle, and natural
selection.

The opposition that scientific creationists see between evolution and
theism follows from their attempts to make the Bible function as a scientific treatise. They take Genesis not only as a religious tract, but also as a
compendium of scientifically accurate information. So we should not be
surprised that conflict appears as soon as an alternative set of scientific
ideas, such as those of Darwin, becomes established. Creationists simply
assume that the Bible is scientifically accurate, while evolutionists think
of it as scientifically inaccurate. Both sides, however, treat it as though its

intention were to give us scientific understanding. One side (creationism) views it as good science; the other (evolutionary skepticism) sees it as bad. But both implicitly conflate science with the Bible, an alliance that inevitably leads to conflict.[9]

So-called "scientific creationism" is objectionable in the first place because from the point of view of good science it refuses to look at most of the relevant data. The scientific evidence in favor of evolution is overwhelming. Geology, paleontology, the fossil record, radio-carbon dating, comparative anatomy, and embryology—all of these and many broader features of current cosmology now converge to support some version of Darwin's theory. Although evolutionary theory is certainly not unrevisable, since there are apparent gaps in the fossil record as well as other problems yet to be resolved, this does not mean that the world and life did not evolve. All it means is that science still has a long way to go in clarifying our understanding of the details of evolution. We fully support scientific efforts to learn more about how evolution works.

In the second place, however, scientific creationism is *theologically* embarrassing. It trivializes religion by artificially imposing scientific expectations upon a sacred text whose objective is in no sense one of satisfying scientific curiosity. It completely misses the religious point of Genesis by placing it alongside *On the Origin of Species* as though the biblical text could provide a superior *scientific* account of the origin of life. Creationism thus fails to focus on the deeper meaning of the biblical account of creation: its covenantal motifs, its fundamental message that the universe is a gift, and that the appropriate human response to this gift is gratitude and trust. Creationism turns a font of holy wisdom into a mundane treatise to be placed in competition with shallow scientific attempts to explain things. To us it is religiously offensive to see the biblical text so thoroughly degraded.

After all, if we address the wrong questions to the Bible we will keep it from speaking to us out of its inner substance. Asking the wrong questions is an unfailing way of cutting ourselves off from the genuine riches contained in any significant text, religious or otherwise. For example, if we approached the writings of Homer, Plato, or any other classic author with the primary intention of learning about, say, ancient culinary habits, we might find out something about the way people used to eat. But if that were our only question the real meat of the text would have escaped us altogether.

Likewise, if our primary question to the Bible is one of scientific curiosity about cosmic beginnings or the origins of life, we will surely miss its real intentions. Since the text was composed in a prescientific age, its primary meaning cannot be unfolded in the idiom of twentieth century science. But that is exactly the demand put upon the Bible by scientific creationism. Needless to say, such an expectation ends up shriveling to prosaic dust a collection of deeply religious writings designed to open us to the ultimate mystery of the universe.

In the third place, scientific creationism is historically anachronistic. Creationists ironically situate the ancient biblical writings within the time-conditioned framework of modern science. They refuse to take into account the social, cultural, and historical conditions in which the books of the Bible were fashioned over a period of two millennia. In doing so they close their eyes to modern historical awareness of the time-sensitive nature of all human consciousness, including that expressed in the sacred texts of religion. They fail to delineate clearly the widely diverse literary genres in the Bible—symbolic, mythic, devotional, poetic, legendary, historical, credal, confessional, etc.—as well as the various time periods in which different texts were composed. Failing to consider the historical and cultural contexts of the biblical writings, they ingenuously superimpose modern scientific expectations on them.

In spite of these problems, however, we can still entertain a certain degree of empathy with the phenomenon of creationism. Creationism is one unfortunate symptom of a much wider effort by traditionally religious people to cope with modernity. At heart creationists and other fundamentalists are sincerely and understandably troubled by all the shortcomings of the post-Enlightenment world. They deplore the breakdown of authority, the diminishment of "virtue," the absence of common purpose, the loss of a sense of absolute values, and the banishing of a feeling of sacred mystery from our lives. For many creationists the notion of "evolution" sums up all the evils and emptiness of secularistic modernity. In battling evolution, therefore, creationism is responding to something much deeper and more complex than just a scientific theory. Up to a point we can easily share its anguish.

Moreover, we are convinced that the phenomenon of creationism also points to serious flaws in the way science has been presented to students and to the general public by some of our most prominent scientific writers. Many scientists—and this point is usually ignored—indulge in a conflation of their own. They too fuse science with belief. In the case of many scientists and philosophers today, to be more specific, the conflation consists of commingling evolutionary theory with materialism, a belief which is indeed antithetical to religion. Scientists of the stature of Carl Sagan, Stephen Jay Gould, E. O. Wilson, and Richard Dawkins, just to name a few, offer the theory of evolution to us already snugly wrapped up in the alternative "faith" of scientific materialism. So in a sense "scientific creationism" is not simply a rejection of pure science, as scientific skeptics usually accuse it of being. It is also an understandable, though ineffective, reaction to an alternative brand of conflation, one that unfortunately makes science appear antithetical to all forms of religious understanding.

Scientific materialists generally write about evolution as though it were inherently anti-theistic. In doing so, however, they are uncritically espousing the assumptions of a secularistic intellectual culture. Their species of conflation may be called simply "evolutionism," an often subtle bonding of Darwinian ideas with hidden premises of secularism, naturalism, and the belief system we have been calling scientific materialism.

One prominent devotee of evolutionism, Stephen Jay Gould, however, is not as subtle as are many others. For he has stated quite openly that the reason so many people cannot accept Darwin's ideas is that, in his opinion, evolution is inseparable from a "philosophical" message, namely, materialism. He says,

> ...I believe that the stumbling block to [the acceptance of Darwin's theory] does not lie in any scientific difficulty, but rather in the philosophical content of Darwin's message—in its challenge to a set of entrenched Western attitudes that we are not yet ready to abandon. First, Darwin argues that evolution has no purpose. Individuals struggle to increase the representation of their genes in future generations, and that is all....Second, Darwin maintained that evolution has no direction; it does not lead inevitably to higher things. Organisms become better adapted to their local environments, and that is all. The "degeneracy" of a parasite is as perfect as the gait of a gazelle. Third, Darwin applied a consistent philosophy of materialism to his interpretation of nature. Matter is the ground of all existence; mind, spirit and God as well, are just words that express the wondrous results of neuronal complexity.[10]

If one is to accept evolution, Gould explicitly claims here and elsewhere, one must first embrace materialism and all of its consequences, e.g. that religion has no basis in reality and that there is no purpose in the universe. Like many of his fellow scientists today, he clearly

the complexity of matter's organization is an undeniable fact of natural history, but it is one that gets lost if we focus only on the branching bush model of biological evolution.

Lately Gould has begun to acknowledge that the scientific study of nature does uncover an overall rise in complexity, but he takes pains to deny that this constitutes "progress" or evidence of any creative principle other than the impersonal laws and accidents of blind natural process. Every slightest opening for a directional or teleological interpretation of nature must be carefully closed up before science has any opportunity to regress to the arcane mysticism and vitalism of the past.

We should emphasize again here that we have no investment in having science shore up our religious belief that there is purpose in the universe. This would be a misuse of science. Moreover, belief that nature embodies a purpose cannot arise from scientific expertise but only from the grace of divine revelation. However, we find it peculiar that skeptics like Gould, while allegedly protecting the integrity of science from bondage to belief, are no less tied to ideology than are the teleological perspectives they renounce so vehemently as "unscientific." Under the guise of presenting a scientific picture of directionless evolution it is not difficult for us to see that in fact these skeptics are harboring a comfortably materialist world view, one without which their whole way of looking at nature would collapse.

Whatever routes life may have taken on its journey toward consciousness, as well as all the hazards it may have encountered along the way, may be scientifically interesting, but to us they are theologically immaterial. The important thing is that in the end we conscious beings are here, and this is a significant enough fact irrespective of *how* we arrived. The particulars of the evolutionary past are useful for scientists to know about, but they are not important for defining who we really are or what our relation to God is. When our species came along, with its capacity for freedom, goodness, and love, it is clear that evolution had leapt onto a new plane altogether. No matter what our evolutionary past was like, the core of our human existence lies now beyond the realm of scientific illumination. So in response to Gould's materialist conviction that human consciousness "is but a tiny, late-arising twig" on the bush of life, we would submit that there are other plausible ways of looking at the same phenomenon, including a religious perspective that points to our inherent and eternal value.

But, you will no doubt ask, can evolutionary science really be extricated from materialist dogma? What about those theologically troubling aspects of Darwinian theory: chance, the struggle for survival, and impersonal natural selection? Do they not refute theism and require a materialist interpretation?

Without getting bogged down in theological conjecture here, we shall be content to show that none of these three items necessarily contradicts theism. Our approach, you will recall, is simply to show that science and religion are not incompatible. We are not interested in drawing speculative theological conclusions from the always changing ideas of science. And so in the case of the apparent contradictions that evolutionary theory poses to theism we would reply very briefly as follows:

1) In the first place, the "chance" character of the variations which natural selection chooses for survival may easily be accounted for on the basis of our inevitable human narrowness and ignorance. Allegedly "random" genetic mutations may not really be random at all. They could very well be mere illusions resulting from the limitedness of our human perspective. Our religious faith convinces us in any case that a purely human angle of vision is always exceedingly restricted. Hence, what appears to be absurd chance from a scientific perspective could be quite rational and coherent from that of God's infinite wisdom.

2) Second, evolutionist complaints about the struggle, suffering, waste and cruelty of natural process add absolutely nothing new to the basic problem of evil of which religion has always been quite fully apprised. The Bible, for example, has surely heard of Job and the crucifixion of Jesus, and yet it proclaims the paradoxical possibility of faith and hope in God in spite of all evil and suffering. Some of us would even argue that faith has no intensity or depth unless it is a leap into the unknown in the face of such absurdity. Faith is always faith "in spite of" all the difficulties that defy reason and science.

As the Danish philosopher Søren Kierkegaard, one of our main sources of inspiration, taught us, too much objective certainty deadens the very soul of faith. Genuine piety is possible only in the face of radical uncertainty. So the objectively troubling evolutionary account of life's enormous struggle and suffering constitutes no more of a challenge to authentic faith than suffering and evil have ever done. In fact, more than a few of our number consider evolution's severity to be quite consistent with the ancient religious theme that the earth is a "soul school" whose often stern lessons make us worthy of eternal life. If life posed no hardships, and if evolution were totally benign, how would we ever be aroused to develop our moral and spiritual character?

3) And, finally, there is no more theological difficulty in the remorseless law of natural selection, which is said to be impersonal and blind, than in the laws of inertia, gravity or any other impersonal aspects of science. Gravity, like natural selection, has no regard for our inherent personal dignity either. It pulls toward earth the weak and powerful alike—at times in a deadly way. But very few thinkers have ever insisted that gravity is a serious argument against God's existence. Perhaps natural selection should be viewed no less leniently.

At any rate, our contention is that humans cannot learn the nature of ultimate reality simply by pondering purely natural laws and occurrences. We too reject Paley's narrowly conceived "natural theology," since it seeks to know God independently of God's self-revelation. Nature itself provides evidence neither for nor against God's existence. Something so momentous as the reality of God can hardly be decided by a superficial scientific deciphering of the natural world. Hence we are neither troubled nor heartened by evolutionary theory.

III. Contact

We allow that the contrast approach has the merit at least of shattering the facile fusion of faith and science that underlies most instances of conflict. Its sharp portrayal of the ideological biases in both creationism and evolutionism is very helpful. Contrast may be an essential step in the process of thinking clearly and fruitfully about the relationship of evolution to religion.

But for many scientists and religious thinkers contrast does not go nearly far enough. Evolution is more than just another innocuous scientific theory that theology can innocently ignore. We need to do more than just show that evolution does not contradict theism. For evolution, in our judgment, may very well be the most appropriate general framework we have ever had through which to express the true meaning of our religious convictions. Indeed, it can deepen our understanding not only of the cosmos but also of God.

Unfortunately, many theologians have not yet faced up to the fact that we live in a world after and not before Darwin, and that an evolving cosmos looks a lot different from the world-pictures that shaped and nurtured traditional religious ideas. If it is to survive in the intellectual climate of today, therefore, our theology requires fresh expression in evolutionary terms. When we think about religion in the post-Darwinian period we cannot have exactly the same thoughts that

Augustine, Avicenna, Maimonides, Aquinas, or for that matter our grandparents and parents had. Today we may need to recast all of theology in evolutionary terms.

Without fusing science with religion, theology is making fruitful contact with the same Darwinian ideas that evolutionists consider antithetical to God's existence. In fact, for many of us, evolution is an absolutely essential ingredient in our thinking about God today. As the Roman Catholic theologian Hans Küng puts it, evolutionary theory now makes possible: 1) a deeper understanding of God—not above or outside the world but in the midst of evolution; 2) a deeper understanding of creation—not as contrary to but as making evolution possible; and 3) a deeper understanding of humans as organically related to the entire cosmos.[12]

Skeptics, of course, will immediately ask how we can reconcile our ideas about a providential God with the role that chance plays in life's evolution. This is a crucial question, and we are not at all satisfied with the contrasters' casual conjecture that chance may not really exist, attributing it as they do to our human ignorance of some larger divine plan. For in our opinion chance is quite real. It is a concrete fact in evolution, but it is not one that contradicts the idea of God. On the contrary, if there exists a loving God who is intimately related to the world we should expect an aspect of indeterminacy or randomness in nature. The reason is simple: love typically operates not in a coercive but in a persuasive manner. It refuses to force itself upon the beloved, but instead allows the beloved—in this case the entire created cosmos—to remain itself, though in such a way as to imply intimacy rather than abandonment.

If, as our religious traditions have always insisted, God truly cares for the well-being of the world, then the world must be permitted to be something other than God. Even if its being is fundamentally derived from God it has to have a certain amount of "freedom" or autonomy. If it did not somehow exist on its own it would be nothing more than an extension of God's own being, and hence it would not be a world unto itself. When viewed in a genuinely theistic perspective, then, there has to be room for uncertainty, i.e. an absence of direct divine determinism, in the universe. We interpret the fact of randomness in evolution as an instance of the necessary indeterminacy required by a world related to a God who cares for its well-being.

In other words, if the world is to be anything distinct from God it has to have some scope for meandering about and for experimenting with different ways of existing. Thus Gould's branching bush is quite accurately representative of certain features of evolution. In their relative freedom from divine coercion, some of the world's evolutionary experiments may work and others may not, but they can all be interesting and significant in widening the dimensions of the cosmos. Moreover, leaving room for such latitude does not mean that there is no divine vigilance, but only that in its respect for the otherness of creation divine love does not crudely intrude. God risks allowing the cosmos to exist in relative liberty. And in the story of life, the world's inherent "freedom" manifests itself through the random variations or genetic mutations that comprise the raw material of evolution. Thus a certain amount of chance is quite consonant with our understanding of God.

If God typically influences the world in a persuasive rather than coercive way, then this may help explain why the random variations or mutations in evolution are allowed to occur. It is because God is a persuading love rather than a domineering force that the world not only evolves, but does so in an indeterminate manner.[13] If God were a magician or a dictator, then we might expect the universe to be finished all at once and remain eternally unchanged. If God insisted on being in total control of things, we might not expect the weird organisms of the Cambrian explosion, the later dinosaurs and reptiles, or the many other wild creatures that seem so exotic to us. We would want our divine magician to build the world along the lines of a narrowly human sense of clean perfection.

But what a pallid and impoverished world that would be. It would lack all the drama, diversity, adventure, and intense beauty that evolution has in fact produced. A world of human design might have a listless harmony to it, and it might be a world devoid of pain and struggle, but it would have none of the novelty, contrast, danger, upheaval, and grandeur that evolution has brought about over billions of years.

Fortunately, the God of our religion is not a magician but a creator.[14] And we think this God is much more interested in promoting freedom and the adventure of evolution than in preserving the status quo. Since divine creative love has the character of "letting be"—which in no way implies a Deistic withdrawal but instead a self-effacing intimacy—we are not at all surprised at evolution's strange and erratic pathways. Nor can we be totally taken aback that an evolving world allows for suffering and tragedy as well. The long creative struggle of the universe to arrive at life, consciousness, and culture is consonant with our faith's conviction that real love never forces any state of affairs but always allows for freedom, risk, adventure—and also suffering—on the part of the beloved.

But why would God want a world that is not completed and perfected once and for all? Why do the universe and life have to unfold (= evolve) in the arduously dramatic way that Darwinian biology describes. Again we have no certain answers, and our ideas on all such matters are themselves constantly in evolution. But might it not be because God wants the world and beings within the world to partake of the divine joy of creating novelty that the cosmos is left unfinished, and that it is invited to be at least to some degree self-creative? And if it is in some ways self-creative can we be too baffled about its undisciplined experimentation with the many different, delightful, baffling, and bizarre forms that we find in the fossil record and in the diversity of life that surrounds us even now? And can't we therefore learn much about the ways of God's creative love by looking at the pictures of nature that evolutionists like Gould are giving us today? For even the model of evolution as a randomly branching bush, while perhaps not completely adequate in itself, at least prevents us from projecting narrowly human conceptions of simplistic directionality onto the natural world.

Ever since Darwin, in fact, scientists have found out things about the natural world that are inconsistent with an innocent notion of divine design such as the one proposed by Paley and lampooned by Dawkins. While a skeptic might interpret evolution's long history of trial and error experimentation to be incontrovertible evidence of an impersonal universe, the emerging cosmic story corresponds just as readily with the infinitely elusive God of religious experience. For ours is a God who wishes to share the divine creative life with all creatures, and not just humans. Such a God renounces from the outset any rigid control over the process of creation, and gives to creation a significant role, indeed a partnership, in the ongoing evolution of the world. Such a gracious self-denying love would be quite consistent with a world open to all the surprises we find in the physical record of evolution. And it would also be logically consistent with (though ultimately intolerant of) the struggle and suffering that we witness in life and its evolution.

Evolution, therefore (along with other new scientific ideas to be examined later), does not demand that we give up the idea of God. Rather it asks that we think about God in a fresh way. Such a requirement is nothing new in the history of religion, since each age faces unprecedented crises that may require dramatic shifts in any given generation's understanding of ultimate reality. Indeed it is generally by facing severe challenges that religious faith sustains or renews its vitality. Like other living and evolving systems, a religious faith also goes limp if no stumbling blocks at all are ever placed in its path.

Thus, a "contact" theology actually looks forward to facing the kinds of obstacles to naive piety that evolution implies. A theology that seriously (and not just half-heartedly) mulls over Darwinian evolution cannot remain completely the same as before. Evolution demands that we think out more carefully how God might influence the world. For, even though the God of evolution is not a dictator, and apparently does not interrupt the flow of natural causation, religious faith implies necessarily that there is still some significant way in which God does influence and interact with the natural world. The religious sense of a God who arrives out of the future, and who comes to meet the world in the mode of a continually fresh promise of new life, is, we think, a most appropriate framework for interpreting the data of evolutionary science.

Thus we are quite comfortable with the idea that a process of "natural selection" is present as a constraining factor in the evolution of earth's biodiversity. However, it is not self-evident that either the fact or the results of evolutionary creativity can be explained exhaustively by appealing to such a nebulous idea as natural selection in the totalizing metaphysical way that biologists often do. For alongside of natural selection, whose relentless workings we do not deny, there may be other creative, and less easily specifiable, factors involved in bringing about just *this* particular world.[15]

Evolution is a highly unpredictable process, and the notion of natural selection merely implies that the best engineered organisms will be the ones to survive. But the standard theory of evolution seems powerless to explain either why matter tends to be self-engineering in the first place or why evolution has moved in the direction of self-conscious beings like ourselves. For the very same theory allows just as readily that life could have come to an evolutionary dead-end in organisms devoid of mind or the capacity for language and love. For such organisms would have been no less "adaptive" than human beings are.

Evolutionists always reply to this that if there are millions and even billions of years involved in evolution, a lot of crazy things can happen—including the emergence of humans—simply as the result of the selection and reproduction of minuscule random genetic changes that turn out to be suited to their environments. However, to make immense spans of time the magician that turns mud into minds, a ploy to which Dawkins resorts, still begs some important questions. Philosophically speaking, new increments of time, no matter how many more you add, cannot constitute the causally creative agency needed to transform dead matter into life and consciousness. Time was needed of course, but the fact and enormity of time are themselves the consequence of a more primordial cosmic creativity, one that cannot be accounted for by the biological notion of natural selection.

We need to remember here that the fact of time, as Einstein discovered, is itself intimately interwoven with the very nature of matter itself. So we cannot talk about time today, including the enormous amounts of it that evolution requires, without bringing the whole physical cosmos into the picture. And we are learning from astrophysics and cosmology today—in an entirely fresh and unprecedented way—how inseparable the evolution of life is from the physical universe as a whole. Any adequate explanation of life's evolution, therefore, cannot arbitrarily bracket out considerations about the nature of the *cosmic totality*. We stress this point because it is especially to the cosmic totality, and not to any specific "gaps" in nature's unfolding, that we wish to relate our understanding of God's influence on the world.

As we are now learning from astrophysics, the material universe must *always* have had a very specifically defined predisposition to evolve into life and mind, long before biotic evolution ever began to occur. In fact scientists today are learning that only a very narrow range of physical properties could ever have permitted the origin and evolution of carbon-based life. And it is not natural selection that accounts for this already existing disposition of matter toward becoming alive and creative. Billions of years before the arrival of life physical reality *already* had a puzzling propensity toward becoming alive and conscious. The creativity of biological evolution, therefore, simply taps into a cosmic stream of creativity whose origins we can now trace back to a time billions of years before the arrival of life.

The real issue then is not why natural selection is so creative, but why the universe *as a whole* tends to sponsor the drama of biological evolution on our planet, and quite possibly elsewhere, at all. It is not inconceivable that if we press this question far enough it may open itself to theological comment, one that in no way supplants efforts to understand the process in a scientifically specific manner as well. As Chapters 5 and 6 will explain in more detail, recent astrophysics demonstrates that the *primary* impetus to biological creativity goes back much, much deeper into the remote cosmic past, and into the very nature of matter itself, than most evolutionary biologists have cared to look until very recently. We doubt that even the metaphysical sense given to the idea of natural selection by materialist biologists can shed any light on this cosmic background.

Moreover, as we shall see again in Chapter 7, according to the new sciences of chaos and complexity the universe already possessed an inherent tendency toward emergent complexity and self-organization long before the first living organisms appeared. This pervasively creative inclination of lifeless matter itself cannot simply be ignored when we attempt to explain why evolution has been so inventive as to produce living and conscious beings.

The epic of biotic evolution, as even materialists must now admit, is inseparable from conditions that occurred in the earliest phases of the cosmic story. However, skeptics usually wield the ideas of evolution and natural selection almost as though the story of life had no deep roots in a more primordial cosmic impulse toward creative adventuring. For most of the past century they have talked about matter as though it were inherently inimical to life, and as though real creativity entered the cosmos only with the arrival of biological evolution. But meanwhile astrophysics has forced us to look at matter and life in a new way. We shall fill in the picture more fully in subsequent chapters, but we must state here that what really begs for an explanation today is not so much why life appeared and evolved, but why the *cosmos as a whole* has *always* had a habit of seeking out novel forms of order. The adventurous leaning of matter toward experimenting with novelty is a feature that life did not invent but merely jumped astride. So what we now need to understand is why the universe itself is so fundamentally intolerant of monotony, and why it has been so, by all recent cosmological accounts, from its very earliest moments. We suspect that theology may not be irrelevant in the quest for this kind of understanding.

Materialist evolutionism, in spite of claims by the likes of Dawkins and Gould, cannot shed any light on the *total* movement of cosmic matter toward increasingly more complex forms of order. Our awareness of the emergent quality of evolution is in no sense the projection of a culturally narrow human desire for progress onto an indifferent universe, as Gould constantly asserts. Rather, Gould's own portrait of an indifferent universe stems from his projecting onto its (imagined) totality his vivid impressions of the indifference he finds in the law of natural selection that sticks out in the relatively short, biotic segment of natural history.

To summarize, then, whether the process of converting hydrogen atoms into brains takes one minute or fifteen billion years, we cannot rule out the possibility that there is something more fundamental about the universe—other than long periods of time and random changes worked over by natural selection—that may be silently, pervasively, and unobtrusively operative in promoting the over-all cosmic movement from simplicity to complexity. It is increasingly clear from science that evolutionary selection joins up with and fosters, but in no way initiates, the cosmic creativity upon which it feeds. Hence it is still an open question as to why the *universe* so generously strives toward creative novelty at all.

Moreover, as we mentioned earlier, the featureless notion of natural selection is likewise too feathery to elucidate any *specific* trajectory that evolution in fact takes. For this reason we propose that the evolutionary process, at the same time at which it adheres to the constraints of what scientists vaguely call natural selection, may very well also be the expression of a divine creativity manifesting itself in a manner that allows for endless diversity and particularity. Evolutionary biology, paleontology, and natural history can help us understand many details of the process, but religion and theology can—without intruding upon the work of evolutionary biology—simultaneously point us to an extravagant Generosity that underlies the whole cosmic process. Thus, there is no good reason for separating religious faith from evolutionary science. The two fit together quite naturally.

In fact, the idea of evolutionary selection, blank as it may be in some respects, may ironically help to elucidate the relationship of science and religion. Evolution, after all, is said to be the story of things struggling to adapt to their environments. Some attempts at adaptation work while others don't. But both science and religion are part of evolution: whatever else they may be, they are among the many ways we humans have hit upon to adapt ourselves to the universe. Consistent with evolutionary principles, we should expect that some of these attempts at adaptation will be successful, and others will lose out in the struggle for survival. We may understand the whole history of science, for example, as a struggle on the part of human intelligence to correspond to its natural environment. Scientists attempt such adaptation by way of experimenting with various "hypotheses," and when these hypotheses fail to conform to the real world, scientists throw them away. Only those scientific ideas which more or less "fit" the natural world can survive.

We may also look at the history of religion as a prolonged series of endeavors on the part of humans to adapt to their environment. However, the environment of religion includes not just nature but also the infinitely creative mystery that religious experience intuits beneath and beyond nature. Religion tries to adapt us to this divine mystery through symbolic, mythic, and credal constructs. But because the mystery is infinitely elusive, and forever evades complete comprehension, our religious symbols, myths, and doctrines will never quite "fit" the ultimate ground of cosmic creativity. Thus, in their attempts to bring our lives into closer conformity with the sacred mystery that grounds the universe, religions themselves will inevitably undergo a tumultuous struggle, and at times even competition, in their long quest to attune us to the true depth of things.

Such a specter, of course, makes the skeptic wonder whether there can be anything to religion—if throughout its history it has undergone so much agitation. If there is any substance to religion, why should it be so messy and so given to instability? But the evolutionary notions of adaptation and selection, in spite of their unspecificity, may give us a helpful new model for understanding the birth and deaths of gods as well as the rise and fall of religions.

Theologian Gerd Theissen speculates that there may well be some "underlying reality" that sifts, sorts, and "judges" our religious hypotheses, separating the fit from the "unfit." We might take "God" as the name for this underlying reality. And as we reflect on the history of religion we cannot but notice that only a few of its constructs ever survive their encounter with this great mystery. The hypothesis of "God" is a plausible explanation, therefore, for the disturbing history of the birth and deaths of "gods."[16]

In summary, the idea of God, taken in consort with (and not as an alternative to) evolutionary theory, can help us account for the increasing complexity and consciousness that evolution has brought about not only in life, but in culture and religion as well. We are suggesting that the idea of a transcendent divine mystery explains not only the fact that the universe has order to it, but also that it has a penchant for novelty and creativity such as we see in evolution.

We understand divine creativity in terms of God's inviting (not forcing) the cosmos to express itself in increasingly more diverse ways. We think of God as the ultimate source not only of the order in the world, but also of the troubling novelty and diversity that always somehow disrupt the status quo. As novelty comes into the world, after all, the present order has to give way. And what we confusedly refer to as "chance," instead of being a "cause" of evolution, may be understood as the *consequence* of a breakdown in present forms of order as novelty enters in.

The ultimate or remote origin of this novelty is one of the things we mean by God. "God's will," in this account, is to maximize evolutionary novelty and diversity. The divine vision of a new creation is gently presented to the cosmos across all of time and space. And since the introduction of novelty and diversity is what makes this into a world of beauty, we may say that the God of evolution is a God who wants nothing less than the ongoing enhancement of cosmic beauty. Thus an evolutionary picture of the cosmos, with all its serendipitous wanderings, corresponds quite well with the biblical understand of an adventurous and loving God as the One "who makes all things new."[17]

However, God's role in evolution is not only that of being the stimulus that stirs the cosmos toward deeper novelty and beauty. Our religious faith tells us that the same God who creates the universe also promises to save it from all its travail, suffering, and death. This would mean then that the whole story of cosmic evolution, in all its detail and incredible breadth, is permanently taken into God's loving memory. The suffering of the innocent and the weak, highlighted so clearly by the evolutionary portrait of life, becomes inseparable from the divine eternity. Our theology cannot tolerate a deity who merely creates and then abandons the world. For us the same God who invites the world to evolve is also intimately *involved* in the evolutionary process. God struggles along with all beings, participating in both their pain and enjoyment, ultimately redeeming the world by an infinite compassion—so that in the end nothing is ever completely forgotten or lost.[18]

This is only a brief sampling of how its encounter with evolutionary science is transforming contemporary theology. Many varieties of evolutionary theology exist today, and we have presented only a small piece of the rethinking going on in theology after Darwin. It is regrettable that so much contemporary religious thought gets hung up in creationism or contrast. For although evolutionary theology is inevitably in need of constant revision—and we do not wish to enshrine for all time any particular version of it—we consider evolution to be, at least provisionally, a most appropriate and fruitful scientific framework within which to think about God today.

IV. Confirmation

We fully endorse the attempts to construct an evolutionary theology. However, we would go even further in establishing the close connection between theism and evolution. Our view is that religious ideas provide much of the soil in which Darwinian ideas have taken root in the first place. There are a number of recent studies that demonstrate theism's fundamental "confirmation" of evolutionary thinking, and we cannot discuss them all here.[19] But one point we should make is that evolutionary theory could hardly have blossomed outside of a cultural context shaped by the biblical understanding of God with its correlative picture of the nature of time.

The Bible understands time in terms of God's bringing about a new and surprising future. When through biblical faith we became aware of a *promise* offered to us by a God who appears out of the future, we began to experience time in a new way. As the promised new creation beckoned us, we no longer felt the compulsion to return to a golden age in the past. Time became directional and irreversible at a very deep level of our awareness. And even when the idea of God dropped out of the intellectual picture of the cosmos in the modern period, the feeling of time as directional and irreversible remained deeply lodged in our sensibilities, including that of secular scientists. It is the originally biblical perception of temporality that made it possible for western science to embrace an evolutionary picture of the universe.

In contrast to this linear-historical outlook, most non-biblical religions and cultures have understood time as a repeating circle. Time's destiny, in both primal and Eastern religious traditions, is not something radically new, but instead a return to the purity and simplicity of cosmic origins. The Bible's emphasis on God as the source of a radically new future, on the other hand, breaks open the ancient cycle of time. It calls the whole cosmos, through the mediation of human hope, to look forward in a more linear way for the coming of God's kingdom, either in the indefinite future or at the end of time.

Only on the template of this stretched out view of irreversible continuance could evolutionary ideas have ever taken hold. Even though evolution does not have to imply a vulgar notion of "progress," it still requires an eschatological, future-oriented understanding of time as its matrix. This view of time, we would like to emphasize here, originally came out of a *religious* experience of reality as promise.

However, there is an even deeper way in which faith in God nourishes the idea of evolution. The central idea of theistic religion, as Karl Rahner (among others) has clarified, is that the Infinite pours itself out in love to the finite universe. This is the fundamental meaning of "revelation." But if we think carefully about this central religious teaching, it should lead us to conclude that any universe related to the inexhaustible self-giving love of God must be an evolving one. For if God is infinite love giving itself to the cosmos, then the finite world cannot possibly receive this limitless, gracious abundance in any single instant. In response to the outpouring of God's boundless love the universe would be invited to undergo a process of self-transformation. In order to "adapt" to the divine infinity, the finite cosmos would likely have to intensify, in a continuously more expansive way, its own capacity to receive such an overflowing love. In other words, it might endure what we know scientifically as an arduous and dramatic evolution toward increasing complexity, life, and consciousness. In the final analysis, it is as a consequence of the infusion of God's self-giving love that the universe is excited onto a path of self-transcendence, that is to say, evolution.[20]

Viewed in this light, the evolution of the cosmos is more than just compatible with theism, as the contrast position argues, or "consonant" with it, as the contact approach might say. Rather, it would not be too much to say that faith in a God of self-giving love actually anticipates an evolving universe. It would be very difficult for us to reconcile the religious teaching about God's infinite self-giving love with any other kind of cosmos.

4

Is Life Reducible to Chemistry?

In his latest book, Francis Crick, who with James Watson discovered the double helix formation of DNA, presents us with what he calls his "Astonishing Hypothesis":

> The Astonishing Hypothesis is that "You," your joys and your sorrows, your memories and your ambitions, your sense of identity and free will, are in fact no more than the behavior of a vast assembly of nerve cells and their associated molecules. As Lewis Carroll's Alice might have phrased it: "You're nothing but a pack of neurons." This hypothesis is so alien to the ideas of most people alive today that it can truly be called astonishing.[1]

The ideas of most people, Crick goes on to say, have unfortunately been shaped by the pre-scientific illusions of religion, with its naive belief in a distinct human soul and the mysterious sacredness of life. "Only scientific certainty (with all its limitations)," he concludes, "can in the long run rid us of the superstitions of our ancestors."[2]

Traditional religion, as Crick is well aware, pictures the universe as a hierarchy of distinct levels of being, each graded according to its degree of importance relative to God. Matter, for example, is generally the lowest level and the least important. Plants, since they are alive, are considered more significant than mere matter, animals more valuable than plants, and humans more so than animals. Then at the highest level of the hierarchy traditional religious instruction typically locates divine reality.

As we move up this hierarchy each level is said to exhibit features that are lacking in those beneath it. We sense an "ontological discontinuity" when we pass from one level to the next. Life, mind and divinity cannot be understood in terms of the rungs beneath them. The higher can "comprehend" the lower, but the lower cannot comprehend the higher.[3]

So how would those who embrace this traditional hierarchical scheme defend themselves against Crick's "astonishing hypothesis" with its denial of the existence of the soul, of any special status to life, and ultimately of the reality of God? Undoubtedly they would reply that if God and the soul exist we should not expect to grasp their reality by the same cognitional methods we use in our knowledge of the lower levels. For whenever we attempt to understand any higher level solely in terms of the levels beneath it, something will inevitably be lost in the translation.[4] Those sciences that teach us something about matter, the ancient wisdom contends, cannot even explain the unique nature of our own being, let alone that of God. Disciplines that might be equal to the task of grasping the lower levels in the hierarchy are by no means qualified to comprehend the higher.

Today, however, scientists are challenging the ancient hierarchical view of the universe. Crick maintains, for example, that the "majority" of neuroscientists "believe that the idea of the soul is a myth,"[5] and presumably they extend the same appraisal to the religious idea of God. Scientific skeptics reject the classical hierarchy because it seems too "mystical." For them it places arbitrary limits on what science can discover or explain on its own. Even though some version of the hierarchical vision has shaped the consciousness of most people on our planet for thousands of years, it now seems hopelessly out of date.

Many scientists today, after all, are confident that they can explain not only life, but also human consciousness in terms of chemistry and other "lower level" sciences. Some of them even question whether we can any longer think of life and mind as more "real" than matter. It seems more likely that the "higher levels" referred to in the traditional hierarchical cosmologies are just epiphenomenal offshoots, frothy derivatives, of a purely material substrate. It is only the physical level that has any real substance to it.

This way of thinking is usually called "reductionism." Reductionism implies that any apparently "higher" levels, such as life, mind, and even religious ideas of "God," can all be fully explained in terms of the "lower level" sciences of chemistry and physics.[6] It will be useful for us, however, to distinguish here between "methodological reduction" and "metaphysical reduction*ism*."[7] The former is simply an illuminating scientific method of breaking things down analytically in order to understand them at the level of their constituent parts. It makes no claims that chemical or physical analysis will bring us closer to the fundamental "reality" of things. It is content simply to investigate the particulars of phenomena without necessarily embracing the belief that scientific analysis can lead us to a *complete* understanding of them.

Metaphysical reductionism, on the other hand, avers that scientific analysis is the *only* way to grasp what things really are. It insists that knowledge of the molecular make-up and activity of living cells, or neurophysiological comprehension of the human brain, is all we need to understand what life or mind really is. In Crick's terms, there is no need for any other kind of explanation than that provided by pure science since there is no other kind of reality than the purely physical. Thus metaphysical reductionism goes hand in hand with what we have been calling scientific materialism. In this chapter the term "reductionism" will be used in its metaphysically materialist sense.

Even though science is moving away from the crude "brickyard" materialism of classical physics, and is beginning to acknowledge matter's amazingly subtle self-organizing tendencies, numerous scientific thinkers still remain thoroughly materialistic and reductionistic in their understanding of life, mind, and cosmic evolution. We need, therefore, to highlight the phenomenon of reductionism in this chapter because, as Crick's book clearly illustrates, it raises serious questions about the validity of religion.

Religion, we must remember, has traditionally claimed that the levels of the cosmic hierarchy become more "real" as we move from bottom to top. The more elusive and mysterious things are, the more important and real they are. Reductionism, on the other hand, implies that the only *real* "stuff" lies at the bottom, at the level of mere matter, fully accessible to scientific conquest. Therefore, isn't Crick correct in thinking of life, mind, the self, spirit, soul, and even deity, as nothing more than fictions?

Here is how our four approaches might respond to this very important question.

I. Conflict

We fully support the reductionist ideal of explaining everything, including life and mind, in terms of chemistry (which in turn is reducible to physics). Science works on the assumption that any reality we encounter, no matter how mysterious it initially appears to be, can eventually be broken down into constituent components and processes that can be completely explained in terms of the more basic sciences. Any opposition to this assumption will only arrest the growth of science. If we leave even the slightest opening for some sort of non-physical "explanation," we fail in our vocation as scientists. As Crick emphasizes, reductionism is "largely responsible for the spectacular developments of modern science."[8] Our job then is to do all we can to explain things naturalistically, that is, without resorting to mysticism.

This means that no territory is off limits to scientific probing. We can competently provide a purely materialist explanation not only of life and mind, but also of ethics and religion. Our objective, in other words, is to "demystify" the universe. We count any recourse to the idea of God to be especially at odds with the advance of human knowledge. And so, regrettably, we are forced once again to conclude that religion conflicts with science.

It is not as though we have no respectable support in the history of human thought for our agenda. Our reductionist program was set forth centuries ago in the materialist atomism of Democritus. This ancient Greek philosopher's declaration that "atoms and the void" are all there is to reality still strikes many of us as powerfully explanatory. Its simplicity and elegance seem so utterly "right" that we find it irresistible; and so we seek to explain all things in terms of their "atomic" makeup, that is, in terms of some lowest common unit of matter. If we can comprehend all life in terms of molecular activity alone, or if we attempt with Crick to explain consciousness in terms of neurons and their interactions alone, what reason would there be to look for supernatural explanations?

Today, of course, we allow that matter is much more subtle than ancient atomism supposed, but we still think that materialist reductionism is the only legitimate approach for a good scientist to take. Likewise, we admit that there is a certain hierarchical character to the arrangement of things in the material universe, but we cannot accept the idea that there are special principles at work in the higher levels that we cannot understand in terms of the atomic components and the purely physical interactions operative at the lower levels.

The push toward reductionism in science also gathered momentum from the classical physics of Galileo, Descartes, and Newton. Science really didn't even get off the ground until these giants began to expel all occult "forces" from the material cosmos and certified that utterly impersonal physical laws are all we need in order to understand our vast and complex universe.[9] Then in the nineteenth century, physicists formulated the laws of thermodynamics having to do with the transformation and conservation of energy; and these laws can now account for everything that happens in nature, including the evolution of life and mind. It is true that the well-known second law of thermodynamics implies that the universe is running down, drifting irreversibly from order to disorder until eventually all life and consciousness will be wiped out. And so for a while some scientists thought that the existence of life contradicted the second law, and therefore implied something miraculously contrary to nature. But we now know that life is simply an expression, and not a violation, of the second law.[10] For every movement in evolution toward more complex forms of life there is a total net loss of "order" (that is, of the energy available to complexify matter) in the cosmos as a whole. The laws of physics and chemistry remain inviolable, and they are sufficient to explain the existence of living beings as well as the "soul" of humans.

Also in the nineteenth century our reductionist approach gained perhaps its most important victory through the arrival of Darwin's evolutionary theory. Presenting us with the picture of the gradual rise of life and consciousness out of mindless matter, his theory implied that living and thinking beings lie on an unbroken continuum with inanimate reality. There are no sharp breaks in the evolutionary process. So there is really nothing mysterious about life and mind at all, since they can be reduced to and explained adequately in terms of the constant reshuffling of inert matter over long periods of time.

Then the complete reducibility of life to material processes was established conclusively in the present century when biology began to absorb the methods of chemistry. Biochemical analysis of the living cell has revealed that the apparent "secret" of life lies in the activity of large molecules of nucleic and amino acids, which are themselves nothing more than chains of lifeless atoms. There is no longer any "secret" here to which theology can appeal in order to make the case for special divine intervention in the creation and evolution of life.

Within any living cell there are enormously complex molecules, the most impressive of which is DNA, the informational code determining the shape and behavior of all organisms. Yet, when all is said and done, DNA is really nothing more than a concatenation of a few ordinary chemical elements completely subject to physical laws. Thus biology is reducible to chemistry. A truly scientific study of life is nothing more than the special application of principles of chemistry to the field of matter that we recognize as living tissue.

Francis Crick, in his earlier book *Of Molecules and Men*, justifiably announced that "...the ultimate aim of the modern movement in biology is to explain all of life in terms of chemistry and physics."[11] This is an honest and clear formulation of the reductionist agenda. Science cannot help but be impressed by the fact that a simple sequence of molecules in the DNA chain determines, when translated, the character of the resultant organism. Life clearly has a chemical basis and can best be understood in terms of chemistry.

But what about human consciousness? Is that most subtle of natural phenomena also explainable in purely scientific terms? We believe it is. Even though we have a long way to go in achieving complete comprehension, we are heartened by the considerable progress we have already made in analyzing the "molecules of the mind."[12] Mind is nothing more than an expression of the brain, and brain is, to put it indelicately, essentially a piece of meat, though an enormously complex one. It is made up of molecules and atoms elaborately patterned into various kinds of tissue, but still utterly material. One of the reasons we think of mind as reducible to matter is that the introduction of certain chemical substances into our bodies can alter the way we feel and think. Hence, as in the case of life, mind must also have a purely chemical basis.

Here is how Daniel Dennett, who proudly calls himself a materialist, puts it in his widely acclaimed book, *Consciousness Explained*:

> ...there is only one sort of stuff, namely matter—the physical stuff of physics, chemistry, and physiology—and the mind is somehow nothing but a physical phenomenon. In short, the mind is the brain. According to the materialists we can (in principle!) account for every mental phenomenon using the same physical principles, laws and raw materials that suffice to explain radioactivity, continental drift, photosynthesis, reproduction, nutrition and growth.[13]

Recently, a few self-styled reductionists, notably E. O. Wilson and his followers, have argued that not only individual human consciousness, but also human culture as a whole, can be explained materialistically. Wilson claims that in the final analysis it is our genes that make us behave the way we do socially. Genetic features may not be completely determinative of behavior, but in some way our genes do hold our social life and all of human culture on a leash.[14] And since the

nevertheless allots a clear and distinct place to the sciences on the one hand and religion on the other, keeping them in sharply defined channels that prevent any mix-up. For example, the proper field for chemistry and physics is the level of matter (**m**). Biological sciences like botany can direct their attention to the province of plant life (**m + x**), and zoology to animal life (**m + x + y**). And the human sciences and humanities may open us up to the specific features of human existence (**m + x + y + z**). Viewed in this way, the upper-level studies are not reducible to chemistry and physics, since something new is added at each level. Each higher level has properties incapable of being grasped by the scientific tools proportionate to the lower levels, but it may still be open to non-scientific forms of knowing. Finally, theology is distinct from all the other sciences since its specific focus is on the most comprehensive level of all, that of divine reality.

This model, sketchy though it is, is a bulwark against all attempts at conflation. It allows us to contrast science with theology in such a way that the two can coexist without having to contradict each other. Theology's business is not to set forth the chemistry of matter, or to do the work of the other sciences. And it is not the role of the other sciences to pontificate on the ultimate nature of things (as in fact metaphysical reductionism does). The hierarchical structure keeps all the disciplines in their proper places, and thus guarantees that there will be no opposition between science and theology.

It is in terms of this set-up that the great centers of learning in the world were originally organized. However, reductionism now flattens the hierarchy down to the bottom level. In doing so it not only destroys the only framework in which a genuinely broad education can take place, but it also opens the floodgates to the sort of conflation that leads to conflict between science and religion. Its insistence that all reality exists only at the lowest, material level is an attempt to have science usurp the tasks of philosophy or theology by making declarations about the ultimate nature of reality. Reductionism, we repeat, is not science at all, but an ideological faith, the product of an unseemly marriage of science with a most unscientific kind of dogmatism. If it gets its way, eventually the only legitimate departments in our universities will be those of chemistry and physics.

Why, though, do so many scientific thinkers capitulate to this doctrinaire reductionism? Why, in other words, is it so easy for skeptics to conflate science with such a constricting kind of belief? It is difficult to answer this question in any particular case, but one hypothesis worth examining is that the main appeal of reductionism lies in its giving to its devotees an exhilarating sense of power over nature. While scientific reduction is an appropriate way to learn about some aspects of nature, metaphysical reductionism is a belief system quietly in the service, not of truth, but of our human will to *control* reality. Humans, as our religions realistically note, have always had a dubious and usually deadening inclination to subject the totality of reality to their own mastery, whether political, economic, military, or intellectual; and today the apparent sense of intellectual dominion that science gives us is almost too much to resist.

Reductionism's fundamental—and completely gratuitous—assumption is that the scientific mind holds an especially privileged position, one of final cognitional supremacy over the rest of the world. Reductionism is the expression of a blind faith in the capacity of the human mind to encompass the totality of being by way of scientific method. The prospect that the human mind might encounter a dimension of reality (e. g. life, the soul, God) that cannot in principle be fully grasped by science is a threat to the reductionist hunger for absolute intellectual rule. Reductionists would sooner deny that a mystical or transcendent dimension exists than surrender in humility to the possibility that science may not be as all-comprehending as they "believe" it to be.

Our contrast approach, on the other hand, allows that *genuine* science comes not from the will to power, but from an unassuming desire to learn something about the universe. Reductionism is a dogma rooted in the will to power, whereas science itself is born in the humble longing simply to understand. Therefore, science's quite innocent method of looking into things to find out their chemical structure is not an act of violence, as some science-haters claim. Probing into the makeup of things such as cells and brains, which is what Crick does best, is entirely appropriate to science as such. What is violent and objectionable, however, is the subtle transformation of the innocuous method of scientific reduction into a program of reductionistic control, one that heartlessly consigns the noblest thoughts of all previous generations of our ancestors to the category of "superstition."[19] The shift from purely chemical analysis to a proclamation that such analysis provides us with a *comprehensive* picture of things is seductively subtle, but altogether unwarranted. Such a totalizing jump takes us out of the field of science and into the arms of an utterly arbitrary faith-system based on questionable—and ironically irrational—human impulses.

Say what you will about the quaintness of our hierarchical scheme, at least it allows science to remain science. Since it requires the modesty to admit that the reductive method of science can tell us only a little bit, and certainly not everything, about the depth and mystery of the real world, it restrains our inclination to hand science over to destructive human tendencies. We agree here with Viktor Frankl when he says that the true problem of our time is not that scientists are specializing, but that too many of these specialists are generalizing.[20]

The "hierarchical principle" embedded in the religious wisdom of countless human generations teaches us that a higher level can comprehend a lower but that the lower cannot comprehend the higher. This means that if there is in fact a spiritual quality attached to life and human existence, or a divine "level" that enshrouds the natural world, it would be more encompassing than the human mind; and so the human mind, no matter how scientifically informed, could not begin to comprehend it or perhaps even be aware of it. The human mind can grasp aspects of what lies beneath it in the hierarchy, and it is the function of science to help us in this effort. But if there is indeed an all-encompassing divine mystery, it would comprehend us without our being able to comprehend it. By definition it would be off limits to scientific verification. Indeed, if science could grasp it, it would no longer be the infinite God in whom we believe, but merely something trivially finite, subject to the poverty of our own limited cognitional dominion.

So science will never be able to settle the question of the reality of the mystical, or the sacredness of life, or the existence of the soul. It is not science's business to do so. Reductionism, however, claims that it is, and by usurping the role of dogmatics, it demands that the "mystical" element, if it is really there, should show up at the lowest level, that of matter. But since the mystical never does show up there, *it must not exist*!

As far as our theology is concerned, however, the divine mystery is the ground and encompassing horizon of nature, not an object that falls within it. It is that which holds the universe in being, not something that could be observed as though it were a mere addendum to the list of finite things that science can comprehend. And we become sensitized to its reality not by trying to master it, or by squeezing it into the lowest level of the hierarchy, but by surrendering ourselves to it in the act of religious worship.

And it is especially in worship that we experience the reality of "soul" as well. The being of God can never be consciously experienced apart from the soul's humble submission in prayer, nor can we come to know what "soul" means apart from a direct awareness of our inherent connection with the eternal. The methods of science do not provide adequate tools for deciding about the existence of a divine presence in the universe or of a soul capable of intuiting that presence. A more direct kind of experience—that of religious faith—is required.

Furthermore, obtaining a clear grasp of the divine presence is neither a possible nor a desirable goal of human understanding. The more comprehensive any level of reality is, the less easily can it be subjected to the authority of the human mind without undergoing a diminishment in the process. Thus, in our hierarchical view the fact that we cannot clarify the divine reality—and must therefore resort to the "vagueness" of symbolic and mythic expression when we speak of it—is completely consistent with the existence of a transcendent and all-encompassing God. If we were to comprehend God, then "God" would no longer be God.

How difficult it is for us to gain a firm hold even of our own mentality, let alone of any conceivable divine reality. For in any effort to grasp our own mind the same mind is trying to do the grasping. But the mind-as-grasping can never slip over into the realm of the mind-as-grasped without losing most of its real substance in the process. Hence the mind always eludes complete objectification by the same mind. This elusiveness, as St. Augustine pointed out centuries ago, provides us with a clue as to why divinity, which is more intimate to us even than our own minds and selves, would also escape any of our attempts to grasp hold of it objectively.

Just as we consider Dennett's project of completely "explaining" mind to be logically impossible, so also we consider all objectifying discourse, such as science employs, to be out of place in religion and theology. For if we cannot even comprehend our own minds objectively, then how could we ever comprehend anything higher than human consciousness in the hierarchy of being? Occupying the highest level of all, God simply cannot fall under the jurisdiction of human knowing. God comprehends us, but we cannot expect to comprehend God.

Since we accept the tenets of faith, however, we believe that God has revealed something of the divine reality to us. Religion even allows that God is humble enough to relate to us on our own level. But it also rejoices that, at the same time, God remains an endless mystery and is not so trivial a reality as to fall under the complete command of our intellectual powers. Our religious sense of an infinite world opening up beyond us fills us with an exhilarating conviction that reality is not a closed box. We rejoice that it remains forever open-ended, and that above us or ahead of us there is always a fresh and unlimited horizon of inexhaustible mystery. Part of what we mean by the human "soul" is our intrinsic openness to this infinity.

In summary, the world of reductionism is too suffocating for us. A world in which our own feeble (scientific) minds are made the upper limit to everything is terrifyingly small. We believe that very little of the totality of things can ever fall beneath our cognitional sovereignty. But the reductionist belief system *demands*, in an utterly arbitrary fashion, that there shall be no aspects of reality that remain off limits to human scientific conquest. We consider this postulate too heavy a burden for us humans to bear. We prefer to be much more moderate in our expectations of what scientific efforts can accomplish. We do not forcefully and arbitrarily insist that reality subject itself completely to scientific reduction. We can accept a certain amount of scientific analysis as one limited way of learning a little bit about the universe. But we consider it both irrational and idolatrous to embrace the creed of reductionism. We need other ways of knowing, in addition to and complementary to science, if we want to get in touch with the real substance and depth of things. The most important of these alternative ways of knowing is religion.

III. Contact

Although the contrast position makes some necessary clarifications, we would allow for a less polemical and more dialogical relationship between religion and the scientific method of reduction. We agree that metaphysical reductionism is a belief system and not a necessary accompaniment to science. Science and reductionism are clearly distinguishable. And yet, we need to think more carefully about the theological implications of the remarkable discoveries made by scientific analysis (methodological reduction) in this age of molecular biology and neuroscience. We are convinced that theology can profit from deeper contact with the new developments in these sciences.

In addition, we have to point out at the very beginning of our presentation that reductionist scientists are not the only ones to question the traditional hierarchical model. Today even some theologians reject it, though for entirely different reasons. The traditional hierarchical way of organizing our understanding of reality seems, at least to some of us, to be a rationalization of the political and male-gender domination that is characteristic of patriarchal cultures. Hierarchical thinking stems from traditions in which males have oppressed women and subjected nature (often simplistically depicted as feminine) to the control of the allegedly "masculine" principle, mind. Ironically, however, metaphysical reductionism, with its implicit will to control reality by way of scientific analysis, is itself a secularized version of the old patriarchal religious view of the universe.

Nevertheless, the hierarchical model does express the important truth that some dimensions of reality are more comprehensive than others. Life is obviously more valuable than dead matter, human consciousness more inherently important than plant life or animal sentience, and God the most significant reality of all. So even though we may wish to dissolve the unyielding verticality of the ancient hierarchies, theology still needs to think in terms of relative grades of importance among reality's various dimensions. Without some, perhaps chastened, sense of hierarchy we would fall into the chaos of relativism. A hierarchy of values, though, does not require a rigidly tiered cosmos. Perhaps the image of concentric circles in which the outer are more encompassing than the inner, or the picture of systems cradling subsystems, is more suitable than the traditional portrait of levels stacked on top of one another.

The term "hierarchy," then, may have some disagreeable connotations, but its intuition that some things are not reducible to others remains a necessary part of the religious, and for that matter any genuinely ethical, perspective. But is it compatible with the recent discoveries of molecular biology and brain science?

Before responding to this question we wish to emphasize that we can fully embrace everything that molecular biology is now telling us about the chemical basis of life, and all that neuroscience is teaching us about the physiology of the mind. Likewise, we are open to the possibility that the sciences associated with "artificial intelligence" can enhance our understanding of some operations of the mind. We consider this new knowledge to be very important. Not only are we not threatened by it; we also think that our theology can be considerably improved by making contact with it.

Scientist and philosopher Michael Polanyi shows us at least one way to bring the findings of the reductive sciences into conversation with a religious interpretation of the cosmos. Born in Hungary in 1891, Polanyi achieved world-wide renown as a chemist at the Kaiser Wilhelm Institute in Berlin. He was forced by Nazism to emigrate, and so he moved to the University of Manchester in England where he eventually became Professor of Social Studies. There he started to think more rigorously about the reductionist program of explaining life and mind completely in terms of the principles of chemistry and physics. While he did not object to methodological reduction, he argued that metaphysical reductionism was not only culturally and ethically debilitating, but also logically mistaken. If biology were reducible without remainder to physics and chemistry, he thought, then we should go straight to the chemist and the physicist to understand life. Obviously, though, we don't; we go first to the biologist. But why?

The answer seems to be that the biologist is *tacitly* dealing with a dimension of reality that is not completely accessible to chemistry and physics, strictly speaking. This dimension comes into the biologist's consciousness only by way of a "personal" kind of knowing, one that cannot be reduced to the more impersonal methods of the harder sciences. Life has about it certain irreducible qualities that only *persons* can grasp. Even without resorting to "mysticism" or a dubious vitalism we can agree that there is something about life that slips through the wide meshes of the chemist's net. The full reality of life can be apprehended only by way of a holistic, as distinct from reductive, mode of cognition. The overall patterning of organisms striving to achieve specific goals—a feature that is part of the definition of life—cannot be known simply by looking at their component material parts and interactions. We need a global, personal intuition of living wholes and the way they act.

However, because it is so thoroughly allied with the impersonal methods of scientism, metaphysical reductionism will inevitably dismiss this "personal" knowledge of living wholes as too fuzzy to be taken seriously. Therefore, it is important for us to point out that *even on purely logical grounds* Polanyi has convincingly shown that reductionism is mistaken. Here we shall provide a very brief summary and adaptation of his argument.[21]

Even scientific materialists allow that living beings are "informed" by an overall arrangement of their constituent parts, that is, by a definite patterning that gives them their specific characteristics. This ordering aspect of living beings, Polanyi notes, is most clearly evident at the level of the DNA molecule. All biologists now agree that DNA in the nucleus of living cells is *informational*, that it carries something like a meaning or a message. DNA, from which the genes of living beings are made, is composed of four chemical "letters" (ATCG) arranged in a *specific sequence* in each living being. When translated and replicated, it is this sequence of letters that determines the general kind and shape of life's various organisms and species.

Thus, even though the DNA code is composed of chemical elements, it is the *specific sequence* of chemical "letters" in the code that causes some organisms to be rats, others frogs, and still others human beings, or that makes one individual within a species unique and different from any other. The specific sequence, however, is not something that the science of chemistry can fully clarify. The concrete way in which the bases in DNA line up in any organism somehow "transcends" pure chemistry. Chemical bonding of atoms is necessary for all of this to occur, of course, but the *particular* succession of elements in any given DNA molecule is not solely and simply the result of deterministic chemical processes. For if the specific arrangement of the letters (ATCG) in DNA were the product of chemical necessity alone, there would be only one species of DNA molecule. There would be only one monotonous "message," whereas in fact there is an endless variety.

Indeed, DNA is able to serve as a code informing so many different species of life and distinct individuals only because its specific order in any particular organism involves something "more than" purely chemical or physical necessity. This follows from the fact that in order to function as the conveyor of information, any code must be capable of an indefinite number of configurations unspecifiable by chemistry. If it is to carry information, the elements or "letters" of a code have to allow themselves to be broken down before they can be reconfigured in an informational manner. Figuratively speaking, they must be susceptible to a mixing or randomizing in order to be put back together into an endless, and chemically indeterminate, variety of sequences.

Thus the code that carries the message of life must be *chemically indifferent* to the message it carries. The message "organizes" the chemical components, but the chemistry does not determine the message.[22] What this means is nothing less than that biology is logically not reducible to chemistry. It does not trouble us that we cannot pin down in precise mathematical terms the informationally indeterminate component in living and thinking organisms. Unlike the reductionists we are willing to allow that every actual, concrete sequence of DNA in living beings escapes the complete specification and mastery of chemical analysis. For if we could master the sequence of DNA in terms of chemical laws alone (even though these laws are certainly a factor), that would mean that DNA would no longer function as informational.

With the contrasters we can therefore embrace the idea that the most important and real things about our world are least able to be made subject to scientific control. However, unlike the contrast approach, we would emphasize along with Polanyi that life and mind still physically *indwell and rely upon* chemical laws and processes. We cannot separate life and mind from chemistry in the dualistic way that the traditional hierarchical view seems to allow. We must logically *distinguish* biology from chemistry, but we cannot so casually *separate* life and mind from matter. For we now know that if the chemical processes in a living organism fail to work properly, then life will not "succeed." Or if the neurons in the human brain fail to function reliably and cooperatively, then thought will be impaired or destroyed. Today we are coming to realize how much more dependent life and mind are on their material basis than we had previously thought. While this awareness does not refute the religious vision, as reductionism maintains, it does force us to think about life, mind, and the "soul" in a new way. It is not helpful to keep theology completely sealed off from developments in molecular biology and neuroscience.

Likewise, we can agree with E. O. Wilson that our genes do in a sense hold human culture "on a leash." Our own genetic make-up, for example, places very real constraints on what we are capable of in the areas of language, affectivity, and behavior. The specific way in which DNA is configured in the cells of each one of us does place limits around us. But we do not need to interpret this circumscription in a reductionistic or deterministic way. For the atomic, molecular, cellular, and neuronal levels of our being still *leave themselves open* to being ordered in an indefinite number of ways by the "next level up."

So (if we may be allowed to revert to hierarchical imagery for the moment) we are not rigidly determined "from below." True, each level indwells and relies upon those beneath it, and it has to operate within the constraints that define the lower levels. In fact, the predictable working of the lower levels is a necessary condition for the unpredictable success of the higher. But while the higher levels depend upon the lower, they cannot adequately be understood by an analysis of the lower. There is something "left over," as it were, at each higher level. It is in those regions left unspecified by chemistry that the emergent freedom of life, mind, and soul are given a very real place in our evolving universe. Reductionists, of course, will deny that such "regions" exist. Their fundamentalist faith assumption is that if science can't grasp something, it has no reality. To us, however, the chemically unspecifiable aspects of life, mind, and soul are their very center and substance.

How could this be so? Are we not failing to cooperate with molecular biology and neuroscience if we insist on allowing for dimensions of reality that cannot be chemically specified? In order to respond to this expected question we must use a couple of analogies.

One way to picture the elusive—but nonetheless very real—dimensions "left over" after purely chemical analysis of life or mind, is to think of a game of chess.[23] The game of chess, as everyone who plays it knows, has very strict, inviolable rules. These rules are operative uniformly in every actual game, and every player must scrupulously abide by them. Their "deterministic," unbending presence places strict "constraints" on any particular player's style of playing. And their very inflexibility keeps the player's moves within those boundaries that define the game of chess.

However, inexorable as the rules of chess may be, they are not so unyielding that every game and its every movement are completely determined "from below." If that were the case, every game of chess would be exactly the same as the others. Rather, the rules still leave a generous opening for an indeterminate number of moves. They are not so restrictive that an individual player cannot develop a unique set of strategies or a personal "style" of playing the game within the "space" left undetermined by the rules.

Now just as we cannot reduce any particular game, or any particular player's style, to the abstract rules of chess, so also we cannot exhaustively understand any *particular* instances of life or mind through an articulation of the chemical "rules" underlying them. The laws of chemistry are no less unbending than the rules of chess, but they too leave open an infinite number of ways in which molecular components may be patterned by living and thinking beings. In fact, usually the real focus of our "personal" interest—both in chess and in living organisms—is on the possibilities that are "left over" after acknowledging the shackles embedded in the rules of the game or the laws of science. Moreover, in the same way that a chess player can express gratitude for the constraints that give the game of chess its formal identity, so also we may be grateful for the fixed laws of chemistry that provide realistic outer limits within which life and mind can become actual.

Science has now forced theology to take into account the intimate relationship that exists between life, mind, or soul, on the one hand, and chemical processes on the other. Reductionism may interpret this intimacy as the complete absorption of the "higher" dimensions into the lifeless and mindless realm of purely material processes. But our point is that while the chemical and neuronal levels are necessary conditions for the successful functioning of life and mind, we need not think of them as sufficient. Physical intimacy and indwelling do not necessarily imply simple identity. Something "additional" may be going on at the levels of life and mind, and chemical analysis alone may not be able to say what it is.

To give another analogy, the chemical laws that allow ink to bond with paper must be working successfully if you are to read the thoughts we are putting down here. The communication of our ideas to you relies upon and indwells the chemical determinism utilized by the printing process. If the laws of chemistry fail, then so does the process of our communicating information to you. In that sense, the chemical level is a necessary condition for our passing on these thoughts to you.[24]

But we hope you will agree that there is much more going on here than just chemical bonding of ink with paper. Chemistry may be necessary, but it is not sufficient to explain the meaning inscribed in the sentences on this page. In fact, knowledge of chemistry alone will not help you at all to grasp the informational content. For the really vital fact here is that you are discerning a specific arrangement of a code of letters (the alphabet) by words, of words by sentences, of sentences by paragraphs, and of paragraphs by our more general intentions. There is a complex hierarchy of informational levels here that your knowledge of chemistry cannot by any means completely penetrate.

You could, of course, choose to analyze this page from a purely chemical perspective, and you might find that illuminating. But in so doing you would miss out on all the other levels of meaning embedded in the black markings on this page. Likewise, with the reductionists you might look at living and thinking beings only in terms of their chemical or neuronal activity. This too would certainly be enlightening, but by so restricting your perspective you might also pass over something very important. Indeed you might miss out on most of what is really going on.

Nevertheless, after thus distancing ourselves from reductionism, we are convinced that theology today must take seriously the close connection between chemistry, life, and mind that recent science has uncovered. What can theologians learn from such consideration?

1) In the first place, the reliance of life and mind on chemical and

physical processes provides us with a new lesson in humility. It under-
scores the theme of our human dependency on the rest of nature. This
sense of dependency lies at the heart of any healthy religious outlook,
and it corresponds well with the doctrine of creation. Although, hierar-
chically speaking, life and mind are not reducible to matter, they nevertheless emerge from the chemical realm. They rely on chemical
processes to such an extent that if the requisite chemical bonding
breaks down, life and mind also perish. Science thus serves theology in
the sense that it gives us clearer reasons for modesty and gratitude in
view of our dependency on the physical universe. We will have occasion to note the ecological implications of this confession in the final
chapter.

2) In the second place, as theology adjusts to the fact of life's (and
the soul's) dependency on chemical processes, it may discover a fresh
way of formulating God's relationship to the universe. According to
religious faith, even though God is traditionally the highest "level" of
all, or the widest circle encompassing the smaller universe, God is also
immanent in the universe. Indeed, as theologian Paul Tillich points out,
God could not transcend the world without also residing within it. To
transcend means to "go beyond," and God cannot go beyond the world
without in some way first being in it. But in what sense is God *in* the
world?

Perhaps in a way somewhat analogous to the gentle and unobtrusive
manner in which life embeds itself in matter.

As life emerges in cosmic evolution it does not in any way violate or
separate itself from the laws of physics and chemistry. We do not discover life by looking for molecular activity that would be exceptional
in terms of the expectations of chemistry. (Likewise we do not learn
about a chess master's special genius by looking for transgressions of
the rules of chess, but by appreciating the creative way in which he or
she exploits these rules.) When in the course of the world's evolution
life enters into the cosmic process, it does so in a way that does no violence whatsoever to the laws of physics and chemistry. It does not suddenly interrupt nature and break its rules in the manner of a vitalistic
intrusion.

From the point of view of rudimentary chemical laws alone, in fact,
there is nothing new happening when matter becomes alive. Life insinuates itself into the evolving material world in the form of a very quiet but
amazingly effective informational ordering of matter, rather than in a
way that alters the laws of science. We notice life not by looking at the

chemical particulars of a system, but by (personally) recognizing an *overall configuration* or "gestalt" comprised of complex relations among physical subsystems and their molecular components.

Perhaps the religious sense of any divine presence in the universe would be given to us through a mode of knowing not entirely unlike the one that leads us to recognize and appreciate the existence of life in the material world. We do not come to know life by scrutinizing the specific molecules in a living organism in quest of some strange, extra-physical element. In fact, the deeper we go in analyzing the particular components of a frog or a worm, for example, the more we lose sight of the quality of its ever having been "alive." For we know something is alive only by relating to it as a whole, through a non-analytical—Polanyi calls it simply a "personal"—kind of knowing.

Likewise, we would not discover the presence of God simply by searching among the particulars of cosmic reality for signs of some dramatic interruption of the natural continuum. This is what the reductionists are looking for, of course, and since they don't find it at the level of atoms, molecules, cells or neurons—or of anything else that science can comprehend—they deny that it exists.

In any case, such a find would still be the old god-of-the-gaps which our theological method has consistently rejected. For in order to be fully present to the world God does not require that physical laws be abruptly suspended. Rather, God can gently "inform" the cosmos in a way analogous to life's unobtrusive informing of chemical processes in an organism. But we cannot expect the reductive method of science to lead us to a sense of any such divine presence. If personal knowing is necessary in order for us to recognize life, how much more deeply personal must our knowing be in order to gain a sense of God.

To go even further, just as the introduction of life into cosmic evolution requires that the laws of chemistry are working reliably and cooperatively, so also the manifestation of God's presence in the world may depend upon the appropriate functioning of the less encompassing levels of mind, life, and matter. The contrast approach rightly emphasizes divine transcendence, but in its simplistic, literalist version of the hierarchical model God is too easily situated outside of nature, rather than being deeply immanent within it. Our own theology, on the other hand, allows for the deep incarnation or indwelling of God. And it suggests that God can be intimately related to the world, analogously to the way in which life is related to matter, without ever being noticed by science. Since science ordinarily uses a reductive method that sees reality only in particulars, and not in informational patterns (although as we shall see later this too is just now starting to change), it cannot quite put its finger on those elusive patternings we call life and mind. It is not surprising, then, that it could not acquire a clear sense of the incarnate presence of God either.

3) In the third place, our new appreciation of the dependency of human consciousness on the chemistry of the brain raises a question about life after death. During our presentation, you may have been wondering, for example, about the prospect of personal immortality. If life, mind, and even "soul" are so dependent upon cellular, chemical, and basic physical processes for their actualization, how can they survive death—as religions often believe they do? Don't we have to go back to the contrasters' dualistic point of view to salvage a coherent notion of life beyond the grave?

Any helpful response to this question would require a separate book, and so we do not pretend that we can do justice to it here. In any case, our destiny and that of the entire universe are matters involving trust in the power and fidelity of a promising God. We do not need to have the specific mode of our redemption spelled out for us in every detail. Demanding absolute clarity on any of the most important questions in life would be tantamount to faithlessness. Faith requires that our trust in the renewing power of God's love be unconditional.

Nevertheless, the perspective of promise does encourage us to formulate tentative hypotheses about how science might at least be open in principle to the seemingly impossible eventuality of a revived conscious life occurring on the other side of death. We may find a way to express the consonance of science with the idea of life beyond death by reflecting briefly on the *informational* quality that biologists have discovered in living beings.

Logically speaking, as we argued earlier, we cannot identify a specific sequence of DNA "letters" with the material substrate in which it is embodied. For as even the hardest of reductionists will admit in an age of computers, in some sense the informational aspect "transcends" the matter in which it resides. We know, for example, that during the course of any organism's life, there is a constant exchange of its atomic and molecular content. Each of us, for example, has an almost completely different aggregation of "matter" in our body today from what we had several years ago. And yet, throughout the process of emptying and replenishing of the material "level," the informational component remains relatively the same, constantly undergoing "re-incarnation."

But if this relatively invariant informational pattern can receive multiple successive incarnations in the course of a single person's or organism's life, can we be certain that an analogous kind of restoration would be impossible beyond the apparent finality of death? Of course, for this to happen there would have to exist an eternally sensitive reality with a capacity to "remember" the countless informationally rich patterns that give form to all things. But such a repository is one of the things our faith tradition has always meant by "God."

The Cambridge physicist John Polkinghorne provides one version of this kind of theological reflection:

> My understanding of the soul is that it is the almost infinitely complex, dynamic, information-bearing pattern, carried at any instant by the matter of my animated body and continuously developing throughout all the constituent changes of my bodily make-up during the course of my earthly life. That psychosomatic unity is dissolved at death by the decay of my body, but I believe it is a perfectly coherent hope that the pattern that is me will be remembered by God and its instantiation will be recreated by him when he reconstitutes me in a new environment of his choosing. That will be his eschatological act of resurrection.[25]

But, to go just one step further, why should we suppose that God could "remember" and reconstitute only *human* patterns and not just as readily the informational aspects of other living beings—and indeed the patterns that constitute the history of the entire cosmos—as well? Indeed, if we accept the new scientific intuition that our own existence is intricately interwoven with the cloth of the whole universe, can we ever again separate cosmic destiny from our own individual hopes for immortality?

IV. Confirmation

The three positions just outlined have overlooked an important feature that underlies the whole project of scientific reduction. At heart, the urge to reduce is an instance of the quest for simplicity and purity that coincides with much that we also find in religion. This urge to find the simplest possible explanation of things is not inevitably a manifestation of the will to control. Rather, it may also correspond, at least in some ways, with religion's own quest for an ultimate unity to things. Even materialist reductionism is a shallow version of the much wider and deeper mystical quest for a foundational unity in which all things ultimately reside.

Religion shares with science a desire to get to the depth that lies beneath the surface of things. And like science it leads us to expect that once we arrive at the heart of things we will find a surprising simplicity. Things are not what they seem; both science and religion can agree on this. Beneath the filmy surface of things lies a resolution that will utterly astound us. At root, then, the impetus behind reductive science is inseparable from the deep human longing for unity that receives its most explicit expression in mystical religion.

Many centuries ago, perhaps somewhere between 800 and 500 BCE, religious mystics, philosophers, prophets, and theologians in several parts of the world began almost simultaneously to tire of the confusion caused by increasingly elaborate forms of polytheism and other extravagant expressions of religion. Their sense of frustration with the unsatisfying consequences of needlessly complicated rituals and strict rules of worship led some seekers to look for a deeper sense of the oneness they felt to lie at the heart of reality. The Hindu composers of the *Upanishads*, Greek philosophers, the Buddha, Chinese Taoists, and the Hebrew prophets all sought during this period to purify religion of its burdensome complexity.[26]

Their goals of purification remain unrealized, for often today religions are as complicated, diversified, and divisive as ever. They continue to worship mutually irreconcilable idols and ideals. Nevertheless, a basic feature of religious consciousness is still the quest for a simplicity and unity that will override all the splintering caused by our worshipping of disparate gods and values. What we wish to highlight here is that even the reductionist agenda of modern science is an oblique expression of this fundamentally religious longing.

As a belief system, of course, reductionism is the enemy of mystical religion. But the quest for simplicity and unity is not. What is theologically troublesome about reductionism is not its quest for a unity of knowledge, but its willingness to settle for a shallow and simplistic atomism as the ultimate ground of this unity. It is its fixation on a disembodied set of atomic, molecular, neuronal, or genetic monads floating on the surface of things that makes materialist reductionism so thin and pallid a faith system.

Therefore, we applaud the reductionist quest for unity and simplicity, and see it coinciding with the religious quest. However, to allow that it coincides with the religious quest is not to say that it is coextensive or

coterminous with it. For it gives up entirely too soon. Scientific reductionism stops far short of the elusive goal of an ultimate unity and simplicity. It ends up enshrining artificially isolated physical units as reality's foundation rather than probing deeper into the fathomless unity
that underlies all the complex patterning of an ultimately mysterious
universe.

The religious perspective might even agree with reductionism that
there is an ultimate simplicity and unity to reality, but it would never
wish to forget all the depth and complexity standing between us and the
final goal of our quest. In its acknowledgment of the endless mystery of
a universe that flows forth from the infinity and oneness of God, religion is much more tolerant of ambiguity and contradictions in our present experience than is materialist reductionism. It realizes that the goal
of real unity and simplicity does not come cheaply and that it lies far
off. The true depth of the universe is too elusive to be skimmed off the
surface and presented to us in the bloodless over-simplifications of
reductionist scientism.

The unity sought by religion includes an inexhaustible plurality and
diversity; it is not one that we can arrive at by subtracting away all the
complexity, nuance, beauty, and value in the actual world. For this very
reason every consistent theology sooner or later recognizes the utter
inadequacy even of our loftiest religious labels for ultimate reality.
Accordingly, many spiritualities eventually insist upon the need for
silence as perhaps the most appropriate form of worship.

For example, Judaism and Islam, as well as significant strains of
Christianity, have an obvious reserve about the use of images. Their
protest against religious images and ideas flows out of a prayerful intuition that no human picture of ultimacy can adequately represent the
inexhaustible divine unity itself. Indeed, an iconoclastic strain is present in much religion, one that shatters our always too paltry images of
God. The religious exhortation to silence is an invitation to acknowledge the inability of the human mind to state once and for all just what
reality is in its depths.

Scientific reductionism is religiously objectionable, then, not
because it seeks simplicity and unity, but because it shouts out too pro-
fanely and prematurely that it has finally plumbed the depths of all reality and brought the long human quest for coherence to its final stage.
Thus its impatience seriously violates the apophatic spirit of silent
waiting that most becomes us humans in the face of a mysterious universe.

Everything, reductionism declares, is now resolvable into material processes and interactions as these can be made known through scientific analysis. Such a claim, we are convinced, imprisons science and renders it subservient to ideology. Our theology of "confirmation" seeks to set science free from this form of bondage. By pointing to the infinite depth and abyss of a unity that transcends the stuff of scientific materialism, a truly religious perspective liberates matter from the burden of having to function as ultimate reality, and science from the terrifying chore of having to function as an alternative religion.

5

Was the Universe Created?

No teaching is more vital to the God-religions than that of creation. This doctrine interprets the universe fundamentally as a gift freely brought into existence by a powerful, loving and personal "Creator." The cosmos, in other words, is not self-originating, but the product of a transcendent goodness. The Hebrew scriptures tell us that "in the beginning" it was God who made the heavens and the earth. And traditional Christian and Muslim theism even maintains that God creates the world *ex nihilo*, out of nothing. What bearing, then, does modern science have on the believability of this most fundamental of Western religious teachings? Does science make the doctrine of creation less or more credible?

The British physicist Peter Atkins bluntly answers that modern cosmology renders the notion of creation by God completely superfluous.[1] And although Atkins himself seems undisturbed by it, his interpretation strikes at the heart of what many consider one of the most important truths in their lives. To religious believers the doctrine of creation is much more than a story intended to satisfy human curiosity about how everything began. Its import goes much deeper, for it speaks directly to a common human concern about whether there are any realistic grounds for hope in the meaning of our lives and of the universe.

If a transcendent power and beneficence brought the universe into being, then this same power and goodness could surely also deliver us from all evils and lead us to the fulfillment for which we long. A God capable of bringing this whole universe into existence would have the power also to bring about salvation for those in despair. A Creator could even bring the dead back to life. The existence of a Creator would mean that there is a reason to believe that the entire universe has a deep significance to it, even though we may not know now exactly what it is.

How momentous a thing it would be, then, if science either gave fresh support to or placed under new suspicion the credibility of this central religious teaching. Is it any wonder that some of the liveliest discussions in science and religion today have to do with the creation of the universe?

The recently formulated "big bang" theory of cosmic origins seems to imply, at least at first sight, that the universe had a beginning. And if it had a beginning would this not perhaps mean that the biblical idea of divine creation as depicted in Genesis makes scientific sense after all? Many scientists, as we shall see, are still uncomfortable with the idea of a universe that came into existence by an act of divine creation. Some of them, for that matter, are not convinced that it ever *came* into existence at all. Perhaps the universe always was and always will be. But today doesn't the "big bang" theory seriously challenge such a notion?

From antiquity philosophers have often taken it for granted that the universe is eternal and uncreated. Plato and Aristotle held this opinion, as did many of the other Greek philosophers. Democritus, long before Aristotle, taught that the universe was made up of "atoms and the void" that have existed from eternity. And, at least until very recently, almost all modern materialists had assumed that matter is unoriginated and everlasting. Science, however, now seems to have laid to rest the idea of an eternally existing universe. Of course it has not done so without a struggle, and there are still many unbelievers. For a long time, we should recall, even Albert Einstein was convinced that the universe must have existed forever, and this is one reason for his rejecting the idea of a personal God. Such a God is simply unnecessary, he thought, as long as an eternally ordered universe is the matrix and source of all things. And so it is not surprising that in spite of all the talk today about the big bang, some scientists still attempt to salvage the notion of a universe without any beginning. They do this either by way of hypothesizing the existence of an endless series of "worlds," or by experimenting with other fascinating ideas that might somehow help us evade the conclusion that the universe had to have a beginning. If they can eliminate any crisp point of cosmic origins they expect thereby to make the notion of a Creator unnecessary.

Some theologians, as noted below, would respond that even an eternally existing universe (whatever that might mean) does not rule out the necessity of a Creator or Originator. But the surprising astrophysical discoveries of this century have by now led most scientists to doubt that the universe has in fact existed forever. The consensus of recent cosmology is that the universe's temporal duration, though unimaginably immense, is still finite.

And so we are left with these questions: If the universe has not existed forever, does its origin require some transcendent cause? And is this alleged cause equivalent to what theism calls God? Or is it possible that our finite universe arose spontaneously, without any cause at all?

Suspicion that our universe did indeed have a definite beginning was first aroused in this century by scientific observations that cosmic space is expanding. But a spatially expanding cosmos requires a discrete starting point, for if we keep going back into the remote past along the lines of cosmic expansion we eventually have to arrive at a tiny point from which the increase in size first began. Observation now shows that the galaxies, whose immense number was also discovered only in this century, are moving away from each other and that the universe is still evolving.[2] So a very long time ago the whole of physical reality must have been squeezed into an unimaginably small and dense grain of matter. Particle physics now even allows that this compact speck may originally have been no larger than an atom's nucleus.

Then fifteen or so billion years ago this incredibly compressed pinhead of matter began to "explode," creating space and time in the process. The resulting fireball is usually called the "big bang," and it is generally associated with the beginning of the universe. In thinking about the big bang, then, we have apparently arrived at the temporal "edge" of the cosmos. And even though philosophers, scientists and theologians tell us to be very careful about raising silly questions about the big bang, it is nevertheless hard to refrain from asking whether anything lies on the other side of it. Is it nothing? Or is it God?

In 1917, while studying Einstein's newly formulated equations on general relativity, the Dutch physicist Willem de Sitter concluded that they implied a changing, expanding cosmos. If the universe were eternal and static, after all, the various masses would by now have collapsed gravitationally upon one another. So the universe must be constantly changing, and this could mean that it also had a beginning. Again in 1922, a Russian mathematician by the name of Alexander Friedmann calculated that general relativity challenges the idea of an eternally unchanging universe. Both De Sitter and Friedmann wrote to Einstein about their suspicions, but the most famous scientist of our century was not ready to accept a cosmology in which the universe arose from a singular starting point. Such singularities are not congenial, he thought, to scientific understanding, for science seeks a universal, intelligible lawfulness. Out of his need for universality Einstein had always clung to the idea that the cosmos must be eternal and necessary rather than dynamically changing. This is why he preferred a universe with no birth, one extending back into the eternal sameness of an indefinite past. And so he responded to de Sitter's and Friedmann's disturbing reports by changing his original computations, introducing into them an artificial and, as it turns out, purely fictitious "cosmological constant." Some constant repulsive feature inherent in the cosmos, he surmised, must keep the stars apart and prevent the universe from collapsing.

A bit later, however, Einstein met the American astronomer Edwin Hubble who provided him with what seemed to be observational evidence of a dynamic universe. Hubble had been looking at several galaxies through the powerful Mount Wilson telescope and had noticed that the spectroscopic lines radiating from some of them were measurably "shifted" toward the red end of the spectrum. This could only mean that the light waves are longer than normal and that the object emitting the light must be moving away from the observer. The best explanation for this "red-shift" phenomenon, he concluded, is that the galaxies are receding from the earth and from each other at enormous speeds. Experimental science was now confirming the expanding universe predicted by Einstein's equations. Einstein was forced to concede the point, and he later admitted that his introduction of the "cosmological constant" was an enormous blunder.

And yet, misgivings about the big bang continued even after Hubble's disclosures. It was difficult for many scientists to break away from their longing for a more stable universe. The new theory was given a considerable boost, however, when in 1965 scientists Robert Wilson and Arno Penzias discovered a low temperature cosmic background microwave radiation which could best be interpreted as the "afterglow" of an initial hot big bang. This radiation was the clearest signal to date that a singular originating cosmic event had occurred some fifteen billion years ago. It was now getting harder to doubt that the universe began with something like the big bang.

But doubts still lingered on, and perhaps for good reason. The big bang theory of cosmic origins seemed to imply that the universe emanating from the initial expansion would be smooth and uniform in all directions. Yet astronomy now makes us realize more clearly than ever that we live in a very lumpy universe. That is, cosmic matter comes together in huge clots in some places while being more thinly scattered elsewhere. Our cosmos is made up of very unevenly distributed galaxies, clusters and super-clusters of galaxies, stars, planets, gases and other not yet fully understood kinds of matter. Immense empty spaces, for example, separate some groupings of galaxies, while others are more intimately connected. If the universe really began with a smooth big bang, then how could it have gotten so far removed from uniform distribution of matter today? To produce all the irregularity that astronomers are now aware of, the universe must have possessed the seeds of such unevenness even at the very earliest stages of its development. But the big bang theory did not seem to take these features into account.

Up until a couple of years ago some scientists were even prepared to reject the theory unless it could explain the ragged dispersal of matter. However, in the spring of 1992 doubts were apparently dispelled. Data carefully collected from a satellite called the Cosmic Background Explorer (COBE) appeared to show that as early as 300,000 years after the big bang, when the universe was still in its infancy, the radiation out of which later forms of matter evolved had already assumed a distinctively rippled character. The primordial wrinkles were probably the "seeds" of the uneven universe we have today. So the big bang theory seems safe—at least for now.[3]

Nevertheless, some scientists persist in their "unbelief." Though admittedly without any evidence, they conjecture that we may live in an "oscillating universe." Perhaps over a period of many billions of years the universe recurrently contracts and expands unceasingly in an infinitely prolonged series of "big bangs" and "big crunches." This provocative hypothesis appeals especially to some scientists who find the idea of divine creation difficult to swallow.

Other scientists, however, have replied that an infinite series of worlds is still a problematic notion in view of the second law of thermodynamics. This remorseless law of physics maintains that the available energy in the universe is gradually winding down irreversibly, like a clock whose spring-tension eventually gives out altogether. So even if there have been many oscillations (big bangs followed by big crunches) the cosmos nonetheless would be slowly running out of available energy over the long run. Hence the law of thermodynamic irreversibility requires that the whole series of hypothetical universes must itself have had a singular beginning, perhaps many oscillations ago.

So the dispute continues about whether the universe ever had a clearly definable beginning. Some scientists are not sure that the same laws of thermodynamics operative in our world today would be applicable in alternative episodes of an oscillating universe. Science has not to everyone's satisfaction definitively ruled out the possibility that the cosmos is eternal. There is no concrete evidence to support the idea that there have been an infinite number of "big bangs," but there is no way to disprove it either.

In the discussion below, a question arises as to whether it is pure science, or rather some very non-scientific "beliefs," that have led a few skeptical cosmologists to cling so tenaciously to such ideas as an oscillating universe and other equally imaginative cosmological theories when there is no empirical evidence that could confirm or falsify them. Perhaps one motive for flirting with the extravagant idea of multiple universes is that it helps to save the idea that the origin of life could have been a purely random event, and therefore one that required no special divine intervention.[4] For in the absence of a Creator, an infinitely prolonged series or proliferation of "worlds" would give life a larger window of opportunity to come about by chance alone. After all, the probability of life's originating purely by chance in a single universe might be very small. But if there were an infinite number of big bangs and big squeezes, then life has an indefinitely wider range of occasions to pop up accidentally during one, or perhaps even several, of these runs.[5]

Science today has shown that innumerable physical coincidences have to come together if life is to be possible at all. But if there were an infinite number of attempts at universes, sooner or later one of them is bound to succeed in having those special conditions that give rise to life. In such a case our own apparently improbable existence would not be so unexpected after all. In fact, it would be an almost inevitable eventual outcome of a gigantic cosmic lottery involving an infinite series of mostly lifeless and mindless worlds.

Nevertheless, until actual evidence of such innumerable worlds comes forth, it seems more appropriate in our present discussion that we look at the relationship of the religious doctrine of creation to the world of current scientific consensus. As it turns out, the cosmos articulated in terms of the widely accepted big bang theory of cosmic origins is fascinating enough, and firmly enough established, to stir some interesting, though quite diverse, reactions. Does big bang cosmology provide a sufficiently substantive basis for a scientific certification of the theology of creation? Here are some possible answers.

I. Conflict

At first sight, nothing in modern science would seem to be more supportive of the idea of a Creator God, and therefore of religion's plausibility, than the big bang theory of cosmic origins. In the Revised
Standard Version, the Bible starts out with the words: "In the beginning, God created the heavens and the earth." And now, after many centuries in which philosophers and scientists have assumed that matter is
eternal, it turns out that science itself is finally leaning toward the
notion that the universe is temporally finite. Could we find a more
obvious basis for reuniting theology and science than in the idea that
the universe had a beginning? For how better than through the doctrine
of creation—and the idea of a Creator God—could we explain how the
cosmos came into existence so abruptly out of apparent nothingness?

A great deal of ink has been spilled in attempts to show that big bang
physics has made the theological idea of creation intellectually respectable once again. Although fundamentalists reject big bang astrophysics
because it makes the universe too old to fit into the narrow time period
(roughly 10,000 years) allowed by their biblical literalism, some other
conservative Christians like Norman Geisler and Kerby Anderson are
now claiming that "the big bang theory of the origin of the universe has
resurrected the possibility of a creationist view of origins in astronomy."[6] The book of Genesis has apparently found conclusive support in
the new cosmology.

As you might have anticipated, however, we scientific skeptics will
need much more than big bang physics to lead us back to religious
faith. For it is not at all self-evident that just because the universe had a
beginning it also had to have a Creator. Quantum physics in fact allows
for the possibility that the universe came into being out of *nothing*. The
cosmos may have had a beginning, but it could have burst into existence spontaneously, without any cause.

The scientific basis for this admittedly counter-intuitive hypothesis
is the following. At one time, according to big bang theory and quantum physics, the universe was about the size of a subatomic particle,
and so we can assume that it behaved the way such particles do. But according to quantum theory the appearance of such particles does not
need to have any antecedent determining cause. The so-called "virtual"
particles of microphysics simply pass in and out of existence—spontaneously. Why then couldn't the primitive universe, in its subatomic

dimensions, also have come into existence in the same way, that is, without any cause whatsoever? Douglas Lackey explains:

> ...the big bang might have no cause. How then did it happen? One explanation provided by quantum theory depends on the fact that in quantum physics the energy levels of particles and systems can never be precisely measured, but oscillate spontaneously between certain levels. For the smallest particles, this oscillation between energy levels may cause the energy to drop to zero, at which point the particle ceases to exist. Conversely, the oscillation can raise a particle from zero to some finite level; that is, it brings a particle into existence. Such particles, usually called virtual particles, are literally coming into existence from a vacuum, that is, *from nothing*....one could explain the Big Bang as a fluctuation in a vacuum, like the fluctuations that bring virtual particles into existence. But if the fluctuations are spontaneous, then the creation of the universe from a vacuum is also spontaneous.[7]

Moreover, the renowned astrophysicist Stephen Hawking recently gave our skepticism a significant boost by theorizing that, though the universe is not eternal, it still might not have had a clear temporal beginning. This is hard for common sense to grasp, but since modern physics emphasizes the close connection between time and space, Hawking submits that it is possible to conceive of time as emerging only gradually out of space, and so there may well have been no abrupt, clearly defined first moment, and therefore no first cause either. He writes:

> The idea that space and time may form a closed surface without boundary...has profound implications for the role of God in the affairs of the universe. With the success of scientific theories in describing events, most people have come to believe that God allows the universe to evolve according to a set of laws and does not intervene in the universe to break these laws. However, the laws do not tell us what the universe should have looked like when it started—it would still be up to God to wind up the clockwork and choose how to start it off. So long as the universe has a beginning, we could suppose it had a creator. But if the universe is completely self-contained, having no boundary or edge, it would have neither beginning nor end: it would simply be. What place then for a creator?[8]

So the new physics does not have to lead to theology after all. Some of us who are skeptical about religious matters have to admit, however, that recent developments in astrophysics (unlike those in evolutionary

ly means in its religious depth. At the same time, it is not the task of religious accounts of creation to give us any details about the physical origins of the universe either. The stories in Genesis have nothing whatsoever to teach science about cosmic beginnings. And although big bang physics may be an interesting and scientifically fruitful way of depicting the origins of the material universe, this is a far cry from telling us anything about the real meaning of creation.

What then is the doctrine of creation all about? Our answer, put in its briefest terms, is that creation is not so much about chronological beginnings as about the world's ontological dependency on God. Ideas about the big bang provide us with provocative scientific theories concerning the birth of the present universe, but the doctrine of creation is about something much more momentous: why is there anything at all rather than nothing? Cosmologists look for a first cause, and we do not object to that; but creation theology is not so much concerned about temporal beginnings as about awakening us to the complete giftedness of all things, regardless of how (or even whether) they "began." Its purpose is to invite us to assume that most fundamentally religious of postures, namely, gratitude for the very existence of the universe.

Thus, nothing that astrophysics can tell us about the early universe will make its existence any more remarkable than it already is to a secure religious faith. Talking about cosmic beginnings does not bring us any closer to God, for the crucial point is not chronological origins but the naked existence of the cosmos. Even if science taught us everything there is to know about cosmic beginnings, we would still not have a "solution" to the encompassing mystery of the world's being.

Moreover, it is not theologically essential that the universe even have had a beginning in time. For, whether it began in time or not, it would still require a transcendent grounding, religiously speaking, in order to sustain it in existence. Hawking completely misses this point in his cavalier suggestion that since the universe may have had no clear beginning, it therefore had no need for a Creator. The theology of creation, as no less an authority than Thomas Aquinas insinuated, is not necessarily dependent on the supposition that the universe had a temporal beginning. Even an eternal universe could be the expression of the primordial love that we call God. By linking the idea of creation so closely to temporal beginnings Hawking duplicates the conflationist superficiality of fundamentalist creationism and Enlightenment physico-theology, both of which try to make science do the job of religion, and vice versa. We repeat: creation is not about chronological beginnings so much as it is about the world's being grounded continuously in the graciousness of God.

Theologian Keith Ward clearly summarizes our position on this point:

> ...it is wholly inadequate to think of God having created the universe at some remote point of time—say, at the Big Bang—so that now the universe goes on existing by its own power. This popular misconception, that "the creation" is the first moment of the spacetime universe, and that the universe continues by its own inherent power, wholly misconstrues every classical theistic tradition. It is irrelevant to a doctrine of creation *ex nihilo* whether the universe began or not; that the universe began was usually accepted because of a particular reading of Genesis 1. The doctrine of creation *ex nihilo* simply maintains that there is nothing other than God from which the universe is made, and that the universe is other than God and wholly dependent upon God for its existence.[13]

It follows also, therefore, that speculations from quantum theory about the spontaneous origins of the universe have no implications for the religious notion of creation either. Lackey's suggestion that the infinitely small early universe could have erupted randomly out of the "nothingness" of a vacuum matrix is not at all relevant to the issue of creation. The really interesting question is: why are there beings at all, including vacuum matrices (which Lackey superficially and erroneously equates with "nothing")?

Incidentally, another word-trick skeptics sometimes use is to identify as pure "nothingness" the hypothetical initial "perfect symmetry" in which opposite charges of primordial physical entities originally canceled each other out mathematically and energetically. Then when this primordial state of zero total energy was "broken," the cosmos is said to have arisen out of "nothing," therefore requiring no creator. It all just happened spontaneously, without any cause.

However, in our view it is in no sense justifiable logically or ontologically to identify a quantum vacuum or the original symmetry of mathematical "zero" with a "nothingness" in any sense remotely resembling the *ex nihilo* of creation theology. No matter how mathematically ethereal or physically subtle the initial cosmic conditions may seem to have been, metaphysically speaking they still enjoy some mode of *being*. And it is the sheer being of things, regardless of how mathematical equations represent them, that evokes the true sense of religious wonder.

In sum, no matter what the specific features of cosmic origins look like to physics, science is not equipped to say anything about the deeper question as to why there is anything at all, or what the ultimate meaning of the universe might be. These fundamentally religious questions are not the same as the question of what caused the universe to appear out of the quantum vacuum or a perfect symmetry. Even if the universe did emerge "spontaneously" and without any determinable physical "cause," the relevant question has to do with the metaphysical fact of the world's "being," not with the interesting sequence of physical events that might or might not have triggered it. Tracing events back either to a first efficient cause, to a vacuum matrix, or to a spontaneously broken symmetry may be scientifically interesting, but it is by no means the same as asking about the ultimate ground of the world's being.

Here we should point out also that Robert Jastrow, who regards big bang theory as a possible victory for the "theologians," shares with biblical literalists the questionable assumption that creation has more to do with beginnings than with ontological dependency. Missing from the "band of theologians" that Jastrow expects to be waiting on the other side of big bang mountain are those (including Thomas Aquinas) who maintain that even an eternally existing universe would not be incompatible with its being grounded in a well-spring of divine creativity. Like many other scientific skeptics Jastrow simply takes for granted that all theologians are likely to be biblical literalists and that "creation" is fundamentally about chronological "beginnings." It is this confusion that we wish to dispel.

In fact, Jastrow is implicitly approving the very same, though highly questionable, theological method that conservative religious writers like Geisler and Anderson employ.[14] It is that of forging a conflationist confederacy between science and religion on the basis of what is *currently* considered the best of science. The problem with this kind of alliance, as we have repeatedly noted, is that it will fall to pieces as soon as the prevailing scientific theory itself proves defective or in need of revision. We should recall always that good science leaves its theories open to falsification. So any theological method that bases its conclusions directly on falsifiable scientific consensus, no matter how secure this consensus may seem to be at present, holds little promise for future relations between science and religion. Even though big bang theory appears to have ousted all conceivable cosmological alternatives, there is no guarantee that it will hold up indefinitely. A permanently sound method of relating cosmology to theology has to dig deep beneath big bang theory and into the perennial truths of metaphysics for more lasting foundations.

We can drive home this point by looking briefly at what in modern times has been the fate of "physico-theology." This is a designation given by Immanuel Kant to those forms of theology that based themselves squarely on physics. In the early modern period, for example, Newton's ideas fostered physico-theology by making the world-machine the primary reason for invoking the idea of God as its divine mechanic. Prominent theologians followed Newton, reasoning that theism had at last hit upon a solid intellectual foundation in the certainties of physics. The "book of nature" even seemed to be a more certain road to God than the Bible itself.

A bit later, however, materialist thinkers like Diderot convincingly argued that physics required nothing other than natural principles to explain itself. It could provide its own grounding. Having no further role to play, therefore, theology became an intellectual orphan. It is no exaggeration to say that theology's taking physics rather than religious experience as its foundation helped lead eventually to the spread of intellectual atheism and to the comparatively low standing the discipline of theology still has in our modern universities. More than once conflation has proven to be theologically disastrous.[15]

Today, while most academic theologians have no use for physico-theology, ironically some scientists are attempting to revive it. One example is the physicist Paul Davies, who constructs his ideas about God quite directly out of the discoveries of physics.[16] Though Davies has little use for religious ideas of God, he thinks good science leads us to the notion of a creating and designing deity. A more recent, and much more bizarre, example of physico-theology is that provided by the respected Tulane physicist Frank Tipler. In his latest book *The Physics of Immortality* he argues with utter seriousness that theology is now a branch of physics. Religion's promises about eternal survival of death, he claims, can now be substantiated much more compellingly by physics than by theology alone. Science itself can now give us mathematical certainty that we will all be raised from the dead to live forever. And not only that: it can also lead us to absolute certainty about the existence of God. In the light of physics there is no more need for revelation and faith.[17]

Many theologians, however, would respond to such efforts by emphasizing that any "God" arrived at through science alone would be only an abstraction, not the God of Moses or Jesus or Muhammad. To read the God of religion directly out of the theories of physicists will eventually lead to conflict rather than cooperation between science and religion. We must seek a more durable theological approach than that of conflation.

III. Contact

Once again the contrast approach provides a clear alternative to the unfortunate commingling of religious and scientific ideas that generates conflict. It rightly resists the strong temptation to identify the big bang with divine creation. However, its severe compartmentalizing of cosmology on the one hand, and the religious teaching about creation on the other, unnecessarily suppresses the prospect of fruitful dialogue. We would argue, as usual, that cosmology *always* has theological implications. If the latter are not made explicit they nevertheless remain implicitly effective in shaping our religious ideas. It seems more honest, therefore, to expose them to the light of day. We need to be very cautious in doing so, of course, since science is always changing (as is religion too in its own way). But current scientific theory is never completely irrelevant to theology. So we should at least look for points of "contact" between big bang cosmology and creation theology.

We do not want to make the same mistakes theology made in the past by basing itself directly on physics. Physico-theology, we agree, has apparently left theology somewhat stranded in the modern intellectual world. But immunizing theology completely against what is going on in science is no less fatal to its intellectual integrity. Theology cannot help but think about God in terms of some cosmology. And today big bang theory, along with all the other things that relativity and quantum physics are implying about our world, must be taken into account when theologians talk about God's relation to the world. Although we do not wish to base our creation faith directly on scientific ideas, our reserve does not mean that big bang cosmology is theologically irrelevant.

One of the immediate consequences of big bang theory for theology is that at the very least it forces us to take the *cosmos* into account once again in our religious thought. It might seem strange that we make an issue of this obvious point, but the sad fact is that the natural world has not been a major concern of modern theology. Even though our creed emphasizes that God is the "Creator of the heavens and the earth," our religious life and practice seem lately to have glossed over this teaching.[18] Theology has been so preoccupied with questions about human existence that it has often left out the fact of our being linked to a much larger universe.

This is not completely surprising, for in modern thought since Immanuel Kant (1724-1804) the universe as an object of theological and philosophical interest had already faded into the background. As far as Kant was concerned, the universe existed only as a kind of construct of the human mind. It was a background notion, not a real, concrete set of interconnected finite things that could be made the object of formal study itself. Thus for the last couple of centuries, especially as the result of Kantian influence, the universe was virtually lost to philosophy and theology, both of which became onesidedly subjective and anthropocentric. It is especially out of Kantian ideas, we must also note, that much of the contrasters' approach to theology was born and nurtured.

However, as Stanley Jaki astutely claims, recent scientific cosmology starting with Einstein has "restored to the universe that intellectual respectability which Kant had denied to it."[19] We can now study the universe more directly, rather than making it only the backdrop of more specific areas of inquiry. The new cosmology, therefore, is theologically consequential simply by virtue of the fact that it brings the universe to the fore once again.

The universe implied by Einstein's theory of general relativity and big bang cosmology is no longer just a vague background for our scientific or theological pursuits, but instead—and notwithstanding its unfathomable enormity—a bounded and limited set of things. It is neither eternal nor necessary, but radically finite. But if the universe is finite, this can only mean, as far as we are concerned, that it is *contingent*. And if it is contingent, this at least opens up the possibility that we may need to go beyond the world itself in order to explain why it does exist at all. Let us unfold this idea a bit further.

To say that something is contingent means that there is no necessity for its having come into existence at all—or for its being the way it is— as there may have been if matter were eternal or infinite. *This* particular universe, even science now seems to imply, need not be here. But since it is here, the question legitimately arises as to *why* it exists if it did not have to. And once we have asked this question we have already brought science into close contact with theology.

We can no longer say, as the contrasters do, that big bang cosmology is theologically unimportant. For the new scientific vision of the cosmos compels us to ask in a dramatically new way the oldest question of all: Why does the universe exist anyway? It is no longer as easy as it was earlier in modern intellectual history for cosmologists to separate "how" questions from "why" questions, as the contrasters would prefer that they do. And once the "why" questions arise, there is no good reason to exclude theology any longer from intimate conversation with science.

After all, the theology of creation understandably maintains that theism provides the most straightforward and uncomplicated answer to the question: "Why does the universe exist at all when there is no necessity that it do so?" And even though the question as to why the world exists arises quite independently of big bang cosmology and general relativity, the fact that today it arises so explicitly out of scientific cosmology inevitably places the latter in a context where close encounter with theology seems wholly appropriate.

Therefore, although we do not run to embrace the extravagant proposals by Robert Jastrow and other scientists that big bang cosmology may have finally bridged the worlds of the Bible and science, neither do we dismiss their overtures as though they were completely pointless. For beneath their efforts to connect the worlds of science and religion we detect strains of an irrepressible sense of awe at the sheer facticity or "thatness" of the universe. Even Steven Hawking seems to hint at times at the need for some metaphysical principle that would "breathe fire" into the abstract mathematics of physics and make this into an actual, concrete universe.[20] It is not difficult to pick up the theological concern in some of his writings, even when he presents himself as a skeptic.

Wonder at the fact that the universe exists at all has been given a powerful boost by current cosmology. And since creation faith is inseparable from this same sense of wonder at the mystery of being, theologians cannot be indifferent to the new scientific developments. While remaining careful about easy liaisons, we can nonetheless be excited that science itself is causing a new wave of what Paul Tillich called "ontological shock," the feeling of being awestruck by the sheer existence of that which need not have come into existence at all.[21]

And there are still other interesting consequences of theology's contact with big bang theory. For example, to a degree that previous theology could not have noticed so clearly, the new cosmology presents us with a world still in the making. Put otherwise, the creation of the cosmos appears far from finished. Especially as a result of its encounter with evolutionary science, but now also with big bang cosmology, theology today has developed a much deeper sense than ever before that creation is far from being a finished product. The universe still surges toward the engendering of ever more novelty and diversity; and we humans are caught up in this ongoing creation (though unfortunately our species also seems intent upon wiping out much of the cosmic beauty that has preceded us in evolution).

When combined with biological notions of evolution, big bang cosmology helps us realize that creation is perpetually new every day. The idea that "creation" is only an originating moment confined to the remote past detracts from the full religious meaning of the term. Jesuit paleontologist Teilhard de Chardin, for example, rejects such a thought as "unbearable":

> The fact is that creation has never stopped. The creative act is one huge continual gesture, drawn out over the totality of time. It is still going on; and incessantly even if imperceptibly, the world is constantly emerging a little farther above nothingness.[22]

This admittedly lyrical declaration sums up the sentiments of a growing number of religious thinkers who have taken seriously the idea of cosmic expansion and evolution beginning with the big bang. It cannot be a matter of indifference to theologians that the universe has probably not existed forever and that it is therefore still in the process of becoming something quite other than what it has been. The big bang, even according to scientists, is not something that is over and done with. *It is still happening.* This brings the fact of creation much more intimately into the immediate present, and it opens up the future before us in a restorative manner.

The event of divine creation is going on within us, beneath us, behind us, and ahead of us. We agree with the contrasters that locating God's creativity only in the past easily leads straight to deism—and eventually to atheism. But a theology of "contact" is still excited about a cosmos that probably began in a singularity, for such an origin helps to dispel the idea of a static, eternal and necessary universe and replaces it with an exciting unfinished world-in-process. It does make a difference theologically if the universe had a beginning, for such a universe seems much more open to new creation than one that is infinitely old.

Consequently, the idea of a big bang rules out any "eternal return of the same." This is the horrifying notion (articulated especially by Friedrich Nietzsche, 1844-1900) that if matter is eternal and unoriginated, everything must periodically be reconstituted in precisely the same way, so that there can never be a completely open future.

However, if the universe has a beginning, or at least a finite past, there is no possibility of eternal recurrence. Nature is open to continually surprising developments in the indeterminate future. According to big bang cosmology, with its implied notion of time's irreversibility, every occurrence is unrepeated and unrepeatable, and so there is always an opening for what our faith looks forward to as a "New Creation." Our hope in the promise of New Creation clearly meshes much more readily with a big bang universe than it ever could with the eternal cosmos of the ancient philosophers or Nietzsche. Many of us would be thoroughly disappointed, we must admit, if science eventually forced us to abandon the idea of a finite and unfinished universe. For that reason we cannot help but be excited by big bang cosmology.[23]

Finally, we cannot avoid the observation that the scientific quest for beginnings, so abundantly evident in recent cosmology, is at some deep level of human existence inseparable from the nearly universal religious search for origins. As much as we might appreciate the contrasters' distinctions between creation theology and big bang theory, our indomitably religious concern for the primordial cannot be completely disentangled from the scientific quest for cosmic origins. Without collapsing one into the other, we would suggest that much of the energy motivating science's look backward into our ultimate cosmic roots stems from the ineradicably mythic orientation of human consciousness.

The scientific sense of "wonder" about cosmic origins is already incipiently religious, and we should be honest enough to admit it. Even though big bang theory is logically and theologically distinguishable from the religious quest for the source of our being, the two are existentially inseparable. Though they diverge in the order of thought, they both flow concretely from a common human concern to discover our roots. We humans are forever haunted by origins.

IV. Confirmation

As you might expect, we shall advance the suggestion here that creation faith is not only consistent with, but also inherently supportive of, science. Scientists are not always aware of how significantly the religious doctrine of creation has assisted historically and logically in the development of their own discipline. But although we cannot be certain of it, a truly empirical method of doing science might never even have come about outside of a cultural and historical context that had been thoroughly imbued with the idea that the world is a contingent creation of God.

To be more specific, the theological notion that the world was created—and is therefore neither necessary nor eternal—gives a stature to empirical science that other ways of looking at the world do not. To understand this point imagine, as some philosophers have actually believed to be the case, that the universe exists eternally and necessarily. That is, suppose that the state of the natural world *has* to be just the way it is and could not have been different. Such universal necessity would in turn imply that every particular thing in the universe is also *necessarily* the way it is and could not have been otherwise. But if this were the kind of universe we lived in, then empirical science would be essentially irrelevant, for every feature of the universe could in theory be deduced from necessary first principles. Observation might be of some practical value in the short term, but it would be cognitionally vacuous. For in principle at least we could logically and deductively reason to the nature of every aspect of the cosmos merely on the basis of an eternal cosmic inevitability. There would be no need for empirical method, other than just to anticipate or confirm what we could come to know through reason alone. We would not have to examine the world's particulars inductively, the way science does, since we could arrive at an adequate understanding of everything on the basis of its relation to the overall necessity built into nature. In other words, there would be no need to *look* at the world to see what it is actually like. Science would be finally superfluous.

Creation theology, however, implies that the actually existing universe is not necessary. It need not have existed at all, and it need not have turned out exactly the way it has. Since its reality and its nature originate in the free decision of the Creator, we cannot come to know it through pure deduction, as Greek philosophy allowed. Creation faith, therefore, implicitly propels us on a journey of discovery to find out *by observation* what the world is like. Since it expels rigid necessity from our view of the universe, creation theology opens us up to the possibility of being surprised by the actual facts. It is especially in an intellectual and cultural milieu molded by the creation theology of the God-religions that the empirical imperative of science, the injunction to attend to what we actually experience, is explicitly confirmed.[24]

6

Do We Belong Here?

Do human beings really belong in this universe? Were we "meant" to be here? We are, after all, beings endowed not only with life but also with a high degree of "mind." And doesn't the fact of mind—in a universe that seems largely mindless—somehow estrange us from that very universe? How do beings endowed with consciousness and self-awareness fit into the general picture of nature that science has given us? Or do we fit in at all?

To put our question more directly: Is "mind" really a part of nature, or is it a quality that sets us apart from the material universe?

The term "mind," of course, can mean many things: the ability to experience, think, reason, reflect, calculate, plan, grasp, or comprehend, etc. All of these features are relevant, but mind means, above all, our capacity to understand, make judgments, and decide. Is mind, taken in this sense, a natural development? Is it the unfolding of a potentiality that has always been present in nature? Or is it a purely spiritual reality that has descended into the material world from a supernatural sphere, as some traditional myths, religions, and philosophies have taught? Is human consciousness an absurd accident that momentarily disturbs the eternal silence of the cosmos? Is it perhaps simply an adaptive characteristic that aimless evolution has hit upon to enable our species to endure a hostile world? Or, on the contrary, is it conceivable that the evolution of mind is what this universe is really all about?

Religious traditions have generally taken for granted that the cosmos is shaped by something like a transcendent "Mind." In prophetic religious circles the universe is the expression of an eternal "Wisdom" or the implementation of a divine "Vision." In the Bible and the Qur'an creation is shaped by God's "Word," while in Platonic thought, which has also greatly influenced Western theology, the cosmos is the reflection of eternal "Ideas."

As long as the cosmos itself was seen as the expression of divine intelligence our finite minds could be said to "belong" in such a universe. Of course traditional theism suggested that our true home lies elsewhere, but at least it allowed that we belong here during our earthly pilgrimage. On the other hand, modern science, one of the most dazzling products ever to spring from the human mind, finds it odd that mind ever showed up here at all. Matter could just as easily have existed indefinitely and even forever without any trace of mind. Thinking beings were apparently absent from the universe for billions of mindless years before the candle of human consciousness began to flicker uncertainly in the cosmic dark. Only after epochs of aimless play by physical determinism and blind chance did matter, according to many of our best scientists, finally give birth—precariously—to mind.

At least until recently, matter seemed inherently hostile or at least indifferent to mind. Science taught us that it was only by way of the most whimsical departure from its entropic slide toward final unconsciousness that the universe, for a flash, puts up with any intelligent kind of existence at all. Science offered no alternative to this essentially mindless universe. It pictured human thought as a mere anomaly, an alien and absurd intruder.

However, a remarkable new set of ideas in science has recently begun to disturb this picture of a pervasively mindless universe. Curiously, a good number of scientists are entertaining once again the notion that mind may be a *fundamental* aspect of nature, and not a merely accidental outgrowth of unconscious evolution. Almost in spite of themselves, they are today making mind an integral part of their picture of the universe. And ironically it is physics, the science that formerly expunged mind so totally from the world, that is taking the initiative in effecting the reversal.

This strange turn of events all started with the birth of special relativity and quantum theory. Einstein showed that in each independent physical framework the speed of light is always the same, but that an event perceived at a given time by an observer in one inertial system would not necessarily occur simultaneously to an observer in another. From his puzzling calculations Einstein was led to the conclusion that there is no absolute simultaneity in the universe. In describing physical events, the situation of the observer makes a very real difference. The observer's mind is much more intimately intertwined with matter, space and time than we had previously thought. No longer hovering somewhere outside the cosmos, as it had been since Descartes' dualism expelled it from the physical realm, mind is once again a respectable citizen of nature itself.

Einstein's science led astronomer Arthur Eddington to remark, perhaps immoderately, that there are theological implications in relativity theory's new picture of the universe. For if our own subjectivity is so interwoven with the objective world, it would be just as easy for a transcendent "Mind" to insinuate itself unobtrusively into the cosmos.

Eddington was no less excited by the implications of quantum mechanics. For here too it seemed that the presence of an observer is inseparable from the scientific description of cosmic reality. Werner Heisenberg's celebrated "uncertainty principle" implied that we cannot simultaneously measure with exactness the position and velocity of a photon or electron. The very act of our observing a subatomic particle's state or activity always puts a kink in our impression of it. Once again, then, how nature manifests itself to science cannot be disentangled from the observer's own mental existence. In quantum physics as well as in relativity theory, scientists now suspect that the observing subject is physically inseparable from the observed world.[1] Mind has become an *essential* aspect of the scientific picture of nature. It is no longer an alien interloper.

Today, however, some physicists are making even more astounding conjectures about why mind may be intrinsic to the cosmos. The suspicion is growing that mind is already subtly intertwined even with the *earliest stages* of the cosmic story. Difficult though the idea may be for traditional scientists, it now seems that the prospect of mind's evolving may have been a factor in shaping the cosmos as early as the big bang. If this speculation turns out to be correct, it would indeed be a most surprising turn of events in the history of science.

Is it possible that physics, which Steven Weinberg took to be the most impersonal of sciences, could now be implying that the existence of matter makes little sense apart from the reality of minds embodied in persons? More than a handful of physicists are toying with this hypothesis. The fundamental features of nature, such as the force of gravity and the rate of cosmic expansion, they say, may have a much closer relationship to the existence of mind than we had ever suspected. Let us now look at the background of this provocative thought.

Both Newton and Einstein formulated theories of gravity, but neither of them was able to say *why* gravity has exactly the amount of coupling force that it does. Likewise, Edwin Hubble showed us that the universe is expanding, that the galaxies are moving away from each other at a rate directly proportional to the distances separating them; but he did not show *why* the "Hubble constant," the rate of expansion of the universe, has the velocity that it does. We do know, however, that the Hubble and gravitational constants had to be pretty much what they are if the universe was to avoid either collapsing too soon or expanding too rapidly to allow for the formation of stars and galaxies. But *why* does it have the precise equilibrium that allows for the formation of stars and galaxies? Scientists, who for so long had restricted themselves to simple *how* questions, can no longer completely suppress these *why* questions.

Before we look at a possible response let us consider some other related points. Astronomers, for example, have calculated that there are about 10^{22} stars in the observable universe. But why wouldn't 10^{11} stars, a staggering number itself, have been sufficient? Exactly why do we have this very immense and very old universe? From the point of view of physics and astronomy, surely a smaller and shorter-lived universe would have been perfectly acceptable. Scientists today surmise that the universe needs just the right amount of matter (that is, its actual density has to be very close to its critical density) to keep it from collapsing too soon or from expanding too fast for life and mind to come about. Is there perhaps some connection between the density of the universe and the existence of living and thinking beings?[2]

And there are many other puzzles. If we look into particle physics, for example, we note that the nuclei of atoms are about two thousand times the mass of an electron. Why not one thousand or three thousand times? From the point of view of physics there is no clearly understood reason why these values might not have been different from what they are. So why are they just what they are and not otherwise?

What we do know is that if the ratio of electron to proton mass had been only infinitesimally different, there would never have been any hydrogen atoms. And if there had been no hydrogen atoms, the heavy chemical elements like carbon, oxygen, and nitrogen could never have been created within stellar furnaces made up of hydrogen and helium. And if there had been no heavy elements there could have been no life and no mind, both of which require the heavy elements (especially carbon) in order to exist. But, in the early moments of the universe, what "decided" that the ratio of proton to electron mass would be exactly such as to allow for the formation of hydrogen—and eventually of life and mind? Is it all a matter of blind chance or impersonal necessity?

Is there perhaps a "principle" that might give us a clear and conclusive answer to all of these questions? Is there indeed some way to answer them all at once? Scientists, as we know, look for explanations that can solve a morass of problems in as straightforward a way as possible. They have a passion for elegantly simple solutions to what started out as very complicated questions. They look for limpid formulas that will simultaneously respond to a wide variety of problems with one elegant sweep of the mind. And the simpler the explanatory principle, the more appealing it will be.

For example, with his model of a heliocentric planetary system Copernicus untied an enormous tangle of astronomical knots that had resulted from centuries of attachment to a geocentric universe. And more recently the theory of evolution apparently swept away many seemingly unrelated problems raised by pre-Darwinian geology, paleontology, and biology with their assumption that the world is static and not very old. Thomas Huxley was so impressed with the explanatory elegance of Darwin's theory that he is said to have remarked: "How stupid of me not to have thought of that." And today some physicists are hoping to come up with a final explanation of the whole physical universe, a "Theory of Everything," that may be elementary enough to fit on a T-shirt.[3]

It is not surprising then that scientists would look for a simple "principle" that can account all at once for the specific features in the macroworld of astronomy and the micro-world of particle physics. It just seems like sound procedure to seek a simple solution, one that can resolve many questions in a flash. Even if such a principle is not immediately testable, it will attract the attention of scientists. For any idea that promises to solve in so straightforward a way such a multiplicity of difficult scientific puzzles may be worthy of close examination, even if for the moment it is resistant to falsification.[4]

Why, then, are the initial conditions and fundamental constants fixed the way they are? Why are there so many stars? Why is the universe so big and so old? Why does it expand at the rate that it does. Why does it have the actual density it has? Why is the force of gravity constantly the same from one end of the universe to the other? Why, in short, is the universe configured the way it is?

The answer some scientists are now playing with—again—is *mind*. It is the existence of mind that makes matter the way it is. The key to the entire nature and history of matter is mind.

One prominent form this kind of "explanation" is taking today is the *anthropic principle.*[5] Derived from the Greek word "anthropos" which means "human being," the anthropic principle maintains that the cosmos, from its very opening moments, was set up in a way that allows for the eventual existence of persons endowed with mind. This sounds hopelessly obvious, for since we are in fact here, the universe must have been "set up" in such a way as to make our existence possible. However, there is as of yet no known scientific reason why it might not have been "set up" in a different way. There is a seemingly "remarkable" congruity between the physics of the early universe and the eventual appearance of mind in cosmic evolution. Doesn't the eventual existence of mind, then, have something to do with the force of gravity, the rate of cosmic expansion, the density of the cosmos, and the relative values affixed to the primordial particles and forces?

This truly "astonishing hypothesis" is receiving an enormous amount of press today. Some scientists consider it outrageously unscientific while others find it intriguing and even compelling. Though it is extremely controversial, talk about an anthropic principle, whatever its merits, at least demonstrates how difficult it is now for science to situate the observing human mind outside of the observed world. Even though formerly it could get by with this expulsion, science itself now forcefully suggests that our minds cannot help casting their subjective shadow over all that we observe, perhaps even over the physics of the early universe.

It seems that our subjectivity is mixed in with everything we try to set forth in purely objective daylight. Mind is at least dimly present even in the earliest phases of cosmic evolution, at a time when we were not supposed to have been present in any way. Along with relativity and quantum theory, discussions surrounding the anthropic principle seem to suggest that the fundamental features of the physical universe might not be completely separable from the existence of observers. And some physicists are now even proposing that the anthropic principle requires the existence of a transcendent, ordering Providence. We are getting perilously close, in other words, to a new version of natural theology's old design argument for the existence of God.

It is important to point out, though, that the anthropic principle has both weak and strong versions. In its "weak" formulation, it sets forth no more than the obvious, namely, that we can see in the cosmos only what the conditions that produced us allow us to see. The Weak Anthropic Principle (WAP) maintains that the early universe looks the way it does to physics because otherwise we wouldn't be here to observe it. We are able to understand only a universe that could produce minds capable of understanding it. In this weak version the principle has no explanatory value and therefore hardly deserves the name of "principle." Nor does it seem to evoke much in the way of theological interest.

But the Strong Anthropic Principle (SAP) goes much further. It holds that the physical character of the universe is the way it is *because* of mind. It is the natural world's impetus toward evolving into beings with minds that has shaped the fundamental features of the universe from the beginning. An acorn's tendency to grow into an oak tree is the best explanation for the seed's properties. Likewise the propensity of the universe to ripen in the direction of conscious beings is the best explanation for why the seedling universe was the way it was.

The eventual production of conscious beings, according to the SAP, is the simplest and most elegant explanation of why the universe began to expand at the rate that it did, why gravity has the force that it does, and why the ratio of electron mass to proton mass was fixed exactly the way it is. Its bent toward producing persons with minds best explains why the universe has so many stars and why it is so vast and old. A younger or smaller universe would never have produced us.

Even if Earth is the only place where mind actually exists, the universe as a whole would still have to be as old and as big as it is for this to happen in just this one place. Moreover, a universe with an actual density that was different from its critical density by as little as a trillionth could probably not have produced us. If the total mass of the universe were not exactly the right amount to keep it from expanding too fast, mind could never have appeared. The existence of mind, therefore, is "exquisitely sensitive" to the initial conditions and fundamental constants that were fixed during the first second of the universe's existence.

The cosmic inclination or "nisus" toward mind explains why the force of gravity, for example, balances so delicately with the rate of cosmic expansion. For if gravity had been only slightly stronger it would have put the brakes on the universe's expansion long before sufficient time—at least several billion years in a stellar oven are needed—to cook the carbon and other heavy elements that go into the evolution of brains. Or if gravity had been only infinitesimally weaker, cosmic expansion would have been too rapid, and the force of attraction between clouds of hydrogen gas too slight, to allow for the formation of stars large enough to bake the heavier chemicals needed for making living and thinking beings.

If there was ever to be anything like mind, therefore, an incredibly delicate balancing of the numerical values of gravity and cosmic expansion was required *at the very beginning* of the universe. Since many possible values could have been assigned to these and other initial cosmic conditions and fundamental constants, the simplest way to explain their "fine-tuning" is that the whole universe must be oriented toward mind. No other explanation is more direct and economical. A Copernicus, Darwin or Einstein could hardly have provided a simpler and more satisfying solution to so many scientific puzzles.

Therefore, since the cosmos has always had an inclination to evolve into mind, it can no longer be said to be indifferent to the eventual appearance of human beings capable of thought. We do indeed belong here.

Or do we? What we have just seen is the argument of those scientists who embrace the Strong Anthropic Principle. But is the SAP really a valid scientific explanation? Or is it just one more instance of the conflation of science with a belief system, in this case the belief that human beings are the central reality in this vast universe?

Before we examine the possible answers, it is only fair to point out that many of its proponents now agree that "anthropic principle" is not a felicitous label for what we are talking about here. Making the cosmic process center so much on *human* mentality smacks of arrogant anthropocentrism. What if there are other intelligent beings in the universe? Or what if our own minds are simply the initial sparks of an eventually wider and deeper kind of mentality (or information processing) that will continue to grow in new and grander ways in the future evolution of the cosmos? Would it not be more appropriate to speak somewhat less immodestly of a "mind-bearing" principle, or perhaps of a "life-and-mind-bearing" principle? This would allow for life and intelligence in other parts of the universe, and it would eliminate criticism that the principle is too provincial and human-centered to be taken seriously.

Let us grant this necessary qualification. Then, is the central idea behind the Strong Anthropic Principle still worth discussing, namely, that mind is an inherent part of nature and not just an evolutionary accident? A good number of scientists and theologians now think the SAP is indeed at least worthy of close examination. Cannot the existence of mind account for all the main physical features of the material universe? Or is it more likely that the idea of a completely mindless evolution of matter, blindly following the laws of natural selection, still contains the best explanation for the apparent fit mind has to nature? Let us look now at how our four approaches might react to the SAP as an issue in science and religion.

I. Conflict

Those of us who have any esteem at all for authentic science will immediately detect something very dubious about the SAP. We smell the aroma of metaphysics and final causes, features that have no place in our discipline. If it were not for the fact that the SAP is being put forth by respected scientists themselves, we would not pay any attention to it at all. It clearly runs against the grain of scientific method by attempting to explain a chronologically earlier set of occurrences (the initial cosmological conditions and fundamental constants) in terms of results (life and mind) that don't appear until much later in time—indeed billions of years later! How can this amount to "explanation" in any genuine sense of the term? To science only those events that chronologically precede or lead up to other events may be called explanatory. The SAP is simply another unscientific instance of teleological speculation, and so it merits no further consideration by self-respecting scientists.

Moreover, the SAP has no predictive value whatsoever, and this defect immediately attests to its unscientific status. As Heinz Pagels argues, the anthropic principle amounts to "gratuitously abandoning the successful program of conventional physical science of understanding the quantitative properties of our universe on the basis of universal physical laws." And he adds:

> Of course there are eminent, if not reasonable scientists who do not share my negative opinion about the anthropic principle. We could debate its merits and demerits a long time. But such interminable debate is a symptom of what is wrong with the anthropic principle: unlike the principles of physics, it affords no way to determine whether it is right or wrong; there is no way to test it. Unlike conventional physical principles, the anthropic principle is not subject to experimental falsification—the sure sign that it is not a scientific principle. No empirical resolution of its veracity is possible, and a debate about whether it is true could go on forever.[6]

As we skeptics have been saying throughout this book, chemistry and physics can adequately account for the existence of living and thinking beings. Through a combination of physical necessity and chance combinations of mindless particles, life and mind will eventually issue forth, if given enough time. And there has been time aplenty. There is no sound reason to fancy that the ten to fifteen billion years of cosmic evolution all happened *in order* to produce humans with minds or any other kind of "mental" realities that might exist. The SAP, no matter how much you try to dress it up, is really nothing more than a rationalization of anthropocentric hubris. It is just another attempt to make our existence seem special and privileged in the face of the universe's unfeeling immensity.

It is not surprising, of course, that the structure of the universe conforms to our existence. Obviously the material circumstances have to be just right for life and mind to come about. So we readily accept the Weak Anthropic Principle (WAP) according to which we can understand only those physical conditions that have allowed our minds to evolve. But this weak version has no explanatory value and is scientifically useless, although it is not wrong. It explains nothing that we did not already know. It is not remarkable that we can become aware only of those physical parameters that have allowed us to exist.

The SAP, on the other hand, is completely repugnant to us. Perhaps it would have more allure if we could be certain that the present universe were the *only* one that has ever existed. For it is undeniable that the physical constants and initial conditions of *this* universe are indeed suited with great precision to the evolution of living and conscious beings. We must admit that if these conditions had been different we would certainly not be here. We can accept all of this. But the real question at issue here is whether the emergence of mind is "remarkable" enough to call forth a theistic explanation.

A few of our number would suggest that no other universe is physically possible than this mind-bearing one, in which case the existence of mind is not anything to wonder about. For all we know, the universe *had* to be the way it is, by virtue of an impersonal necessity that we do not yet fully understand. Still, in the light of big bang cosmology, most of us are now willing to concede that the physical properties of this universe are not necessary and that they could well have been other than the mind-bearing variety.[7] As far as we know, most other sets of cosmic conditions and constants would not have permitted life and mind to evolve. But contemporary physics allows for a multiplicity of worlds, even an infinite number of them. And most of these worlds would probably be stillborn and mindless. If there are an infinite number of universes, most of which are not fit for mind, then it is not so arresting that at least one of them, just by accident, would favor the evolution of beings like ourselves.

There could very well be an indefinitely large number of other worlds, some of which came into existence serially, big bang followed by big crunch; or they may exist as parallel branchings or "bubbles" born out of some mother universe. Our point is that in all this mathematical immensity the probability that *one* or even several of the innumerable worlds would contain mind increases as more universes are added. In an indefinitely broader bundle of worlds the evolution of life and mind might not be so amazing after all. In such a scenario the idea of a designing deity would be superfluous, for mind might be nothing more than the outcome of accident and natural selection.

In fact, as John Gribbin argues in his recent book *In the Beginning*, cosmologists should follow the lead of Darwinians like Richard Dawkins who make natural selection the principal explanation of all physical phenomena.[8] There may be *countless* universes competing for survival—in the same way that living species have always struggled for existence in biological evolution. According to Gribbin's evolutionist perspective, the existence of our present mind-bearing world is the product of nothing more than random variations and blind natural selection involving numerous worlds. Perhaps mind-bearing worlds like our own are simply better adapted to the rigors of existing and are more capable of surviving than mindless worlds.

The point is, we do not have to invoke the hypothesis of some supernatural influence behind our present universe. Our existence in this mind-bearing cosmos can still best be explained as the result of an unimaginably lengthy and vast, but still essentially mindless, process of trial and error. Such a universe is still wonderful, even if mind is not essential to it.

II. Contrast

We are not enthusiastic about the SAP either. Unfortunately, well-intentioned but theologically naive scientists and believers are likely to seize upon it and use it as a "proof" of God's existence. They will argue in the fashion of natural theology's dubious design argument that only a divine Creator could have arranged the world in so delicate and harmonious a fashion that matter would lead eventually to mind. They will seek in the SAP scientific support for their religious faith, a faith which loses its intensity and depth as soon as it begins to rely upon any such rational or scientific props.

It is primarily on religious and theological grounds that we distance ourselves from the barely disguised form of conflation known as the SAP. We have previously shown how "unreligious" such attempts at scientific validation of God really are. For even if scientists concluded that some intelligent being had tinkered with the initial conditions and cosmological constants, pointing them in the direction of life and mind, this "being" would still be an abstraction, and not the living God of religion. It would be a great empty plugger of gaps, and not the personal God of Abraham, Jesus and Muhammad. The SAP is no more capable of confirming or deepening our religious life than are the old arguments for God's existence. The realms of science and religion are radically distinct. Once again, then, in the interest of maintaining the integrity of both religion and science, we refuse to derive any theological consequences or religious comfort from this spuriously "scientific" theory.

Moreover, we have learned from past experience how theologically suicidal it would be to base our religious ideas on the ever shifting sands of scientific conjecture. What if next century's or even next year's physics leads us to a purely naturalistic explanation for the initial physical conditions and fundamental constants? For all we know, Alan Guth's inflationary hypothesis has already done so. This hypothesis holds that it was not any initial (divinely ordained) conditions, but a rapid inflation of the cosmos during the earliest nanoseconds of its existence, that fixed the cosmic constants. So we can only agree with George Smoot's recent assessment:

> Many things that cosmologists thought in 1974 were miraculously fine-tuned to allow life and human existence are neatly and powerfully explained by inflation....I think that a fuller set of observations will lead to models and theories that will gracefully and easily explain why things are the way they are. Whatever these future discoveries are, I am confident that, like inflation, they will astound and delight us with their elegant simplification and unification of nature.[9]

Or what if those skeptics are right who insist that, physically speaking, this is the only kind of universe that could possibly exist? What status would our theology then have if we now bind it too tightly to the SAP? We simply do not need science—and it is highly improbable that the anthropic principle can even be dignified as part of science—when religious faith is sufficient by itself to lead us to God.

Therefore, we can only applaud those scientists who dismiss the SAP because of its transparently theological implications. Even though they often reject it out of a purely naturalistic scientism, they are really doing theology a service. By purging science of any contamination by final causes or teleology they implicitly hand the whole business of purpose and meaning over to religion and theology where they belong. Physics can tell us nothing about our reason for being here or about the world's meaning. If you want to know the deepest essence of the universe you will find it displayed more fully in an act of human kindness than in all the elaborate formulas of physics.[10]

Finally, it would not be such bad news to us even if science concluded that mind does *not* fit very comfortably into the cosmos. At the core of our being, faith tells us, we don't really belong to this world anyway. Our home is elsewhere. Look at all the religious texts that instruct us to accept our situation as only pilgrims in a foreign land. We are no more than "strangers and exiles on the earth" as the Christian author of the Epistle to the Hebrews puts it (11:13). So we are not impressed by cosmological thinking that makes mind and personality too much a part of the "natural" order. Such a shallow synthesis trivializes humanity by absorbing us into the material dimension and loosening the eternal connection that our souls have with the transcendent world. For this reason also, then, we are not interested in pursuing any possible religious implications in the SAP.

At the same time, however, we are not impressed by the implicit materialism that lies behind much scientific debunking of the SAP. This usually takes the form of imaginatively multiplying worlds, as Gribbin does, so that the present mind-bearing universe would only be one of perhaps an infinite number of worlds, most of which remain mindless. The idea here is that if there are countless possible universes to choose from, the fact of mind existing in this one would not be quite so "remarkable" as advocates of the SAP maintain. Given an infinite number of "attempts" at shuffling and dealing in the cosmic poker game, it would not be surprising that one of the hands dealt would eventually be a royal flush.

What are we to make of such extravagant speculation about innumerable worlds? We think that even though you might plausibly interpret some equations of quantum physics in terms of a "many-worlds" perspective, it is ideology rather than observation that attracts skeptics to it. From the perspective of empirical science there is no evidence at all that many parallel or sequential worlds exist, and the hypothesis appears no more testable than the SAP. Pagels' observations about the unfalsifiability of the anthropic principle are also applicable here.

Gribbin, we should note, proposes that since the physical properties of black holes are theoretically similar to the singularity of the big bang, they could be openings into alternative "universes."[11] Perhaps this idea would be open to experimentation at some later time in scientific history; it is too early to tell. But even if there were many separate "worlds," they would altogether still constitute a *single* universe. Even if physical laws place observational barriers between them, there would nevertheless be some deep relationship of these worlds to one another so that altogether they would comprise *one* overarching totality. For at the very least they would all share "being" or "existence," and from a philosophical point of view this is enough to give them an overall unity. There can really be only *one* universe, even if it has many separate facets and phases.

Moreover, even within the lavish aggregation of worlds that Gribbin and others conjure up, the fact of mind, like that of the universe itself, would still be an unexplainable mystery. Even in an infinity of universes spanning an infinity of time there would still be no absolute necessity for mind to come into existence. Time and immense numbers alone can never be the metaphysical cause or explanation of anything. Some other principle(s) would also be required to explain anything so intense in being as the human mind. Making mindless matter, natural selection, and long spans of time the exhaustive explanation of mind, as materialists attempt to do, violates the basic principle of causality without which all of our thinking is reduced to insanity: no cause can produce an effect greater than itself. Regardless of how much time they have at their disposal, blind material processes could never account by themselves for the existence of mind with all its cognitive and spiritual propensities.

We cannot help suspecting, therefore, that the speculation about numerous, and perhaps an infinite number of, "worlds" often has nothing whatsoever to do with science. Rather it is a desperate conflationist attempt by a materialist belief system to ally itself with science in such a way as to diminish the plausibility of any non-materialist, religious interpretation of the cosmos. Beneath the multiple worlds hypothesis there is an implicit, though very telling, confession that if our present big bang universe is in fact the only world-phase that has ever existed, materialist and reductionist explanations would be in serious trouble. For the existence of only this one fine-tuned universe would not provide a statistically broad enough base to allow for the purely random origin of life and mind that skepticism requires. So in order to avoid the obligation of responding to our existence with the gratitude appropriate to such an improbable gift, skeptics must find a way to show that in the final analysis there is nothing "remarkable" or improbable about our being here at all.

At a time when the universe was held to be eternal and necessary, such a belief would have been quite congruent with cosmology. For, given an infinity of cosmic time, our unique species was bound to come about sooner or later, purely by chance and physical necessity. But in an age of big bang physics—where our present universe is taken to be temporally finite, a "mere" ten to fifteen billion years old—the only way to take the surprise out of our being here is to multiply worlds *ad infinitum*. This is the only option left. In an unending plurality or succession of worlds the probability of one of them being finely tuned enough to bear life and mind increases to the point where we can expect it to show up inevitably somewhere in the whole batch. Then there would be no need to go outside the materialist framework for an adequate explanation of either life or mind.

In brief, the multiple-worlds hypothesis provides skeptics with a convenient way to avoid an interpretation of the universe that would call forth the religious response of gratitude for its truly gracious existence. How easily ideology clouds over the "objective" world of science and then presents itself to us as though it were pure, unadulterated scientific truth! The very attempt to exorcise the need for wonder about our universe is itself a wonder to behold.

Likewise we suspect that those who try to get around the SAP by appealing to Alan Guth's still highly speculative, though scientifically plausible, idea of an inflationary universe may sometimes be governed more by ideology than by science. Their efforts are a throwback to the old longing by philosophers for a *necessary* universe. They want to rid the universe of any contingency. Thus they find the inflationary universe compelling not simply because it responds to very real scientific problems in the standard big bang model, but also (at least in the case of some scientists) because it apparently irons out any wrinkles of contingency and implies that the universe just *had* to be the way it is. In the absence of any belief that the universe is the free creation of God skeptics are forced to appeal to either chance or necessity as its "explanation." They appeal to chance in the case of the multiple-worlds view and to necessity in the case of the inflationary hypothesis.

We suspect that neither of these two choices is always motivated purely by science itself.

III. Contact

The contrast position is partially valid, but it always plays too safe. It fails to take advantage of the exciting theological opportunities provided by new developments in scientific cosmology. Discussions surrounding the SAP are, we think, of considerable interest to theology. Of course we do not want to make too much of the principle either, and we have no investment in defending its allegedly scientific status, at least according to the generally accepted sense of what science is. But to ignore it altogether is not fruitful either. As is our habit, we would like to probe it, at least tentatively, to see if there might not be some substantive way in which the cosmological reflections surrounding the SAP can contribute to our theological vision of the universe.

Why do the conflict and contrast approaches simply dismiss the SAP out of hand? Is it for purely scientific reasons in the first case, and for purely theological reasons in the second? We suspect that more is involved in each instance. Scientific skeptics throw it out not only because the SAP's flirtation with teleology is unscientific, but also because it doesn't fit materialist and reductionist ideas of what the universe *should* be like. If there were anything to the SAP's thesis that mind somehow causally shapes the evolution of matter so as to bring conscious beings into existence, this would shatter the reductionist claim that emergent mind is fully explainable in terms of lower and earlier levels of physical reality. What is at stake in skepticism's dismissal of the principle, then, is not always just the integrity of science, though this is the case with many good scientists, but the validity of materialist and reductionist ideology. To this extent we are sympathetic with the contrasters' critique.

At the same time, however, the contrasters' abrupt rejection of the SAP is also, at least in many instances, the consequence of certain arbitrary assumptions that they too are unwilling to abandon. They dismiss the SAP not only because it threatens to confuse science with theology, but also because to embrace it would mean that the whole cosmos is somehow inseparable from mind. Such a synthesis would be offensive to the dualism so characteristic of contrast theology. You will note that throughout this book the contrast approach has consistently segregated physical nature from conscious personality and human freedom.

Contrasters maintain the same divorce between consciousness and cosmos that we find implicit in scientism. They allow for divine influence in the arena of private freedom and personality (and also in human history), but they ignore the possibility that God is intimately related to the whole of nature or that humans are themselves inextricably connected to the universe. They fear that if we insert humanity too deeply into the cosmos we might forget that we also transcend nature.[12]

Thus the SAP is obviously a threat not only to the materialist interpretation of science, but also to the dualistic leanings of traditional theology. The SAP is one of several recent cosmological developments that hint at the inseparability of the human subject from the natural world, and this is an intimacy that has little appeal to the contrast theologians. For if the cosmos and humanity are as mutually interwoven as the SAP implies, then contrast theology, which insists on being so logically clean, precise, and acosmic, would no longer be appropriate to the real complexity of the universe. The SAP clearly puts mind back into the physical universe, and we think that both science and theology need to take this connection more seriously.[13]

In our view, therefore, the SAP (or even the WAP) cannot be ignored in any discussions of science and religion today. Our sentiments are very close to those of the science writer Eugene Mallove:

> It can only be a guess—an article of faith supported by the latest cosmological findings—but the mysterious universe seems in some unfathomable sense "destined" to support organization and life, with the ability to reflect on itself and its relation to the unthinking part of the cosmos. How much of that "purpose" is programmed in the very structure of elemental matter? How much of that "purpose" later transformed its program to the more complex structures of primitive life and then again to the unimaginably more complex structures of the brain? Is the ultimate "goal" to ignite that cosmic fire that then bodily and mentally seeks the universe? These are mystical feelings...but they seem to converge at a lightning-quick pace with the conclusions of modern science.[14]

If it does nothing else, the anthropic principle may at least force us to recognize the dramatic shift now taking place in discussions involving scientists and theologians. For many decades the central question in science and religion was that of how to explain the improbability that life and mind would emerge out of what seemed to be completely mindless matter. Scientists had assumed (more on the basis of ideology than scientific investigation) that matter is inherently unsuitable to mind. Given entropy's apparent hostility to order of any kind, it seemed that the only possible way life and mind could make their appearance in cosmic evolution would be either as the result of a most unlikely series of accidents, or as the consequence of a miraculous intervention by a supernatural force.

In either case the evolution of life and mind gave every appearance of being a reluctant, evanescent, and thermodynamically improbable reversal of the laws of physics. In order then to explain the evolution of life and mind, scientists were divided between advocates of the "chance" hypothesis, which appealed to materialists, and devotees of the "vitalist" hypothesis, which made the most sense to religiously or "mystically" inclined scientists. Even today discussions in science and religion often choose up sides roughly along the lines of these same mutually exclusive alternatives.

Although the chance hypothesis and vitalism are incompatible with each other, they share the common assumption that matter is inherently mindless. But the anthropic principle brings to our attention the refreshing possibility that matter is inherently suited for, and not at all inimical toward, the evolution of mind. Even in its weak version the principle suggests that the main issue in science and religion is no longer that of how to explain the emergence of life and mind out of mindless matter. Rather, the really interesting question is how to explain matter's puzzling hospitality toward the evolution of life and mind—when things could very well have been physically otherwise.

What is remarkable is not that mind would crop up in a material world that only grudgingly allows it to flourish for a brief season. We have now learned that matter is not so stingy after all. Rather, what arouses our wonder today is that the physics of the universe is so generously disposed in the first place toward bringing mind about at all. In spite of great resistance the anthropic principle, in both its weak and strong versions, has already shifted the focus of many discussions in science and religion away from evolutionary biology and toward the physics of the early universe. After all, given the initial conditions and fundamental cosmological constants, it is no longer very surprising that evolution would eventually bring conscious life into existence. What still remains to be explained, though, is that the cosmic dice would have been so loaded in the first place.

As noted above, by immersing their cosmology in the acids of the multiple-worlds hypothesis, many scientists hope to dissolve any possibility of our being so surprised. We agree, of course, that science should explore every possible natural explanation for what we take to be mysteries. Methodological reduction and naturalist explanation should be pushed as far as they can go. Even Gribbin's intriguing proposal that natural selection is appropriate to cosmology as well as biology cannot be dismissed. As we have learned from history, natural occurrences that we had formerly attributed to a god-of-the-gaps can usually be explained eventually by purely scientific exposition. This is why we have to take into account also how the inflationary model might challenge the SAP.

And yet, in the present instance it seems that we are dealing with something more fundamental than just another gap that will eventually yield to a naturalistic accounting. The SAP asks us to consider the possibility that there is a *globally* mind-oriented impetus at work in the cosmos, one that scientific abstraction, intoxicated as it is by the reductionist need to interpret mind in terms of mindless matter, has no room for in its own picture of the universe.

We are willing to concede that the SAP is not conventionally acceptable science, and that scientists have every reason for being suspicious of its teleological nature. But we cannot simply brush it aside as though it has nothing to offer. We see it, at the very least, as a protest against a reductionism that pretends to explain the more (mind) in terms of the less (matter). Although the SAP may not be purely scientific, it may nonetheless be explanatory. Of course, in order to accept the possibility of there being non-scientific ways of explaining phenomena, one would have to give up the scientistic belief system that rules out all other ways of arriving at knowledge.

If there is any over-arching significance to the universe, it would be too elusive for science to grasp all by itself. So even if the anthropic principle were an accepted scientific idea it could still not be sufficient to place us in touch with God. To this extent we can agree with the contrast position. However, if we look at the universe with the eyes of a faith that instructs us to see promise in all things, it comes as no surprise to us that science now discerns the prospect of life and mind already latent in the finely tuned early universe.

Without rooting our faith directly in science, we are yet heartened by the emerging sense in biology and cosmology that the universe is by no means the enemy of mind but from the beginning has been more than willing to bring about the countless conditions for its creation. And we are grateful that theology is now making contact with the new developments in astrophysics that correspond so well with our conviction that the universe is and always has been the embodiment of a promise of future surprises.

IV. Confirmation

The confirmation approach looks not only for ways in which religion may cohere with scientific ideas, but also for how it may support the scientific adventure. We have been arguing in the previous chapters that in many respects religion and theology nourish rather than inhibit scientific knowing.

Thus we are somewhat disturbed about the rather abrupt way in which some of our fellow theologians have dismissed the "multiple-worlds" hypothesis that is now favored by an increasing number of physicists. Although we concede that so far there is no scientific evidence to support it, we shall make the case here that it is entirely plausible on theological grounds. In addition, we shall propose that a wholesome theology confirms the overwhelming scientific suspicion that the SAP is too anthropocentric.

First of all, then, from a theological point of view the idea that there might be a plurality of "worlds" is quite compatible with the idea of God. Given the extravagant graciousness that religion attributes to the Creator, God could quite conceivably bring about a great abundance of worlds. The God of prophetic religions is anything but miserly, and we are instructed by faith to expect that the Creator's works far surpass any cosmic immensity that we humans can imagine. Consequently, contemporary scientists' luxuriant speculation about a plurality of worlds is not at all inconsistent with a healthy religious openness to the overflowing abundance of an infinite love. Religion, after all, invites us to keep our imagination of the divine munificence fully alive, and never to allow the cosmos to close in upon us. And while it may be simpler to think both scientifically and theologically in terms of only one world, it is certainly also appropriate from a religious point of view to be suspicious of any unnecessary narrowing in our cosmologies.

Hence when scientists express their sense of the possibility of many worlds or world-epochs, speculation on such a grand scale—at times approaching infinity—is not as opposed to religious sensitivity as some theologians and skeptics maintain. Even though the multiple-worlds hypothesis is at times the product of a materialist longing to make the origin of life and mind seem purely natural and "unplanned" accidents, the extravagance of cosmic creativity is also a thoroughly religious motif. It has its roots in the long religious quest for limitless horizons. And though the physical universe is finite, its unimaginable magnitude—and the possible plurality of its branchings or epochs—remains a vital religious metaphor of the divine infinity. In any case it is ironic that some kinds of theology, whose purpose is to open our minds to the infinite, would gratuitously exclude the possibility that there is an enormous expanse of worlds.

In the second place, a theocentric (God-centered) perspective may also confirm the suspicion many scientists have that the anthropic principle is too narrowly focused on human existence. We would agree that talk about an "anthropic" principle, or any principle that focuses only on "mind" in the sense of *human* consciousness, lacks sufficient cosmic breadth. The anthropic principle is indeed too anthropocentric if taken in that limited sense.

Our theocentric perspective, on the other hand, requires that we considerably broaden the anthropic principle, to give it a wider cosmic scope. We find intriguing, therefore, a proposal made by eminent physicist Freeman Dyson.[15] In his somewhat sympathetic discussion of the anthropic principle Dyson argues that we might speak more magnanimously about a "principle of maximum diversity." The physics of the early universe may or may not have been biased toward the evolution of consciousness. But what does seem obvious—and scientifically irrefutable—is that the cosmos has always been somehow intent upon diversifying into as many experiments with form as possible, one of which (fortunately for us) turns out to be human consciousness. To answer the question that titles this chapter, we do indeed belong here, but so also does much else of great interest.

Another way of putting this is to say that the universe, no matter how many worlds or cosmic epochs it includes, seems to be influenced by what might be called an "aesthetic" cosmological principle. We do not need to think narrowly of a cosmic striving toward life and mind. It is remarkable enough that the universe is bent upon expanding and intensifying its inherent beauty. We would include the evolution of life and mind, therefore, within a more encompassing cosmic adventure toward an ever greater breadth of beauty.

The God of our religion is, in fact, best understood as One who wills the maximization of cosmic beauty.[16] As scientists and theologians continue to make sense of our vast universe, only small parts of which have yet been opened up to us, they may eventually be able to agree that a God who wills adventure, beauty, and diversity corresponds more closely to the nature of things than one whose only concern is with humankind. As the Book of Job reminds us, we humans may be important, but the universe is immeasurably vaster than anything our own finite minds can conjure up or comprehend.

7

Why Is There
Complexity in Nature?

Science keeps changing our pictures of the universe. As it comes up with new methods of exploring the natural world, the cosmic landscape itself seems to shift. Early in the modern period, for example, scientists began using the machine as a model for understanding nature, and this made the world look—not surprisingly—like machinery. Today's new scientific machine is the computer, and it too is giving nature a strange new face. Computer imaging is allowing scientists to pay more attention than ever before to what they are now calling "complexity" and "chaos."

The sciences of chaos and complexity are still so new that thus far little attention has been devoted to their implications for the subject of science and religion. In this chapter, however, we shall hazard a guess as to how our four typical approaches might greet the new sciences.

"Chaos" and "complexity" are familiar words, but their meanings to scientists are somewhat technical.[1] Whenever science borrows human language it almost always gives ordinary words a new twist, and this can cause a great deal of confusion unless we examine carefully just how the terms are being used. What then do the terms "chaos" and "complexity" mean?

Chaos, in common discourse, means "disorder." However, science is primarily interested in order. In fact, only the assumption that the universe is in some way organized gives scientists the incentive to search for its inherent intelligibility. In what sense then can science be interested in chaos? It is interested in chaos because many natural processes start out with a simple kind of orderliness, move through an incalculable phase of turbulence, but then end up manifesting surprisingly rich forms of unpredictable order in the midst of chaos, an order that can best be mapped by computer imagery.

Even without computers, though, we can get a sense of chaos. For example, a pot of soup is sitting cold upon the stove, its molecules resting in a state of relative equilibrium. If you turn the heat on, the molecules in the soup start moving excitedly all over the place, and wild commotion rules for a while. But then something remarkable happens. Under appropriate conditions hexagonally shaped convection cells begin to form in the liquid as it gets hotter. When energy is fed into an unstable system, puzzling kinds of order often "emerge" unexpectedly out of it. Today this is the cause of much scientific wonder.

Countless happenings in nature exhibit the same feature: order emerging "spontaneously" at states far from thermodynamic equilibrium—or at the "edge of chaos." Thus, when scientists today talk about "chaos" this term includes not simply disorder or randomness, but the often incalculably complex patterns that arise unaccountably out of turbulence.

There is much more of this "chaos" in nature than previous science had ever noticed. Scientists used to assume that physical reality, based apparently on timeless natural laws, follows rigidly causal pathways. They were convinced that if they observed any deviations from deterministic conceptions of natural processes there must be something wrong with their measurements. Nature itself could not at bottom waver in the slightest from their mathematical ideals. But now chaos theory implies that causally determined processes with completely predictable outcomes seldom occur in nature. They typically exist only in the mathematical abstractions of scientists, not in the real world.

If science is about the real world, as it claims to be, then why doesn't it examine what actually happens in nature? Why doesn't it admit that its mathematical calculations are nothing more than rough approximations? The new turn to chaos and complexity is in fact causing many scientists to rethink their discipline. Chaos and complexity constitute an implicit rebuke to the excessively abstract character of modern science. More than that, they may even be bringing about a dramatic shift in our whole understanding of what science is all about.

They are forcing us, for example, to take more seriously science's empirical imperative, that of closely observing all of the data, and not just those that fit *a priori* mathematical schemes. The new kind of science is more open to surprise and less obsessed with exact predictions. Through the use of computer imaging the researchers in chaos and complexity hope to represent more approximately how natural processes *really* unfold in nature. Just as religious fundamentalists have to give up their naive scriptural literalism in order to see the rich layers of meaning beneath the surface of texts, so now scientists are called upon to give up their cosmic "literalism" and look more penetratingly into the actual universe.

What will they see? They will see that nature is composed largely of intricate, spontaneously self-organizing patterns. Many of these patterns exhibit a quality known as "complexity." When scientists speak of "complexity" today they mean elaborate, emergent, adaptive, self-organizing systems. Examples of "complexity" are cells, organisms, brains, ecosystems, economic systems—and even religions.

Science, of course, has always seen order in nature. But the kind of order it has customarily "discovered" is only a thin mathematical facade masking an inexhaustibly rich tapestry. Until recently physical science, for example, has been almost exclusively preoccupied with bringing to light only the kind of order that can be calculated in *linear* terms represented by straight lines on a graph. "Linearity" refers to processes that can ideally be traced back along a sequence of causally related steps, so that the final outcome could have been accurately predicted if we only knew the starting conditions. For example, if we measured in advance the distance an object has to fall from the top of a tower to the ground below, we could map out, on the basis of our knowledge of the laws of gravity, how long it would take to reach the ground. And we could inscribe a series of points on a graph that would specify exactly where the stone would be at any particular spot in the duration of its fall. This is linear science, the kind that many of us learned in high school and college physics classes.

The key to linear science is knowledge of the initial conditions (e.g. the distance from the ground, the rate of acceleration by gravity, the resistance of the atmosphere, etc.) with some degree of exactness. If we knew all these initial conditions it would be relatively easy to predict the future simply by extending the line on our graph. This kind of predictability is what makes most engineering and technology possible. It is linear thinking that allows us to launch satellites, to rendezvous with them, or to send astronauts to the moon.

Scientists who study chaos and complexity do not wish to trivialize or dismiss linear science, for without it we would have little control over our technological projects. Today, though, they are realizing how limited linear science is in its ability to represent any but the simplest happenings in nature. For the initial conditions of many natural processes cannot be specified with the degree of exactness that could make our predictions completely accurate. It is nearly impossible to map many processes beyond their first few steps. For example, the exact way in which a thunderstorm takes shape is still quite incalculable. The same goes for the way a plant, an embryo, an immune system, a living species, or an economic system evolves. Even the rotation of planets or the falling of a brick cannot be determined as precisely as we used to hope. It would take little less than omniscience to specify all the initial conditions we would need to master in order to determine in advance exactly how most events in nature will turn out. Precise prediction of future outcomes is quite impossible in most cases.

This is not what we had come to expect from Newton and Laplace, or even from Einstein and most other scientists of the past. For three centuries we thought the business of science was to make accurate predictions of the future states of all natural occurrences. Obviously science never succeeded in actually doing this except in the case of some rather standard physical processes. But its limited success in these areas gave scientists the confidence that one day predictive kinds of explanation could be carried over into other areas, even those of life, consciousness and human culture. Now, however, science is going through an identity crisis. It is beginning to acknowledge its inability to predict accurately what will happen in the case of nature's most fascinating phenomena, from turbulence in the atmosphere to the evolution of new species.

But if science is severely limited in its ability to predict exactly the outcomes of so many natural processes, then what good is it? What is the purpose of science? We thought it was to explain and predict, not just describe. We thought science should be able to determine the future, not just wait around to see how physical processes turn out. But scientists who study chaos and complexity are less inclined to claim that science explains than that it describes. They still have no satisfying explanation of much of the order they see in nature. They are bedazzled by the fact that complex order can arise "spontaneously" out of chaos, or that apparently simple, calculable processes can suddenly give rise to turbulence. They are puzzled by the way in which patterns called "strange attractors" tend to pull chaotic processes toward unpredictably intricate and often beautiful forms of order. But so far very little that resembles explanation has come forth.

Explanation in science has traditionally meant the reduction of complex phenomena, like living organisms, to simpler ones such as those studied by chemistry and physics. But chaos and complexity seem somewhat impervious to reductive kinds of explanation. They consist of a kind of formal organizational bearing that is irreducible to something more fundamental. And they are so super-sensitive to initial conditions that they cannot possibly be explained from the bottom up. Thus they are a challenge to the whole way we used to do science.

Without computer imaging, of course, we could scarcely have noticed the many processes that start out simply and deterministically, then become turbulent or chaotic, and finally cascade toward surprisingly complex states. Computer technology has finally brought the fact of incalculable patterning at "the edge of chaos" to the attention of scientists. By mapping on computer screens the phase-space "attractors" (which function as geometric basins toward which dynamical systems gravitate) the sciences of complexity and chaos are quite possibly ushering in a whole new epoch in the history of science. For the first time, science is systematically paying close attention to the complex adaptive systems in the natural world. Since classical science was so analytical and atomistic, it failed to discern clearly the remarkable fact that the universe unfolds in the shape of self-organizing *systems* striving to adapt themselves to the universe. The sciences of complexity and chaos are telling us that we can no longer ignore these systems with their strange, unpredictable patterns.

The favored examples of such incalculable natural patterns are weather formations. Although weather forecasting can make roughly accurate predictions of climatic conditions over the next few hours or days, it cannot do so over longer periods. It cannot conceivably nail down all the conditions it would have to know with precision in order to forecast weather patterns in the distant future. The slightest variation in present conditions would have to be taken into account as a factor. Attention to every single relevant detail, of course, is simply impossible.

Chaos theory shows us that two series of events that start out very close to each other can lead to vastly divergent outcomes. A crude but common example is that of placing two paper cups very close to each other at the top of a water rapids. Although their initial conditions are nearly identical, the very slight difference between them at the start becomes dramatically amplified as the cups float down through the turbulence of the rapids. They can easily end up at increasingly greater distances from each other as they move further downstream. Their subsequent positions are thus said to be "extremely sensitive to initial physical conditions."

We used to think that we could eventually graph and master everything natural in a linear way. This would give us scientific control over the future. But now scientists are starting to recognize how exquisitely sensitive most natural outcomes are to their initial conditions. That is, even the most minute, unmeasurable fluctuation at the beginning of certain processes, such as in the development of a hurricane or the growth of an embryo, causes enormous differences at a later stage in the unfolding of the process.

In the realm of legend, minute genetic modulations gave Helen the beauty that brought down Troy, and in the sphere of history something as small as Cleopatra's nose contributed to the reconfiguration of the Roman Empire. Now it seems that even in the natural world the shape or trajectory of a hurricane may be determined in considerable measure by something so insignificant as the flapping of a butterfly's wings at the beginning of its development. Amazingly, even to predict the position of a billiard ball accurately after only one minute of movement would require that we take into account the gravitational attraction of an electron at the outer edge of our galaxy.[2]

This is why some scientists today are talking less about predictability and more about the "butterfly effect." Many things in nature are said to be "exquisitely sensitive" to initial conditions. Even the possibility that our cosmos would bring forth living and thinking beings may have required that the initial physical conditions at the time of cosmic origins were very precisely and delicately configured. The evolutionary emergence of life and mind is contingent upon the most infinitesimal variations in the universe's initial conditions and fundamental physical constants. For if the rate of expansion, the force of gravity, or the ratio of proton to electron mass had been just slightly different, the countless physical conditions essential for life would not exist, at least in the present universe. The butterfly effect seems to apply to the whole cosmic story.

Are there any theological implications in all this new scientific talk about sensitivity to initial conditions, strange attractors and complex patterns? Why, for example, do we live in a universe so intent upon diversifying into innumerable forms of order? Can science alone explain the world's tendency toward diversity, unpredictability, and complexity? And why is there not only complexity, but also, at least over the long haul, a habitual inclination toward increasing, or *emergent* complexity along the edge of chaos? Why is the universe like this? These are questions that not only theologians, but scientists themselves are now asking.[3]

For a century or more the second law of thermodynamics has dominated both physics and intellectual culture—leading usually to cosmic pessimism. The universe seemed to be heading down the slopes of entropy toward an abyss. But there is nothing in the notion of entropy itself that helps us understand why the cosmos, from its very beginning, has also moved toward increasingly various and more complex forms of order. Science has simply slurred over one of the most interesting features of our "unfinished" universe, namely, that it has such an irresistible tendency to seek out the "edge of chaos" so that from there it may branch out into endlessly interesting and novel patterns. Neither physics nor the evolutionary principle of natural selection can tell us exactly why the cosmos is put together in such a way that it keeps "breaking symmetry" and reaching toward richer modes of ordered novelty. Why has it not rather remained stuck in the more likely groove of sheer physical equilibrium? Or why, as its total energy level runs down, does it wend its way through the apparently needless detour of so much beauty?

Without in any way violating the second law of thermodynamics, the cosmos has clearly entertained an endless array of complex systems that "emerge" unpredictably at states far from thermodynamic equilibrium. It is especially in living organisms, apparently arising out of "chaos" and then curdling into systems of incalculable "complexity," that the cosmos discloses its mysterious potential for emergent order. So many systems in nature, from cells, to organisms, minds, and civilizations, appear and stabilize for varying periods of time at states far from physical equilibrium. And it is there—at the edge of chaos— that the most interesting things happen.

Why science has ignored this fact for so long would make an interesting study in itself. But, whatever the reasons, some scientists are in fact finally taking notice of nature's complex adaptive patterning with its defiance of linear mathematics. They are now asking *why* nature tends toward emergent complexity. Doesn't this new "why" question bring science to the brink of theology? Here are some possible responses.

I. Conflict

Proponents of the old design argument in natural theology would have enjoyed all the new scientific attention now being given over to the study of intricate patterns in nature. Natural theologians would surely have seen the hand of God behind the surprising order and strange attractors that science is uncovering in processes that on the surface seem chaotic. But those of us who are intellectually most at home with scientific skepticism find nothing whatsoever in the new scientific emphasis on chaos and complexity that would lead us to religion. In fact, the utter spontaneity of matter's self-organization, a major emphasis in the new science, would seem to render more superfluous than ever the idea of an ordering deity. As it turns out, matter itself is *inherently* self-organizing. Hence there is no need for an extraneous, supernatural designer who would put the stamp of order on chaos. Chaos gives rise to order *spontaneously*, and nature blindly selects those systems that are most adaptive. Self-organization is an irreducible property of matter, so the phenomenon of ordered complexity needs no explanation beyond itself.

Obviously, if nature is composed of complex adaptive systems, we can no longer base our science on the crude mechanical models of the past, even though these are still applicable in engineering. We admit that the physical universe is much more subtle than scientific skeptics used to think. But, for all that, we can still easily remain materialists. Granted, matter is more puzzling than we had ever suspected, and we may not be able to reduce and analyze life and consciousness in the same way that previous scientists aspired to do. But in all its complexity life arises as a purely material process, and even consciousness is no more mysterious or magical than digestion. If we stopped struggling for a purely natural explanation of all complex phenomena it would be a cowardly flight from science, a childish capitulation to mysticism.[4]

Furthermore, the science of complexity does not deny that all events are materially caused and determined. It simply states that, since we are not omniscient, we cannot specify in advance all the conditions that we would have to know in order to comprehend most natural occurrences. In principle we could model the universe computationally. It's just that the computation is so complicated that it cannot be carried out completely in advance. Any natural process is its own computation, but for all we know, it may still be as deterministic as classical physics proposed.

In short, chaos and complexity provide no new warrants for a religious interpretation of the universe.

II. Contrast

The fact that matter is self-organizing, or that order arises spontaneously out of chaos, is in no way disturbing to our theological vision. In fact, if matter is inherently self-organizing this gives us all the more reason to repudiate the superficial God that natural theologians with their physico-theology have always tried to slip into the gaps of human ignorance.

Natural theology invents a divine designer to "explain" the complex order in nature. William Paley, for example, argued that intricate order could not have arisen spontaneously, and so he brought in his pallid divine Watchmaker to fill the gap—to account for the order in nature. But we have always been suspicious of natural theology. Any God humans try to arrive at through the devices of paltry science and reason has little if anything to do with the God of revelation.

Therefore, by excluding any supernatural designer who intervenes to impose order on randomness, the skeptics have actually done our kind of theology a great service. They have allowed us to speak of God where it really matters—in relation to human freedom and the quest for meaning—and not simply as a way to satisfy our scientific curiosity. So we agree that the new sciences of chaos and complexity have no theological implications. The God who speaks to us only through a revelatory "word" does not have to await developments in science in order to gain appropriate credentials. The reservations we expressed in the preceding chapter with respect to the anthropic principle are no less applicable here.

III. Contact

By abolishing any contact between theology and cosmology the contrasters diminish both disciplines. They are rightly concerned that we avoid making room for any insertion of a god-of-the gaps into the dark regions of human ignorance that naturalistic explanation may eventually illuminate. However, the new emphasis on chaos and complexity brings into our field of vision an aspect of nature that had been ignored by the kind of science that gave rise to modern skepticism. The new sciences (if we may call them that) focus our attention in a fresh way on the pervasive fact of patterning. In doing so they are dealing with something as fundamental as being itself, and not with just another gap that could conceivably be filled in by fresh scientific discoveries.

After all, can we really separate the deep question of a thing's existence or "being" from the fact of its patterning? For anything to exist at all would it not have to possess some degree of organized structure? Without at least some internal ordering of its components could anything even have actuality? Our position, as articulated by Whitehead, is that things simply cannot exist without being ordered in a definite way.[5] Indefiniteness would be equivalent to non-existence. No order means "no thing"—which we usually spell "nothing." Thus, the question scientists are asking today about *why* there is complexity in the universe is only a hair's breadth away from the theological question concerning why anything exists at all. Consequently, the new sciences cannot be so neatly segregated from religious questions as could the atomistic and mechanistic abstractions of classical physics.

The very possibility of doing science in the first place *presupposes* the fact of patterning as science's field of exploration. Science teaches us interesting new things about the specifics of cosmic order, and the new sciences dealing with chaos and complexity are doing just that. But science cannot by itself explain the naked fact of patterning. True, it is *discovering* complex designs that it never noticed before. And with computers it can model more closely than ever the strange forms of order that emerge along the border of chaos. But can scientists ask the very deep question as to why there is any patterning at all and pretend that they are not thereby steering perilously close to metaphysics? And when they wonder why complex patterning has the features of diversity, emergence, adaptability, and interactivity, can they pursue such inquiry to the very end without making contact with theology? Our own approach wants to avoid any conflation with science, but we cannot ignore some suggestive features in the current preoccupation with complexity and chaos.

1) In the first place, it is not inconsequential, theologically speaking, that the new sciences enlarge our picture of a universe remarkably generous in allowing order to arise even where we would expect more disorder. It is noteworthy that something about the cosmos—a feature that science itself has not yet specified—graciously holds randomness within bounds. Stable systems that become turbulent when they experience a

new influx of energy do not always avalanche precipitously toward further chaos. Surprisingly, they take on even richer patterning and stability at states far from equilibrium. Why does the universe have this wondrous, and we would add generous, habit of turning confusion into complexity and order? And why is there an overall increase, or emergence, in complexity as evolution moves forward in time? Scientists deftly cover over a multitude of mysteries by an all too cavalier use of the expressions "spontaneous" and "self-organizing"—as though these adjectives could conceivably stave off our craving for understanding.

We cannot suppress the question raised by previous generations of scientists who followed the second law of thermodynamics: What right do we have to expect that the universe would unfold so extravagantly in novel patterning rather than simply abiding at a monotonous and homogeneous mode of existence? So far the so-called "science" of complexity has given us very little that is truly explanatory. We are of course grateful that it has placed new emphasis on the neglected facts of patterning and emergence. But by its own admission it has been more descriptive than explanatory.

On the other hand, in our quest for explanation we are not ready for an abrupt return to natural theology, although the new sciences' accent on organization might easily tempt us in such a direction. Rather, we find in chaos and complexity an invitation to construct a fresh "theology of nature," which is by no means the same thing as a natural theology. Our theology of nature does not try to prove God's existence from science, but instead looks for ways of integrating the new picture of a universe comprised of complex, chaotic, adaptive, evolutionary systems on the one hand with our belief in the creative and promising God of our religious faith on the other.

It is no secret, of course, that such an idea of God has not sat well with the linear science of the past. Scientific skeptics, resting comfortably on scientism, materialism, and reductionism, have confidently dismissed all ideas of God as illusory. However, the sciences of complexity and chaos may have something to teach us about the intellectual plausibility of scientific skepticism today. For the new orientation of science seriously challenges, and perhaps even demolishes, the fundamental beliefs out of which scientific skepticism's judgments against the idea of God arose in modern times.

At the present time, for instance, science is questioning its former obsession with the linear abstractions that constituted the intellectual core of modern materialist atheism. Our new scientific awareness of the prevalence in nature of non-linear systems places under suspicion the scientific respectability of the materialism and reductionism that have usually been based on a naive conviction of the absolutely linear character of natural processes. Science itself is now rocking the very foundations of modern scientific skepticism. This remarkable turn-about cannot help being of interest to theologians.

Even more dramatically, however, chaos theory delivers a fatal blow to the scientistic epistemological ideology underlying both materialism and reductionism. For chaos theoreticians all emphatically deny the possibility of our *ever* being able to specify fully the initial conditions in most natural processes that would give us complete scientific control over them and their future states. Accordingly, chaos theory also frustrates the horrifying expectation—exemplified by the likes of Weinberg and Hawking—that by giving us a conclusive grasp of the "fundamental" levels of nature, some "final theory" in physics will make science triumphantly complete. Furthermore, if indeterminate quantum effects can be factored into the initial conditions to which dynamical systems are said to be so sensitive, science must despair all the more of ever fully comprehending physical reality.[6]

In this respect, then, the new science is bringing us face to face with mystery once again. Far from demystifying the world, as the reductionist agenda proposed to do, science is now opening up the horizon of an inexhaustibly indeterminate universe. There is no danger, then, that science is getting us any closer to an exhaustive understanding of the world. Refuted by science itself, scientism is less believable than ever. The universe was kind enough, apparently from its very beginning, to see to it that science would never realize the dream of a totalizing completeness, and that we would never run out of interesting new things to explore and explain.

2) In the second place, there are theological implications in the fact that patterns appear in dynamical systems that at first seem utterly random. In terms of the history of scientific expectations it is enormously puzzling that the most intricate and complex forms of order arise out of non-linear, chaotic processes. It was not hard for an older science to see the connection between linearity and order, and for an older theology to claim a close relationship between mechanical order and a religiously irrelevant clock-making God. What is so baffling and exciting now, though, is that the richest types of natural order seem to emerge out of chaos. Formerly physico-theology connected God primarily to the fact of linear order. But what happens to the cosmic Designer now that lin-

earity gives way to a kind of order that arises "spontaneously" out of apparent disorder? Doesn't this different world require a new cosmology and a new theology of nature? Doesn't it demand that we think in a fresh way about any Creator we wish to associate with this world?

Chaos and complexity are stimulating to our theology because they correspond so well with a religious experience that pictures God not only as the source of cosmic order but also as the source of surprise. God in our traditions is, after all, the ultimate origin of the *novelty* that causes chaos or turbulence in the first place. The religions descended from Abraham, whose faith consists of openness to an indeterminate promise, think of God not just as an orderer, but as One who brings about an always new future. This means, however, that we expect the future to be always open to surprise—and therefore to the chaos that surprising new developments can cause.

Chaos, in our metaphysical perspective, is an essential feature of a universe created in such a way that it remains unfinished. A universe still in the making is by definition always open to a freshness and novelty capable of disrupting any present state of cosmic order. For as novelty enters into any ordered situation, it inevitably stirs things up. Chaos ensues, but the chaos novelty brings with it is not just the dead end of disorder. Rather, it is the opportunity for new creation. Creativity happens "at the edge of chaos" because it is at this adventurous juncture, rather than in rigid states of stagnant equilibrium, that novelty can slip silently into the world.

So if we think of God as the ultimate source of this novelty, as the "One who makes all things new," then God must be nearer to chaos than the old natural theology would ever have allowed. If we thought of God exclusively as the source of order (and not of novelty also) then the fact of randomness and chaos might occasion skepticism about God's existence. But the God of our religion is the author not only of order and life, but of *new* order and *new* life. Hence, our theology (as intimated in the biblical accounts of creation) finds divine creativity hovering very close to chaos.

This gives a new meaning to entropy, the former companion of cosmic pessimism. For whenever something new enters into an already ordered arrangement, the present state of order tends to break down, to slip toward chaos. To be receptive to novelty, rigid orderliness has to give way. It is a habit of nature, as it seeks wider and more intricate patterning, to veer entropically toward the "edge of chaos." The world's atomic, molecular, and organic structures first have to loosen up if they are to make way for more intricate configurations. If natural order were absolutely inflexible there could be no emergent novelty of patterning, no growth, no life, no process of adaptation. Isn't entropy then at heart the opening of the universe to new creation?

Chaos, non-linearity, and randomness are not signals that the world exists without the care of God, as scientific skepticism has always argued.[7] Rather, to us at least, they are consonant with a God who cares that the world become something more than what it already is. We take the fact of chaos to be the consequence of a divine discontent with the status quo—signals of a Creator who is still creating and who invites our own participation in making the world new. Chaos and complexity are marks of an unfinished world, one that remains always vulnerable to the infusion of novelty. Nature—and, one might also add, the human spirit—seek out the edge of chaos, for that is where new growth and new creation take place. Theologically speaking, then, chaos and complexity follow from a divine longing that the world become ever richer, more diverse, and more beautiful.[8]

However, we want to make it clear once again that our theology is by no means just another attempt to prove God's existence through a more subtle kind of physico-theology. We are only trying to show the *congruity* that we perceive between faith's idea of a creative God who is full of surprises, and the emerging scientific picture of chaos and complexity in the cosmos. We do not wish to base our theology on the new science, which is constantly changing anyway. But the sciences of chaos and complexity cannot help catching the attention of theologians whose religious tradition educates them to look into all things for signs of promise and new life.

Shaped as we are by the figure of Abraham and his trust in the divine promise, we understand "faith" as an invitation to look for signs of promise even in the most inauspicious beginnings. The sciences of chaos and complexity exhibit a universe remarkably conformable to the theme of faith's promise: many processes in the natural world (a) begin with an amazing modesty and simplicity, (b) unfold into a turbulence or chaos, but then (c) eventually burst out into the richest and most beautiful of patterns. Such a universe is remarkably congruent with the basic outline of religious faith.

Though turbulence seems to reign supreme at times, there remains the possibility of surprising outcomes—for which we usually must wait with patience. We cannot calculate the specific character of emergent natural beauty in advance of its actual arrival, but we have grounds for expecting it to emerge in surprising ways nonetheless. This universe, we have learned at last, is remarkably different from the one we saw through the lens of classical science, and it may not fit the older idea of a designer deity. But a world so full of promise corresponds very well with our faith in the unfathomably surprising God of prophetic religion.

3) In the third place, the sciences of chaos and complexity are theologically (and we might add, ecologically) significant because of their emphasis on "sensitivity to initial conditions." This fact brings out the significance or value of everything in the world, no matter how incidental it may seem to be. For even the tiniest modulations in the patterning of initial conditions in any evolving system render the profoundest of differences as we follow the course of its unfolding. The slightest initial inflection is not at all inconsequential with respect to the future state of affairs. This fact should have implications for interpreting the unique and special character of every existing thing, including ourselves and our lives and actions. It is not just abstract universal laws that possess significance, for every concrete thing and every person makes a difference in shaping the whole character of the universe. Ours would not be the same world if even the tiniest part of it did not exist.

4) Fourth, the universe of complexity and chaos suggests an understanding of God's power as gentle and persuasive rather than coercive. A world which, as a whole, is so sensitive to the initial conditions from which it has evolved is one that seems to be guided more by tenderness than by brute force. The delicate sensitivity of cosmic processes to their initial conditions gives theology new metaphors for interpreting the notion of divine providence. God apparently does not force the world into some final shape in an instantaneous display of magic. Nor is God a linear mathematician, deterministically directing the world in the manner of a cosmic ruler. But still the universe does exhibit, from its very beginning, the character of being influenced by some gentle, noncoercive quality of self-ordering that allows it to proliferate into an amazingly creative diversity of adaptive systems. The kind of creator we might associate with this spectacle is not the same as the narrowly conceived divine mechanic of classical natural theology.

The specific steps in chaotic cosmic evolution are not evident in the initial conditions. There is a great deal of freedom in the unfolding of the story. But we cannot help speculating that there is nevertheless a gentle constraining of the initial conditions, so that the cosmos will at least tilt in the direction of becoming more and more interesting. Given

God's self-restraining character, one that is fully compatible with an infinite love, we do not expect the cosmos, or any of its particular processes, to unfold in a rigidly deterministic way—as though it were being forced to fit a pre-existing scheme. Instead, there is room for experimenting, meandering, and even straying far from the possibilities available to it. It is not beyond the range of our theological presuppositions, then, that the cosmos would give birth to the kind of structures and patterns that the sciences of chaos and complexity are now bringing to our attention. Though chaos and complexity may not be compatible with certain rigidly construed conceptions of God, they seem to correspond favorably with the idea of a God whose omnipotence (i.e. capacity to influence all things) consists essentially of persuasive love rather than mechanical coercion.

In the now obsolete cosmology of scientific materialism a combination of blind chance and impersonal physical necessity governed everything. But the notions of chance and necessity, at least as scientific materialism wields them, now seem so abstract that they do not correspond accurately to the concrete cosmic realities to which they clumsily refer. Chaos and complexity leave us with a picture of nature in which we do not have to choose between a rigid determinism on the one hand or blind randomness on the other, as most scientific skepticism has done. For the actual world is not comprised of abstract chance and necessity but of a balanced synthesis of *reliability* on the one hand and openness to *surprise* on the other.[9]

If we sever nature's reliability from the element of surprise we end up with the misleading impression that the universe is made up of impersonal necessity. Or if we separate the element of surprise from its concrete connection to nature's inherent reliability we reduce everything to blind chance. However, the notions of chaos and complexity invite us to put reliability and surprise back together, even though there is always going to be some tension between them. They allow us to see that both pure chance and absolute necessity are weak, abstract notions that fail to capture the concrete character of nature as a complex and unstable blending of lawful consistency on the one hand and creative openness to the future on the other.

Chaos theory, furthermore, shows that exceedingly complex patterning can arise out of the simplest laws of nature and that order is latent even in the most aimlessly meandering and apparently random of processes. The cosmos, as it teeters on the edge of chaos, is influenced by the past but also open to an interesting future. The new scientific picture of a universe comprised of reliability and openness is harmonious with the understanding of God given to us in prophetic religion. Nature's reliability points us toward the theme of God's fidelity; and its openness to novelty seems to augur the surprise we anticipate from our trust in a God of promise. The God of our religious experience is faithful to the divine promises, yet always surprising and incalculable in fulfilling them. The world of nature now seems remarkably consistent with this picture of God.

5) There is yet a fifth way in which chaos theory and the new science of "complexity" may catch the attention of theologians. It has to do with the interpretation of creativity in evolution. What is the cause of life's extraordinary inventiveness and creativity? In his book *Ever Since Darwin* and elsewhere Stephen Jay Gould responds with the usual Darwinian line: blind natural selection is the only and sufficient cause of creativity in evolution. Richard Dawkins expands on this postulate in *The Blind Watchmaker*. Like many other evolutionists, Gould and Dawkins both argue that natural selection of numerous small variations over a long period of time is sufficient to account for all the new things that appear in evolution, including eventually ourselves. If variations arrived already "pre-packaged in the right direction," Gould admits, then evolutionary selection would have no creative role to play.[10]

Recently, however, complexity science has proposed that organisms do indeed arrive in a "pre-packaged" form. Stuart Kauffman, for example, has argued at great length that even before nature has a chance to select some few species for survival and reproduction, living systems have already organized themselves spontaneously. Creativity in evolution takes place primarily in the self-organization that occurs *prior* to selection. Thus natural selection by itself cannot account for all the creativity in evolution.[11]

Kauffman's theory of evolution bears no direct implications for theology. It does nothing, for example, to disturb his own skepticism. Still, it does raise questions about the skeptics' appeal to the notion of natural selection as a forceful refutation of religion. In order to bludgeon religious interpretations of evolution, skeptics have constantly assumed that an aimless process of selection is sufficient to account for all of life including the human species. However, if we are to trust Kauffman's interpretation, nature now turns out to be much more inherently creative than the conventional materialist interpretation of evolution had ever suspected. Nature is in fact more than eager to provide the stuff for selection in "pre-packaged" form. The pervasive phenomenon of self-organization provides further hints that our universe is not one that only grudgingly allows living and thinking beings to appear. Rather, nature goes out of its way to make such momentous occurrences possible. Chance and natural selection may still have a role to play in evolution, but they no longer seem to be as all-important as science previously supposed.

In sum, what the new scientific attention to chaos and complexity suggests to theology is that the religious intuition of order prevailing over disorder is a sensible one. Chaos surprisingly conceals strange but rich patterns of order. Isn't there at least a hint here of a more benign universe than materialism allowed? That complex pattern would appear spontaneously in surprising ways, even where we least expect it, runs counter to the icy vision of physical reality upon which scientific skepticism was erected. If skepticism is to have a future in the intellectual world it will have to be of a different species from that which purged theology from intellectual culture in modern times. For, lurking beneath what physics takes to be a cosmic trend toward maximum thermodynamic disorder, there may be nothing less momentous than the surprise of a *final* patterning whose beauty we are not yet able to fathom, but for which we have every reason to hope.

IV. Confirmation

What we find most intriguing about the sciences of chaos and complexity is nature's capacity for *self*-organization. That the universe seems to be creating itself is of great theological interest to us. Old-fashioned natural theology would probably have been disturbed by all the new scientific talk about nature's self-organizing capability. After all, a self-organizing universe would apparently leave little room for a creative and designing deity. Does the world no longer depend on God? Is it really so autonomous that it can actively organize itself?

The science of complexity thinks of nature as actively self-creative at all levels. Living cells, ant-hills, immune systems, ecosystems, and even economic systems seem to come about simply as the result of unspecifiable internal organizational impulses. There is no evidence of any outside designer. It all seems to just happen as the result of an experimental, adaptive and creative impetus built into nature from the start. Even the emergence of life and mind in all their complexity now appears to science as simply the unfolding of a potential always resident in matter. No miraculous intervention is necessary.

How then can we continue to talk about God or divine care in terms of a universe comprised of complex, adaptive, self-organizing patterns?

Our response is that the fact of a self-organizing universe allows us to bring to the center a way of thinking about God that has long been present in religion, but which for too long has been marginalized. And this conception of God, in a sense, anticipates and "confirms" the scientific idea of a self-organizing universe. The God of whom we are speaking here is one who is concerned that the universe through and through, in all of its dimensions, possess a self-coherence and capacity for self-creation that makes it appear, at least at first glance, as though it does not need God at all. Yet, if we think about God in terms of some of theology's deeper and more radical reflections, the autonomous, self-organizing universe of complexity science is just what we should expect.

The theology to which we are referring thinks of God as infinite, self-emptying love. Such a God is said to be "kenotic." In Greek, "kenosis" literally means "emptying," so a kenotic God is a "self-emptying" God. In this theological perspective, it is only because of God's self-emptying love that a self-organizing universe can come into being.

Remarkable as it may seem, if God is to create a world truly distinct from the divine Self, such a world would have to have an *internal* "self-coherence" or autonomy. Simply in order to be the "world" and not God, the creation has to be different from its Creator. This implies, then, that divine creativity allows the world to be itself, and so we may understand divine "creation" here as a "letting be." Thus the creation of the world is not a coercive, direct divine designing of things. If it were, then the universe would not be truly distinct from God, nor would God transcend the universe. If the universe is to be clearly not-God, or if it is to be something other than God, as all forms of theism require, then it would not be totally surprising that it has a propensity for the kind of self-organization that the sciences of chaos and complexity highlight.

To put all of this another way: in order to create a distinct universe God freely "withdraws" the exercise of divine power and expansive presence. The creation is not an expression of divine might, but a signal of divine humility. God freely undergoes a self-emptying (kenosis) so that something "other" than divine reality can come into existence. At the heart of the divine life, so to speak, there is a deliberate self-contracting, a reduction of God's expansiveness to "nothing," a self-emptying withdrawal of the infinite presence and power. It is this kenosis that allows God's "other," the universe, to emerge. And it is out of God's humility and loving concern for the integrity of this "other" that the universe is endowed, from its conception, with an inherent capacity for self-organization. It is only because we have not thought extensively about divine love as a self-emptying that we find ourselves surprised that a divinely created universe is a *self*-organizing one.[12]

Yet even in human relations we are most responsive to others whose love takes the shape of a non-interference that gives us the slack to be ourselves. We feel most liberated, and most alive, in the presence of those who risk letting us be ourselves, whereas we feel cramped by those who force their presence upon us. We tender our deepest devotion to those who by restraining their powers allow us to unfold our lives at our own pace, and we resent those who cannot curb their coercive impulses and are constantly running our lives. Unfortunately we often think of God as wielding this crude kind of might rather than bestowing a love that is mighty precisely in its restraint.

It is only because God is not only infinitely loving, but also infinitely humble, that the self-organizing universe can come into being. Theologians have ignored the divine humility and have presented "God" as powerful in a very coarse and at times tyrannical sense. Too often we have understood the conception of God as "all-mighty" in a way that leads to theological contradictions, many of which have been pointed out quite rightly by scientific skeptics. Our view, however, is that God's "power" (which means "capacity to influence") is more effectively manifested in a humble "letting be" of a *self-organizing* universe than in any direct display of divine magicianship. A world capable of self-organization is surely a more integral world, one more intense in being, than a world thought of as merely passive in the hands of its Creator.

Using the ideas of chaos and complexity, however, we may still hold that the universe is fully dependent upon and sensitive to the presence of its self-emptying Creator. The world's ongoing creation is a cooperative enterprise whose dynamic self-organization is ultimately made possible by the non-interfering love of God. We suggest that it is the self-outpouring of divine love that both invites the world into being and that continually challenges it to raise itself ever further above indefiniteness and nothingness.

8

Does the Universe Have a Purpose?

More than sixty year ago the famous British physicist James Jeans wrote that modern science has given us the distressing picture of a universe hostile to life and consciousness, one destined for death at the hands of entropy. This specter, he went on to say, raises an unavoidably harsh question regarding our own status:

> Is this, then, all that life amounts to—to stumble, almost by mistake, into a universe which was clearly not designed for life, and which, to all appearances, is either totally indifferent or definitely hostile to it, to stay clinging on to a fragment of a grain of sand until we are frozen off, to strut on our tiny stage with the knowledge that our aspirations are all but doomed to final frustration, and that our achievements must perish with our race, leaving the universe as though we had never been?[1]

Isn't Jeans making an important point here? Is it not the case that science does indeed nullify the ages-old belief that we live in a purposeful universe? This, of course, is the real issue underlying each of the preceding chapters, and it is one that we must now bring more nakedly out into the open. No question in science and religion is more to the point, or strikes more directly at the heart of human concerns, than that of cosmic purpose or "teleology."

And if the universe holds no purpose overall, what does this say about who we are, and about what sort of destiny awaits us individually? Einstein himself once said that the most important question each of us has to ask is whether we live in a friendly or an unfriendly universe.

We could paraphrase: the most important question each of us has to ask is whether the cosmos we inhabit is purposeful or not. Is there any "point" to the universe? What possible significance or meaning might there be in the cosmic story that science has lately been telling us? Or is there perhaps no point to it all?

In the first chapter of this book, while pondering the question of the validity of religious faith in an age of science, we were already implicitly asking whether scientifically educated people today can still embrace—in any substantive sense—the ancient religious intuition that the cosmos is an embodiment of a transcendent meaning. And in subsequent discussions about such issues as the personality of God, the implications of evolution, whether life and mind are reducible to matter, whether the world was created, whether we humans really belong here, and how we are to interpret the fact of nature's emergent complexity—in all of these we were simultaneously raising the global question of whether the universe has any purpose to it.

But isn't this a tediously academic sort of inquiry? What does it have to do with my own personal existence? Why should I worry about cosmic purpose? What difference does it make to me if the universe is friendly or unfriendly, as long as I can carve out my own destiny, find a gratifying career, or achieve something significant in my own life? Why should the question of the world's general disposition be of any importance to me at all?

There was a time perhaps when we could casually separate the question of the meaning of our individual lives from the apparently indifferent universe of modern science. It was possible for both religious and skeptic to view the cosmos itself as inherently purposeless as long as the individual could find some personal significance in spite of that. The absence of meaning in the objective world provided a blank slate upon which we creative human subjects could inscribe our own meanings. Philosophers could even claim that an inherently vacuous universe actually renders human life and creativity all the more splendid.

Perhaps no more compelling rendition of this belief may be found than in the words of the American philosopher E. D. Klemke:

> From the standpoint of present evidence, evaluational components such as meaning or purpose are not to be found in the universe as objective aspects of it....Rather, we "impose" such values upon the universe....An objective meaning—that is, one which is inherent within the universe or dependent upon external agencies—would, frankly, leave me cold. It would not be mine....I, for one, am glad that the universe has no mean-

ing, for thereby is man all the more glorious. I willingly accept the fact
that external meaning is non-existent...for this leaves me free to forge
my own meanings.[2]

Such a perspective still appeals to many. Stephen Jay Gould, for
example, recently argued that a purposeless universe is "exciting" and
"uplifting," for the fact that we cannot find any purpose in nature
means that "we will have to define it for ourselves." The absence of
cosmic teleology is not a misfortune but an opportunity.[3]

And yet, modern evolutionary science and contemporary physics,
as Jeans himself was already aware in 1930, no longer permit us to separate our own existence so neatly from the rest of the cosmos. Our personal lives and minds are so intertwined with all of physical reality and
the story of its unfolding that the status of the universe as a whole is
deeply determinative of our own private identities. Recent cosmology
does not allow us to flee into some acosmic haven of "subjectivity" and
pretend that our minds or our personal ideas of meaning have no connection to the rest of the universe. In a Cartesian world such dualism
might have been plausible, but it does not sit well in the world of twen-
tieth-century physics or—as we shall see in the next chapter—ecology.
The thrust of science today is that I and the world constitute an inseparable unity, so that if the cosmos as a whole has no point to it, then surely this says something about who I am. On the other hand, if there is
after all a teleological dimension to the universe it too would enter into
the definition of my own being.

I might, of course, still persist in arguing that my individual life can
have significance even if the universe is "sound and fury signifying nothing." But if I were fully convinced, at every level of my consciousness,
that the universe itself is utterly pointless, then, short of reverting to an
absolute dualism of mind and nature (a stance which today is highly
problematic scientifically speaking), such a conviction would inevitably
place in question the meaning of my own existence. It is only artificially—and by ignoring contemporary cosmology altogether—that I can
separate the question of who I am from the larger issue of cosmic purpose.

But what do we mean by "purpose"? Minimally we mean "oriented
toward a goal or toward a value." A process is called purposeful or
"teleological" if it tends toward the realization of some good, rather
than just meandering blindly about. A teleological process need not be
coercively driven, nor need it be a straight-arrow thrust toward a prede-

termined goal. But it somehow has to transcend sheer aimlessness. It must fall along at least vaguely directional lines. Something of significance must be "going on," and we must be able to have some idea of what it is. But does our evolving cosmos qualify as purposeful even in this "loose" teleological sense?

The God-religions, Judaism, Christianity, and Islam, maintain that the universe does have a purpose, and their faith stands or falls on this claim. Although they have diverse formulations, theistic religions consistently cling to a teleological understanding of the universe. They are convinced that the cosmos, and all the entities within it, are here for a reason. Devotees of such a faith may not be able to state very clearly what this reason is, and reverence for the fathomless ways of God warns them not to expect absolute lucidity on such an important matter. But religious symbols, stories, doctrines, and rituals give believers a deep, albeit often cloudy, impression that their lives and the whole universe are embedded in a mysterious movement toward beauty, or love, peace, new life, and communion with an eternal goodness. The main concern of this book, however, has been to ask whether—in the light of what science is now telling us—we can still honestly embrace this religiously teleological understanding of the universe.

Doubts arise in great measure because modern scientific method seems to have turned its back on any concern about purpose. Indeed its expulsion of teleological kinds of explanation is what makes modern science so dramatically different from ancient ways of knowing. In European intellectual culture prior to the seventeenth century, any full understanding of the cosmos required knowledge of what Aristotle called "final causes." The "final cause" of something is its purpose or the goal for which it is intended. To understand something fully you had to know *why* it existed, and this applied also to the universe as a whole. But as scientific aversion to teleology has penetrated our thought processes and our universities, the ancient attribution of purpose to the universe has become more and more intellectually suspect.

Aristotle had taught that a satisfactory understanding of anything consists of mastering its "four causes." First you must know a thing's "efficient cause" or the agent that brings it into existence. Second, you need to know the "material cause" or the stuff that makes it up. Third, there is the "formal cause," the mold, essence, or "whatness" into which the agent shapes the material cause. But most important of all, knowledge means awareness of a thing's "final cause," the end or purpose for which it exists or toward which it tends. In Aristotelian science there can be no comprehensive understanding without knowledge of final causes. Before the modern scientific revolution Western "science" consisted mainly of exploring all four causes, but especially the last. Cosmology itself was a search for the four causes of the universe, and both philosophy and theology simply assumed that the cosmos as a whole had a final cause: God. God was not only the ground but also the end of all things. Prescientific consciousness, shaped by philosophy and religion, nestled snugly in the impression that we live in a purposeful cosmos, and that our individual lives need only conform obediently to the designs of God if we are to find ultimate happiness. It was within the framework of a teleological cosmology that theism received its classical expressions.

Modern science, however, has challenged all of this, renouncing teleological or final causal explanations as unworthy of science. In his *Novum Organum* (1620) Francis Bacon argued that experimental observation of efficient and material causes, not "sterile" speculation about final causes, is the way to genuine knowledge. Indeed, ever since its formal debut in the seventeenth century, modern science has concerned itself almost exclusively with efficient and material causes, that is, with the question of "how" things work and what they are made of. It has wanted nothing to do with final causes, or with "why" things are the way they are.

At the present time, as we noted in the preceding chapter, there are signs that science is once again flirting with formal and final causes. It shows a fresh interest in pattern and in questions about why the world is arranged the way it is. But for the most part scientific thought still avoids any suggestion that questions about the purpose of things can lead us to true or useful knowledge.

This brings us then to this chapter's topic: to embrace modern and contemporary science are we not obliged first to reject the idea of cosmic purpose, and along with it the God-religions which have always instructed us that the universe is the momentous carrier of a divine meaning? What follows here is a summary of the ways in which each of our four contestants might interpret science's distaste for teleological explanation.

I. Conflict

It was only when scientists dropped the Aristotelian and Medieval theological concern about "why" objects fall, and started investigating the laws that determine "how" they fall, that physics was finally emancipated from its suffocating conflation with religion. By breaking free of the religious obsession with purpose, physics could at last become a truly illuminating science. And only after biology dropped its formerly mystical habits, and turned its attention to the chemistry of life, did it experience a truly scientific birth in the present century. As long as vitalism ruled the day, leading us on the futile search for some mysterious or supernatural "life-force," biology made no progress. As long as we were governed by the illusion that life tended toward some goal, there was no truly scientific biology. Only after the life sciences began to base themselves on mechanistic explanations and the hard science of chemistry did their practitioners become rigorously scientific.

As far as we are concerned, therefore, a major criterion of genuine science is its distance from teleological explanations. And this applies as much to cosmology, the study of the cosmos as a whole, as to any particular branch of science, such as biology or physics. Cosmologists today, unlike the Aristotelians and the theologians, are justifiably embarrassed when any of their associates even so much as hint that there may be some purposive influence shaping the universe. Please understand our reservations about questions of purpose. We are not trying to be spoilsports, but if we so much as let teleology get its foot in the door of science once again, our cosmology will inevitably grow too murky to be useful or enlightening.

Science, as the Harvard biologist Ernst Mayr indicates, has not found any "teleological mechanisms," even in living organisms, and so there are simply no evidential warrants for our thinking about cosmic purpose at all.[4] Moreover, even if they were really a factor, teleological goals would be realized only far off in the distant future, and so we could not really know anything about them here and now. How could a future eventuality have any influence on present reality? Science can make predictions about the future only on the basis of what it has already observed about the way nature works. By tracing chains of efficient and material causation from the past we have been able to explain a great deal more about how nature works than could Aristotle's fuzzy doctrine of final causes.

You can see then that we prefer not even to get into the messy subject of teleology. We have never observed any cosmic trends from which we could extrapolate an ultimately purposeful destiny for the cosmos. And so, we must stick to the facts and avoid making wild guesses about the meaning of the whole universe. For us science is the only trustworthy guide to truth, and since it has not come close to find-ing any evidence of cosmic purpose, we must conclude that it is quite unlikely that there is any.

A sober examination of the data available to us, as we have implied in the preceding chapters, should lead the honest and informed person toward cosmic pessimism. Cosmic pessimism is the sober conviction that the universe as a whole lacks any purpose whatsoever. We think this is a much more reasonable interpretation of cosmology than the unempirical imaginings of religion. We freely admit that humans are meaning-seeking beings, but the universe of modern science is clearly indifferent to this search. Just look once again at the impersonal cos-mos uncovered by physics and evolutionary biology. Or survey the chilling immensity of the heavens and our own insignificance in all the empty cosmic vastness. Even the nearest stars and galaxies care not a whit for us.

We may be able to give some local and temporary meaning to our individual lives, often by working with others to combat suffering or to improve life on this planet, or to advance the cause of science. But sci-ence gives us no reason for thinking that the whole universe puts any final stamp of approval on our ethical, intellectual and aesthetic efforts. All the data available to us simply confirms the world's indifference to our human projects. Physics, evolutionary biology, and astronomy actu-ally provide solid reasons for our not trusting that the cosmos tends toward any meaningful destiny. The conflict of religion with science, therefore, is fundamentally rooted in the fact that religion uncritically embraces some version of cosmic teleology whereas science rules it out.

Toward the end of his book *The First Three Minutes* physicist Steven Weinberg states ironically that as the universe becomes more comprehensible to science the more "pointless" it also seems to be.[5] Many of us agree with this sentiment. When asked whether she has ever thought about whether the universe has a point to it, astronomer Sandra Faber, for example, replied:

> ...I think the universe was created out of some natural process, and our appearance in it was a totally natural result of physical laws in our par-ticular portion of it—or what we call our universe. Implicit in the ques-tion, I think, is that there's some motive power that has a purpose be-yond human existence. I don't believe in that. So I guess ultimately I agree with Weinberg that it's completely pointless from a human per-spective.[6]

Again, responding to the same question, physicist Marc Davis stated:

> I try not to think about the question too much, because all too often I agree with Steven Weinberg, and it's rather depressing. Philosophically, I see no argument against his attitude, that we certainly don't see a point. To answer in the alternative sense really requires you to invoke the principle of God, I think. At least, that's the way I would view it, and there's no evidence that He's around, or It's around. On the other hand, that doesn't mean that you can't enjoy your life.[7]

Perhaps many of us scientific skeptics would feel most at home with astronomer Margaret Geller's thoughtful reply to the question about whether there is a point to the universe. One may be a cosmic pessimist, she says, and still feel that life is well worth living:

> I guess my view of life is that you live your life and it's short. The thing is to have as rich an experience as you possibly can. That's what I'm trying to do. I'm trying to do something creative. I try to educate people. I enjoy seeing the world, and I have as many broad experiences as I can. I feel privileged to be able to be creative. But does it have a point? I don't know. It's not clear that it matters. I guess it's a kind of statement that I would never make. I figure, thinking in the small way that I think as a human being, well, okay why should it have a point? What point? It's just a physical system, what point is there?[8]

We realize that some physicists, even of the stature of Freeman Dyson, are now suggesting—on the basis of the anthropic principle— that the universe does have a kind of point to it after all. However, we do not think there is sufficient evidence to confirm such a quasi-religious hypothesis. Cosmic pessimism seems to be the most realistic position to take, even if it sometimes hurts to do so.

The Cornell professor of natural history, William Provine, has recently written a clear summary of the stance of scientific skepticism vis-à-vis the question of cosmic purpose. His words aptly depict our position:

> [Modern evolutionary biology] tells us (and I would argue that the same message flows in from physics, chemistry, molecular biology, astrophysics, and indeed from all modern science) that there is in nature no detectable purposive force of any kind. Everything proceeds purely by materialistic and mechanistic processes of causation or through purely stochastic processes....All that science reveals to us is chance and neces-

sity....modern science directly implies that the world is organized strictly in accordance with mechanistic principles. There are no purposive principles whatsoever in nature. There are no gods and no designing forces that are rationally detectable. The frequently made assertion that modern biology and the assumptions of the Judeo-Christian tradition are fully compatible is false.[9]

II. Contrast

The idea that the universe is "just a physical system" (as Margaret Geller states) or that it "proceeds purely by materialistic and mechanistic processes" (Provine) is not the consequence of science but of the beliefs we have been calling scientism, materialism and reductionism. It is these and not science itself that conflict with teleology. Cosmic pessimism is the comprehensive viewpoint of modern scientific skepticism, arising as the logical consequence of the three other components of the skeptic's belief system (scientism, materialism, and reductionism). At the deepest level beneath cosmic pessimism there is the *belief* that the only evidence that counts is scientific evidence (scientism). Then there is the naturalist *belief* that matter is all there is to reality (materialism). And finally there is the *belief* that only physical analysis can give us a satisfactory understanding of matter (reductionism).

Once again we must emphasize that these are faith statements and not knowledge gained from scientific experience. They are unfalsifiable, quasi-religious assumptions. Cosmic pessimism is no less rooted in belief than is religious teleology. It is the result of conflating science with suppositions that have nothing to do with science itself. If one believes that the universe is "just a physical system" then obviously one will also have to believe that there is no point or purpose to it either. But these are beliefs *about* some of the results of science, arising from outside of science, and not an inevitable consequence of scientific observation itself.

Nevertheless, we "contrasters" think that it is entirely appropriate that scientific method itself deliberately steers clear of any association with final causes. As most scientists will agree, science simply has no business talking about purpose. It does not fall within its province either to affirm or to deny it. And so when cosmic pessimists argue that it is scientific knowledge that justifies their skepticism about cosmic purpose, they are going beyond science itself, implicitly forcing science to answer a question for which it is naturally unqualified. Cosmic pessimism, which has deep and mysterious roots in all sorts of temperamental, cultural, ethical and historical factors other than science, seeks intellectual approval for its denial of cosmic purpose by appealing to the authority of *science*. But this appeal to science as the basis for pessimism is itself quite unscientific. At the same time, science is unable to establish that the cosmos is teleological either. Science itself is not equipped to deal with such questions.

Cosmic pessimism, we repeat, springs not from science, which is inherently innocent of any considerations of purpose or purposelessness, but from the three-headed ideological monster comprised of scientism, materialism and reductionism. By conflating science with these spurious and unscientific beliefs cosmic pessimism persistently presents science to a predominantly religious public as though scientific method were inseparable from anti-religious beliefs. In addition to being utterly arbitrary, this is a disastrous public relations procedure for the scientific community. Is it any wonder that there is so much public aversion to science? If scientists want to promote the cause of scientific knowledge, then they should ardently avoid mixing it up with pessimistic ideas that most human beings, for whom hope in ultimate meaning and purpose is essential to their very vitality, will never be able to swallow. For the very sake of science's own survival and flourishing, then, we call once again for its complete divorce from all ideologies, whether religious or secular.

This is why we entirely approve of the *scientific* avoidance of final causes. For we are fully aware that underneath the so-called "conflict" of science and religion there is a long and unfortunate history of scientific ideas being "contaminated" by teleology. So powerful is the human need to see purposes in things that our teleological impulses keep jumping over their properly religious boundaries and invading the world of science. This transgression is somewhat forgivable since it is nearly impossible for us humans completely to suppress the burning question "why?" And since scientists are also human beings it is not totally unexpected that they too occasionally slip into teleological modes of thinking, often without realizing it. (This is especially the case with the spurious anthropic principle.) But we agree with the skeptics that science as such should leave out any consideration of final causes. We only wish that they would themselves refrain from amalgamating it with cosmic pessimism.

However, to say that science must remain mute on the question of cosmic purpose is not to say that we humans can say nothing about it.

As you will no doubt have surmised by now, our position is that it *is the task of religion, not science, to deal with the issue of purpose*. We are awakened to the ultimate meaningfulness of this universe only through the kind of communion with the whole of things that characterizes religious faith. Since any conceivable cosmic purpose would be a global, overarching influence pervading and transcending the *entire* universe, we should never expect to capture its presence by way of scientific investigation of physical particulars. From the very outset science deliberately—and rightly—exempts itself from any concern for purpose and loses itself in analysis of the simpler aspects of things. Precisely because it has to simplify in order to understand, it cannot deal with anything as complex, sweeping and cloudy as cosmic purpose.

Thus Provine's complaint that science has not yet found any "teleological forces" in nature is not to the point. Science, whose methods are generally reductive and analytic, can focus our attention only on specific properties of the physical universe. It cannot, by definition, give us a sense of the meaning of the whole. To attain such a perspective we need to be gifted by an alternative way of looking at things. We consider it to be the role of revelation and religious faith to attune our consciousness to this wider vision of the universe. And so, our religious trust in cosmic teleology in no way conflicts with science, only with cosmic pessimism.

III. Contact

It would be most convenient if the relationship of science to religion were as crisp and clean as the contrasters see it. However, in the real world things are not that uncomplicated. And so here once again we are compelled to point out that the particular discoveries of science cannot but have a bearing on the question of cosmic purpose. In an age of evolutionary biology and big bang physics we cannot help asking how *this* particular universe could be said to have any point to it. We cannot protect a simplistic religious faith in cosmic purpose from facing the new challenges that come from science. And so, unlike the contrasters, we have no desire to divert the questions about cosmic purpose that arise out of new scientific ideas.

We agree that cosmic pessimism is a fabric woven out of a few tantalizing scientific threads mixed up with a lot of unfounded stoical, rationalistic, and other sorts of belief. But we also think that even in its purest formulations science still poses questions about cosmic purpose that theology must address. Fortunately, where it has undertaken to do so, theology has not only met the challenges but has undergone considerable growth in the process. It is very much to the advantage of theology that it engage in vigorous dialogue with scientific discoveries rather than incarcerate them in separate quarters where they can do no mischief. At the same time it is entirely appropriate for cosmologists to point out to us the serious religious questions they think arise with their new findings about the universe.

Isn't it a fact that some scientific ideas, even independently of their spurious alliance with materialist beliefs, do challenge our religious faith in cosmic purpose? We have already seen this to be the case, especially with the Darwinian emphasis on randomness and natural selection. And didn't the idea of entropy, at least for a while, raise serious questions about cosmic teleology? Furthermore, doesn't the ecological crisis, which science has helped us to see more clearly than we ever could otherwise, demand that we think over again just what it means to be religious in a world threatened by the collapse of its life-support systems? Or suppose, as is quite possible, that someday science will discover beings more intelligent and ethical than ourselves in other parts of the universe. Could our religions, with their terrestrially based and humanly shaped God-images, simply go along as before, completely unshaken?

We could multiply examples of ways in which science, even apart from the unfortunate spin put on it by cosmic pessimism, does indeed offer challenges to a religious belief in cosmic purpose. At the same time we could point to the many instances where theology has been enriched by taking on these challenges. For that reason we want to keep the lines of communication open between science and religion, perilous as that sometimes appears to be.

But what about the issue of cosmic purpose? What contribution to its general vision of things can theology glean from conversations with physics, evolutionary biology, geology, astronomy, chaos theory, etc.? At the very least, we would answer, science has already helped us widen our teleological outlook. In its moving us away from narrow concepts of the cosmos it has implicitly forced us to abandon unduly cramped concepts of God's designs. It has caused us, in the process, to change in significant ways our very understanding of the divine. The pre-Copernican pictures of God, for example, are clearly too cosmically provincial for us today. As the world-picture of science has expanded, theology has been challenged to move away from its formerly naive, and generally anthropocentric, articulations of nature's possible purpose.

In the process of facing what scientists like Darwin and Einstein have told us about the universe we were perhaps momentarily disoriented. Some of us perhaps were even tempted to doubt the plausibility of our inherited religious schemes. The latter, after all, were originally cast in the molds of prescientific cosmology, and the traditional doctrines of faith settled into our lives accompanied by images that have little in common with current cosmological thinking. But as we have gradually made room in theology for developments in scientific cosmology we have found—often to our surprise—that they have given our religious faith an exciting new horizon within which to ponder the possible meaning of the cosmos. Many of us have no desire any longer to return to pre-scientific conceptualizations of God, even though we acknowl-edge that these are still significant theological resources and repositories of enormous power and wisdom. For evolution, relativity, the big bang, chaos, complexity, and ecology have given us fresh and fruitful ways to think about the possible "point" of the universe.

Of course, it takes a considerable amount of reflection and readjustment of our religious sensibilities to think through consistently what God's purpose for the universe might be in the light of modern science. Such an undertaking, it seems, is probably too much for many religious believers. A large majority of them have never allowed evolutionary theory or big bang physics deeply to affect their consciousness, let alone their religious imaginations. For many genuinely religious people the kind of revision we have in mind is simply impossible, and we have no wish here to belittle their faith which is often generous and deep. But our point is that, without baptizing any particular aspects of current science, recent theology has shown that the cosmological features of modern science are no less assimilable to a deep religious trust than were the cosmologies of the past.

From ancient times the outward expression of inner religious confidence has almost always assumed one cosmological framework or another. We are convinced, then, that contemporary scientific cosmology, provisional and revisable though it may be, is no less suitable to conveying a religious trust than the now obsolete cosmologies in which the God-religions first came to expression. Unlike some of the contrasters, we prefer that theology not be thoroughly de-cosmologized, but that it be carefully re-cosmologized.

How then can we draw out the possible correspondence between current science and a religious trust in cosmic teleology? We would begin an all too brief answer to this question by having you observe that science itself now clearly presents us with the picture of the cosmos as an unfolding story. And since it is in the form of story that religions have always expressed the meaning of things, it is not inconceivable that, without "forcing the facts," we could somehow assimilate the scientific story of the universe to the narrative pattern that has always shaped our religious consciousness. Our faith's trust in an eternal love, or our traditional hope for a final cosmic fulfillment, can take up residence no less convincingly in the framework of evolution, big bang physics, and chaos theory than it did earlier in the three-storied universe of prophetic religion or in the geocentric cosmologies of Plato, Aristotle, Ptolemy, and Dante.

We are not advocating here any new conflation of cosmology and religion, nor do we wish to force the data of science into any pre-existing theological scheme. But we cannot help noticing that the results of evolutionary biology, particle and relativity physics, astronomy, and chaos theory—major ingredients of the new cosmology—can be meaningfully contextualized by the *story of promise and hope* through which Abrahamic religious tradition has already shaped our way of looking at the world.

Science up until recently has been very abstract and law-oriented. It has not taken into account the *story* underlying the laws. And as long as the universe was seen as essentially storyless—as unoriginated, eternal, and necessary—it was difficult for science to think of it as having any possible point to it. Today, however, the universe has taken on a discernibly narrative mien. The laws of nature are themselves not the offspring of an underlying eternal necessity but the contingent outcome of a definite story with a definite past. We do not yet know all there is to know about the origin of the cosmos, for example, but at least we can say that it is no longer completely lost in the mists of an eternally remote past. Even if the beginning of our universe is still somewhat cloudy, science has by now reached a virtual consensus that the world's past is at least a finite one. Even if there were "many worlds" prior to this one, a possibility that we cannot absolutely rule out, it is sufficient for our purposes here that at least this present big bang universe, since it began in a singularity, has a relatively "clean" point of origin.

If, then, the cosmos has a finite past, its evolutionary unfolding will inevitably be expressed in a narrative form. And if the cosmos is fundamentally a story, then it is difficult for us to suppress completely the question Steven Weinberg raises about the "point" of it all. Stories inevitably have a way of making us ask such questions.

We do not think, however, that the only reasonable answer to the question is that the story is pointless. Although we cannot claim any degree of finality, we think that part of our own human purpose in the larger scheme of things is to seek out the larger "point" of the universe story—and of our own existence. We do not expect our search to terminate in any definitively clear conclusion, but we are convinced that our human vitality depends on our perpetual pursuit of an answer to the question. Moreover, if we allow both science and religion to contribute to this ongoing adventure of discovery, we may find that we do not have to acquiesce in skepticism or pessimism after all. The reason for our confidence is that science has recently brought to our attention some surprising ways in which the cosmic story corresponds with the basic religious sense of reality as rooted in a promise that invites from us the response of hope. It is now possible to connect this hope to the cosmic story.

Hope is not possible, of course, without the experience of promise. And it is only a sense that the world is in some way the embodiment of a promise that invites human consciousness to assume the response of hope. But it is especially religion that awakens us to, and continually nourishes in us, a trust that reality is pregnant with promise. The God-religions in particular are characterized by a kind of trusting and hoping that expects the future to be new and fulfilling. They reject the idea that the past is fully determinative of the future, and they view the present as always open to unexpected kinds of fulfillment.

Of course, in these religions the stimulus to hope has been primarily the contingent (and therefore unpredictable) events of history rather than the more regular and invariant features of nature. Historical events, such as the unexpected liberation of Israel from Egypt, or the early Christians' experience of the unanticipated compassion of Jesus, or the prophet Muhammad's unique experience of the absolute oneness of deity, are the basis of religious trust. The confidence of these faiths is based on the assumption that if such surprising events could occur in the historical past, then newer marvels may also arise in the indeterminate future. It was their sense of the complete openness of history to surprising future outcomes that made their hope possible. And, although the beauties of nature could also at times be the source of their religious inspiration, it was essentially the indeterminateness of historical process, rather than the repetitiveness of nature, that aroused their religious confidence in the promise of universal fulfillment.

Today, however, it is of great interest to us that science is now opening up the natural world to a reading that is also essentially "historical." The new story of the universe increasingly shares with history the contingent features that allow us to read nature as a great promise. As a result of scientific developments such as evolutionary biology, geology, astrophysics and chaos theory, nature itself is now assuming a historical, narrative quality that invites us to assimilate it to the theme of religious promise and hope much more deliberately than we ever could before.

Looking back, for example, at nature's birth and evolution with a sensibility shaped by participation in the story of our common father Abraham, we cannot help but see the entire unfolding of the universe as one long story of promise. From the first moments of the cosmic dawn, for example, the physical organization of matter—though there was no known physical necessity that it do so—already fell within the almost unimaginably narrow range of numerical possibilities that would allow it to become hydrogen atoms, galactic clusters, supernovas, carbon, life, and eventually minds. Science itself now confesses that it could never have predicted such outcomes at the time of cosmic beginnings. It could at that point have had no mathematical certitude that matter would end up in all the various forms of life, immeasurable biodiversity, and complexity that would lead to consciousness. The various episodes in this amazing story all came about in ways that could never have been anticipated, even in principle.

Yet nature, as it turns out, had always been pregnant with such promise. And who knows what else it may still have in store for the billions of years of evolution that probably lie ahead of it? Recent scientific innovations such as those of quantum physics and chaos theory have alerted us in totally unexpected ways to nature's perpetual openness to indeterminate outcomes. We realize now that cosmic pessimism was believable only because it was based on the non-narrative, abstract oversimplifications of a purely linear science. The simplistic formulas of modern science, mostly innocent of the narrative depth of the natural world, made the cosmos appear absolutely determined by the dead necessity of the past, utterly closed off to unpredictable modes of new patterning. All the morose modern ruminations about the remorselessness of the second law of thermodynamics and final cosmic doom were plausible only so long as science had fixated on emaciated mathematical abstractions that ignored the contingent openness of nature's *de facto* historicity.

However, science is now beginning to realize that its linear over-simplifications had indeed left the inherently unpredictable, chaotic, and open character of most natural processes completely out of the picture. Even entropy, the notion that had formerly led to so much despair, is now being given a new reading. Instead of signaling only the heat death of the universe, entropy is now positively embraced as an essential condition for matter to realize new possibilities. For without an entropic cosmic tendency toward disassembling or fragmentation, the most primitive forms of order would have dominated indefinitely, keeping the world stuck in an inflexible sameness from age to age. There would have been no room for emergent complexity, since the cosmos would have permanently solidified into triviality.

Without entropy there could be no information, and therefore no possibility of the cosmos carrying a meaning. Entropy is what allows the universe to cool, primordial physical symmetries to be broken, atoms to emerge out of the plasma, and acid bases in DNA to be jumbled. Without the breakdown of trivial instances of order there could be no reconfiguration into newer forms of emergent complexity. Matter could not realize its promise. Entropy guarantees that the cosmic story will avoid repeating forever the same old refrains, and permits it to wend its way toward an always open and often surprising experimentation with novelty.

It is such openness to an indeterminate future that the new scientific accounts of the universe are now generously setting before us. A theology that makes contact with this cosmic openness will be immeasurably enriched. Materialist reductionism, on the other hand, still tries—almost in defiance of the inner logic of current scientific discovery—to suppress the obvious fact of nature's inherent openness. In its obsession with "explaining" emergent new phenomena (such as living and thinking beings) only from the bottom up, or only in terms of already mastered principles of chemistry and physics, reductionism damps out any appreciation of the world's future indeterminacy. Rooted in this dour reductionism, cosmic pessimism then interprets the apparent novelty in cosmic process as fundamentally no more at best than an interesting reshuffling of the same old stuff that has been there forever. Matter is forced to be eternal or necessary so that the cosmos cannot open itself up to a truly new and creative future. It is not science but a fundamental denial of the possibility of surprise that underlies this pessimistic posture.

Moreover, as we saw in the previous chapter, the new sciences of chaos and complexity (along with other developments in contemporary physics) have put an end to the idea of a necessary, closed universe determined only by the dead past. They have set before us the horizon of an unpredictable cosmic future. No longer, therefore, is there any scientifically compelling reason for a doctrinaire and pessimistic exclusion of future cosmic outcomes that might correspond to the shape of our religious hopes. There is no solid reason any longer to force the world's future trajectory into the narrow tunnel of a despair based on an obsolete scientific materialism.

Cosmic pessimism, in fact, no longer seems nearly as "realistic" as it used to in the old days when science ignored anything that could not be expressed in the form of linear mathematics. Scientific honesty itself now compels us to acknowledge that we can know the natural world in its actual concreteness only by watching and waiting to see how things turn out. The modern pretense of completely predictive scientific control over the future has been effectively deflated. The cosmic future seems more open today than it has at any time since the birth of modern science. Our conviction, then, is that in such a universe there is room (once again) for surprise, promise, and hope. There is at least the *possibility* that the nature of things, in the final analysis, runs more closely along the lines of hope than of tragedy.

This opening to possibility, we are convinced, means that there is room once again in a scientific age for religious faith. We are not suggesting, of course, that we can base the certitude of faith on any particular scientific hypotheses. But, at the same time, we cannot ignore the general demise in science of those exclusively mechanistic and deterministic doctrines that made modernity so suspicious of religious aspiration. It is a rather dramatic development that science can no longer decisively claim, through the voice of scientism and mechanism, that the future is indifferent to our hopes. Science has indeed changed things for theology.

In our faith-and-hope perspective the "point" of the universe, therefore, is closely tied up with a cosmic openness to the implantation of new forms of order. Another way of putting this is to say that the cosmic story seeks to express itself in continually more diverse forms of beauty. By beauty we mean what Whitehead and others have meant: "the ordering of novelty." And since beauty is a high "value"—having the same status as other transcendental values such as goodness and truth—we can say that its orientation toward ordered novelty, or beauty, is what gives the cosmos a "directional" character. Although the aim toward beauty is not necessarily realized in a progressive fashion, it is not difficult for our new scientific-historical reading of the cosmos to detect its disposition to unfold in ever new forms of order.

This aim toward beauty harmonizes well with our faith's sense that a God of promise and fidelity is the ground and artisan of the elaborate cosmic story. As we have noted before, a truly creative God is not coercive, but persuasive. If God is creative love, the world will not be forced to fit into some preconceived plan. It will be gently lured toward such beauty as we see in atoms, cells, brains, and societies. But the process does not need to be directional in any rigid sense. If we speak of the cosmos as purposeful we do not mean that it is compelled toward a specific pre-established goal. For the cosmos to have a "point" to it, it is sufficient that it be open to future outcomes that take the shape of unanticipated beauty. We are convinced that the universe which science is now laying out so richly before us is truly open to this kind of teleological interpretation.

IV. Confirmation

Without taking anything away from honest attempts to articulate the "point" of the cosmos, we prefer to highlight our faith's own reluctance, and even aversion, to saying very much about such a colossal matter. Along with the contrast position we agree that it is not the business of science to tell us anything about the point of the universe. However, we wonder if it is religion's business to do so either. It's not that we suspect that there may be no point to the universe. Rather we are skeptical of any human attempts, whether scientific or religious, to say anything that would come close to capturing just what cosmic purpose might be. Such matters are best left shrouded in silence.

The difference between our hesitancy and the contrasters' is that we suspect that even religion cannot say much about cosmic purpose. A radically theocentric perspective not only confirms the modesty of scientific method and its refusal to get involved with final causes; it also compels us to ask whether even our religions and theologies can make it their business to give "answers" to the question of cosmic purpose.

The contrast position correctly allows science to bracket out questions of final cause. This avoidance of teleology is not a defect, but a strength of science. Thus any transgressions of the imperative to avoid discussions of purpose are not to be laid at the feet of science itself but at those of us frail human beings who have a tendency to bite off more than we are capable of theologically chewing. Both cosmic pessimists and theologians are inclined toward pretensions of omniscience. Cosmic pessimists tell us that their judgments about the indifference of the world come directly from science, even though science itself is ill-equipped to give us any information of this kind. And theologians tell us that religion's task is to awaken us to the cosmic meaning beyond the particular facts. However, our own position—and here is where we differ from the contrasters—is that even religion and theology are unable to articulate the "point" of things with anything approaching substance and clarity.

Genuine religion, after all, always has an "apophatic" aspect, that is, an inclination to silence. Silence in religion is essential in order to betoken the inadequacy of all our responses to the large questions of life. The silence of religion cautions us against trying to state in a clear and distinct way what the "point" of the universe might be. In this sense, then, religion "confirms" the reluctance of science to talk about purpose. And the scientific refusal to enter into the issue of teleology is consistent also with the religious inclination to keep still about matters that are simply too big for us. In this sense science joins with the deepest elements of religion in keeping us firmly tied to our own proper sphere, restraining our flights into things we can know nothing about.

This sharing of silence could well be one of the reasons why some deeply religious women and men have entered quite naturally and enthusiastically into scientific work. There is a humility about authentic scientific research that corresponds very well with a religious perspective on the limits of human knowing. For religion, by entrusting to God's mysterious providence and love the answers to all the big questions, liberates the finite human mind so that it can concentrate day by day on issues more proportionate to its finite capacities. Science is one way in which the human mind finds its proper groove, and so it thrives best under the umbrella of a theocentric vision of things.

A theocentric faith allows us to relax into scientific pursuits because it instructs us that the big issues such as cosmic purpose need not become our own worry. Therefore, we have a great deal of respect for those scientists who, in their role as scientists, refuse to get sidetracked into answering questions about the "point" of the universe. Their reticence is not always a sign of cosmic pessimism. Perhaps just as often it is a quiet protection of the great mystery they implicitly sense at the heart of the universe. Theological attempts to articulate the point of the universe inevitably sound flat and inconsequential, and so it is sometimes refreshing to see scientists diverting the issue with humorous or irreverent remarks.

Teleological discourse, then, is not something we should casually enter into. The wisdom of our religious traditions almost unanimously instructs us that it is not necessarily our business to know the purpose of the universe. Here we might once again take our lead from the Book of Job:

> Then the Lord addressed Job out of the storm and said: Who is this that obscures divine plans with words of ignorance? Gird up your loins now, like a man: I will question you, and you tell me the answers! Where were you when I founded the earth? Tell me if you have understanding.[10]

9

Is Religion Responsible
for the Ecological Crisis?

The world's ecological crisis gives new urgency to discussions in science and religion. Unless people of differing perspectives can arrive at a shared concern for the natural world, our planet's life systems are in danger of irreversible collapse. A recent conference of scientists, religious leaders, and theologians recognized the need for consensus on this matter, and it worked out a common statement encouraging all parties to attend more closely to ecological issues.[1] The final declaration of this "Joint Appeal by Science and Religion on the Environment" noted the past hostilities between scientists and theologians, but it argued that we must now put such differences behind us and work together to save the Earth. Perhaps, then, in no other area than ecology is it more pragmatically important that we keep conversations between scientists and theologians alive.

However, to some secular ecologists such discussions may prove to be quite difficult, for religion and theology have the reputation of not caring very much about the welfare of the natural world. The churches, synagogues, and mosques have traditionally paid little if any attention to the main ecological issues, and until recently theologians have ignored them as well.[2] The classic texts of religious traditions have precious little to tell us about the destruction of rain forests, the erosion of soil, the loss of sources of fresh water, the spread of deserts, the pollution of land, water and air, the alarming rate of extinction of species, global warming, or the thinning of the stratospheric ozone layer. Moreover, some religious teachers still ignore the burgeoning human population which con-

siderably exacerbates every one of the environmental threats just mentioned. How then can religion be said to have ecological relevance?

Russell Train, who chairs the World Wild Life Fund and has been a
leader in the environmental movement for over thirty years, finds it
extremely puzzling that religion and theology have been so unresponsive
to the present crisis. He also laments the fact that government, big business, and academia have failed to speak out. But religion's lack of concern in this area, he says,

> ...has been nothing less than extraordinary. Here we have had one of the
> most fundamental concerns to agitate human society within living mem-
> ory. Here we have issues that go to the heart of the human condition, to
> the quality of human life, even to humanity's ultimate survival. Here we
> have problems that can be said to threaten the very integrity of Creation.
> And yet the churches and other institutions of organized religion have
> largely ignored the whole subject.

Why, in so pressing a matter, have our religious institutions
remained "silent and on the sidelines"?[3]

Any serious discussions in science and religion today must attend to
the business of ecology. These transactions will feature an ethical
intensity that has not surfaced in the topics we have considered up to
this point. Moreover, there is room for a wider range of opinions on
such a controversial topic. Nevertheless, we may usefully organize the
various positions—at least in a rough way—by placing them in the four
categories we have been using throughout. Here, then, are some possible answers to the question of whether religion (in the theistic sense to
which we have restricted our deliberations in this book) is ecologically
significant.

I. Conflict

Scientific skepticism maintains that religion is at best an unnecessary
distraction from, and at worst a serious obstacle to, a healthy ecological
concern. Nevertheless, before we give the reasons for our suspicion of
religion's ecological value, we should emphasize that some of us, like
Carl Sagan, Stephen Jay Gould, and E. O. Wilson (who all endorsed the
Joint Appeal mentioned above) do indeed allow that religion can bring a
robust moral fervor to ecological activism. We skeptics welcome the
religious community's somewhat belated participation in the ecological
movement. Even though from a scientific point of view religions are

mere illusions, what is important ecologically is not so much their truth-status as the assistance they can offer in the common moral endeavor of saving our planet. With its massive educational networks and its ability to penetrate to the grass roots, religion can become an integral part of the ecological movement today.

However, we must question here whether a religious outlook provides a more solid grounding for ecological ethics than does our own materialistic cosmology. We do not think that it does, and we have good reasons for this negative assessment. Even though we may deny that the universe as a whole has any point to it, most of us scientific skeptics are still passionately concerned about preserving life and consciousness here on the earth. Probably the most moving ecological literature today comes from morally sensitive skeptics who have no investment at all in anything beyond nature. This leads us to suspect that there is a much more substantial foundation for ecological ethics in our pure naturalism—a view that renounces any trace of cosmic teleology—than can ever be found in the comforting fantasies of super-naturalism.

That we see no ultimate point to the universe does not mean that our earthly environment is undeserving of our care. In fact, the very hostility or indifference of the universe at large is what makes this precious earth, by way of contrast, so special in our eyes. Since the appearance of life in the cosmos was utterly improbable in the first place, its perishable delicacy is all the more to be treasured. Although there may be pockets of life and intelligence elsewhere in the universe, the massive deadness and mindlessness of most of the cosmos simply accentuates the importance of our own fragile biosphere. The precariousness of our ecosystems, then, is enough to make us cherish them. The loneliness of terrestrial life in a silent universe makes it so privileged in our estimation that we have no need for a God to ground our ecological ethic.

Moreover, religion with its orientation toward the world of the supernatural has, by virtue of that very fact, too little regard for the value of life on this planet. Because religion worries so much about the "next world," or about some hidden cosmic purpose, it pays insufficient attention to this world's welfare. Obsession with some far-off, final cosmic meaning takes the urgency out of our present moral commitment to the earth's survival. Religions that hope for a future divine deliverance even allow us to abandon concern for the immediate world. When they look pathetically for some ultimate cosmic purpose, they too easily tolerate an indifference toward the present state of the earth's ecology. The consolation of a final destiny actually makes room for ecological abuses in the present.

John Passmore, an Australian philosopher and environmentalist, accurately presents our point of view when he says:

> Only if men see themselves...for what they are, quite alone, with no one to help them except their fellow-men, products of natural processes which are wholly indifferent to their survival, will they face their eco-logical problems in their full implications. Not by the extension, but by the total rejection, of the concept of the sacred will they move toward that sombre realization.[4]

Keep in mind that a fundamental axiom of ecological ethics is that unless we learn to experience the earth as our true home we will have little if any inclination to take care of it. Religion, however, cannot embrace this world as our home. You don't need to look very far into the teachings of religion to observe that they typically locate our true home elsewhere—in the realm of the supernatural. Religion tells us that we are only pilgrims or sojourners on earth. How could such an unworldly perspective ever claim to take ecology seriously? The cos-mic homelessness that religion entails cannot provide sufficient moral energy to help the ecological movement. On the other hand, a purely naturalistic philosophy, with its sense that the natural world is all there is and all there ever will be, is an appropriate foundation for ecological ethics.

Let us not forget also the well-worn thesis of Lynn White, Jr., name-ly, that the present ecological crisis originated in the Bible's giving humans "dominion" over the earth.[5] The arrogance of this anthropocen-tric belief has granted humans religious permission to subject nature to their control and abuse. Likewise, the apocalyptic religiosity of many believers allows them to view this world as headed for destruction. For them, our present natural environment is not worth saving if it is des-tined for doom anyway. In these and so many other ways religion has shown that it has too little concern for the non-human natural world. Therefore, we find it ecologically hollow.

II. Contrast

It is tempting to attribute the world's ecological ills to a single cause. This is what Lynn White, Jr. does when he argues that these evils origi-nate in biblical religion's emphasis on our right to exercise dominion over the rest of the earth. In fact, however, the Bible encourages us to practice "stewardship," that is, to take care of nature. And biblical scholars tell us that "dominion" does not mean domination, but rather our proper human role of standing in as God's representatives to non-human nature. This means that since God is the sustainer of life, the Bible implicitly commands that we imitate God in this respect. There is no justification whatsoever in the Bible for our dominating and abusing the earth. On the contrary, there are numerous passages in the Psalms, the Wisdom literature, and traditional theological sources that impose on us the obligation of respecting and nurturing the natural world.

But these exegetical clarifications are still somewhat beside the point as far as secular ecologists are concerned. For the latter's principal objection is that religion is simply too otherworldly to be ecologically helpful. It is true, of course, that we accept the existence of a supernatural realm. However, we are convinced that it is only by practicing the ethical virtues pertaining to this supernatural realm that we will ever make any headway in alleviating the ecological crisis. We need, for example, to learn a religious humility and detachment that will allow us to "live lightly upon the earth." Only thus will creation be granted intrinsic value rather than being simply the object of our arrogance and greed. We must cultivate a sense of holy justice if we are going to heal the global economic inequity that causes impoverished peoples to cut down rain forests and pollute their lands in order to survive. We should also cultivate that most characteristically religious virtue, gratitude, giving thanks always especially for the beauties of creation. And above all else we need to practice the supernatural virtues of compassion and love—not only for our fellow humans but also for animals and other living beings.

In short, then, it is not religious influence but the lack of it that has allowed us to destroy the earth's ecosystems. The banishment of God by modern secularism has made it possible for rationalism, humanism, and scientism to rush in and fill the void; and these all thrive on the assumption of our human supremacy over nature. If anything, the ecologically disastrous anthropocentrism of our culture, intensified by the emergence of "secular humanism," has become even more vehement in the wake of the "death of God." At least our own position, because it is theocentric (that is, God-centered), implies the overcoming of anthropocentrism.

So we regard the thesis that religion is the cause of our ecological problems as exceedingly lame. Our view is that without the recovery of

a religious vision—and along with it a renewed commitment to humility, detachment, justice, gratitude, and compassion—the earth's ecosystems will be irreversibly ravaged.

In any case, the real causes of the ecological crisis are immensely
complex, and most of them have nothing to do with religion. Runaway
greed, industrialism, individualism, nationalism, belief in unlimited
economic progress, massive poverty caused by the maldistribution of
wealth, militarism, consumerism, over-population, and gross materialism are more likely the real causes. It is hardly likely that a religious
belief in the sacred could be the root cause of the crisis. Indeed, only
the religious affirmation of an eternal source of values can help us con-
quer those evils that are now moving the earth's life-systems toward
their death. In other words, too much this-worldliness is more ecologically damaging than is religious other-worldliness.

On the other hand, we are equally opposed to those who accuse science of being the cause of the ecological crisis. It is true that the crisis
would not have come about without the technology and industrializa-
tion that science has made possible. But this does not mean that science
itself is the culprit. According to our contrast approach the problem lies
not in science as such, but in the conflation of science with ideologies
and beliefs that have led to our draining the earth of its substance.
Perhaps the most important of these assumptions is that the earth has
enough resources to fuel our secular obsession with limitless economic
growth. The secular myth of economic progress has corralled and
exploited scientific expertise and technology, as well as some aspects
of religious messianism, to produce a climate that is inherently inimical
to the earth's own well-being.

This is most unfortunate not only ecologically speaking, but also
because it gives science an undeservedly negative reputation. For the
scientific approach to the world is not inherently and inevitably tied to
the premises of materialism, pessimism, or the secular myth of
progress. If it is set free from them it will not have to take the blame for
promoting pictures of the universe that drain it of its inherent value, a
value that originates—as do all values—in the realm of the sacred. A
retrieval of our classic spiritual traditions and their sense of a radically
transcendent God can free science and ecology from imprisonment in
materialism and other spurious forms of naturalism.

We need, therefore, to contrast science sharply with all kinds of
assumptions, both religious and otherwise. This means that we have to
question the ecological value of the coalition that scientific skeptics

have uncritically forged between science on the one hand and material-ism on the other. We seriously doubt that materialism, which is the metaphysical underpinning of most scientific skepticism, is able to arouse adequate ethical concern for the natural world. In fact, scientific materialism and the cosmic pessimism that goes along with it are inher-ently antagonistic to ecological ethics. Whatever personal ecological concern scientific skeptics themselves might have emerges not because of, but in spite of, the materialist belief system in which they have encased their scientific thinking.

A long time ago William James expressed the inherently anti-eco-logical implications of scientific materialism:

> ...in the vast driftings of the cosmic weather, though many a jeweled shore appears, and many an enchanted cloud-bank floats away, long lingering ere it be dissolved—even as our world now lingers for our joy—yet when these transient products are gone, nothing, absolutely nothing remains, to represent those particular qualities, those elements of preciousness which they may have enshrined. Dead and gone are they, gone utterly from the very sphere and room of being. Without an echo; without a memory; without an influence on aught that may come after, to make it care for similar ideals. This utter final wreck and tragedy is of the essence of scientific materialism as at present under-stood.[6]

Implicit in this eloquent depiction of the implications of scientific materialism is the question of whether we can consistently value any-thing at all unless it has something of the "eternal" in it. If everything is destined for "absolute nothingness," could we truly treasure it? And since materialism views the universe as ultimately a "final wreck and tragedy," how can such a philosophy ever motivate us to care for the earth's beautiful treasures? We doubt that it can.

A much firmer basis for ecological concern may be found in the reli-gious sense that everything earthly somehow participates in the eternal. All the beauty that surrounds us is an invitation to link our own lives and the glories of nature in gratitude to the Eternal Beauty that never perishes. If we deaden the glow of nature around us, we shall thereby blunt our sense of the God who transcends us. At the same time, if we relinquish belief in God, the natural beauty around us will be robbed of the sacred depth that gives it its true splendor. These elemental reli-gious principles are more than enough to motivate us to save the earth and its ecology.

III. Contact

The contrast approach once again makes some obviously valid points. Unfortunately, though, it is so busy defending the classical religious world-view that it fails to take advantage of the opportunity for spiritual and theological renewal afforded by the present ecological crisis. Our own proposal is less apologetic and, we think, more constructive than the one you have just heard. In this book we have allowed our theology to undergo the shock of revolution and reformation as it makes "contact" with new scientific ideas. Science, we have claimed, does make a considerable difference to our thinking about religious matters. So here also we shall expose our theology to the new emphasis on ecology; and we shall find that ecology can be no less enriching for theology than evolution and astrophysics have been.

The current situation in fact calls for a whole new way of thinking about some of the basic teachings of the God-religions. The ecological crisis is really unprecedented, and so we cannot expect either that our religious classics will have ready-made solutions to it, or that after becoming aware of our perilous ecological predicament we can any longer look at the ancient texts in the same way we used to. Indeed, it is quite likely that the current threats to nature provide us with one of those special historical moments when our religion is invited to undergo a radical transformation. We do not see this as a defeat for our faith, as do the traditionalists, but as an opportunity to bring to it a new vitality.

In order to make room for such a dramatic change, however, we have to take seriously the accusation that religion may indeed have been a factor in permitting some of the ecological derangement of our times. We have to face up to the possibility that traditional understandings of God, salvation, and human destiny may not, in their classical modes of expression, be fully adequate to the emerging ecological sensitivity. At best, many of the ideas of conventional religion are ecologically ambiguous. They need to be revised in accordance with an ecologically sensitive cosmology and its new emphasis on the inherent relationality of all things.

We agree with the contrast position that ecological morality should be rooted in a sense of the eternal, but we must take care that our longing for the eternal does not lift us prematurely out of the earth-community to which we belong. Such a dualistic separation of humanity from the earth has dominated religious thinking in the past, and the result has been the "cosmic homelessness" which skeptics have rightly censured.

Ecological concern demands that we treat the earth as our home rather than as a hotel that we can simply trash at will. But religion's focus on the supernatural seems to have tolerated a kind of diffidence toward our natural surroundings. We have accepted too literally the idea that this world is not our home.

It seems, then, that we have an irresolvable dilemma. On the one hand, religious teachings tell us to live homelessly. They exhort us to cultivate a spirit of detachment from "the world" so that we will gain the freedom that brings us to God. But, on the other hand, an ecological ethic demands that we put our roots down deeply into nature. For only if we cherish our connectedness to the wider community of life, and fully appreciate our interdependency with the rest of nature, will we be inspired to respect it. We are torn—or so it seems—between two equally attractive sets of values. We still want to embrace the essential religious ideal of living without clinging to things that will diminish us and ultimately disappoint us; and so we are reluctant to make nature itself an ultimate concern—for we know that in the final analysis the physical world is destined to perish. But, at the same time, we are just as deeply attracted to the ideals of ecology, to the sentiment that nature is our home, and to the demand that we conserve our natural habitat for future generations. Is there any way, then, in which we can hold these two persuasions together? Does the ideal of religious homelessness, in other words, have to contradict a hearty ecological sense that earth is our home?

Fortunately science itself can help us out here. It can show us how to link the religious adventure of homeless detachment with the ecological requirement of remaining firmly fixed to nature. For if science has taught us anything over the last century and a half it is that the natural world is itself a restless adventure. Nature is not static, eternal, and necessary, as scientists formerly thought it to be. Though many still do not believe it, the cosmos is most certainly an ongoing process; it is not a stationary set of things frozen in essentially the same way from age to age. The universe, as noted in the preceding chapters, is an unfolding story. Hence, for us to embrace the universe means that we must also welcome its inherent restlessness. Taking the scientific picture of the world seriously allows—even requires—that we embed our own unsettled lives within the much larger context of a cosmic restlessness. Only by accepting its own homelessness can we be at home in *this* universe.

Ages before we humans came along in evolution the universe had already been on the move—for some billions of years. Science during the past century has filled out in remarkable detail the various episodes of this story. Now, we are persuaded, there are both ecological and theological implications in the accounts of this cosmic adventure. For in order to accept our own restlessness and fundamental freedom, which is what religion tries to get us to do, we do not have to uproot ourselves from nature. We do not have to make the cosmos a victim of our religious restlessness. Instead, our belonging to nature is the very condition of our religious homelessness. By linking ourselves to nature we are already sojourning. We are on a long pilgrimage not *from* the universe but *with* the universe.

There are many other features in the new cosmology that seem congenial to an ecological theology today, including its emphasis on the holistic, organismic character of the evolving universe. But here let us simply point to a couple of features in contemporary physics that put our species back into nature in a way that also satisfies our need for transcendence. First, there is the new scientific suspicion that the cosmos is not eternal, that it quite possibly had a beginning and hence a finite span of duration. And second, there are new ideas in physics and astrophysics that seem to make *mind*, our most characteristically human attribute, an *intrinsic* part of nature. These two sets of physical reflection make it quite possible for us to think of ourselves once again as fully belonging to the universe; and at the same time they allow us to think of the cosmos itself as a homeless sort of wandering, a fact that speaks in a deeper way than ever to our religious need for transcendence—this time in an ecologically wholesome way. Let us look more closely at each of these developments.

In the first place, it is especially big bang cosmology that has challenged the ancient assumption that the universe is eternal. At first glance you may wonder what ecological-theological significance could possibly be squeezed out of this new way of understanding the cosmos. But if the universe has a finite past—and quite likely even a definite beginning—then it becomes possible for us to understand the *whole* of the universe as a still unfolding story.[7] This would mean that it is not just the human spirit that has embarked upon an immense journey. Rather, the entire cosmos may be understood as an itinerant passage.

Therefore, we don't need to abandon the universe in order to follow the religious advice to live homelessly. Indeed, we may even be permitted to say that the universe's own adventurousness is the very root system of our religious restlessness. We satisfy our religious longing for the beyond by immersing ourselves in the cosmic journey, not by extricating ourselves from nature. The new scientific cosmology allows us fully to belong to the universe without our having to sacrifice the ideal of religious sojourning. We are not lost *in* the cosmos (which is the anti-ecological assumption of religious dualists), but instead we are lost *with* the cosmos: there is a kinship or togetherness in our mutual forlornness, in our common distance from destiny. Religious homelessness, therefore, does not have to entail an ecologically noxious cosmic homelessness.

Second, several developments in physics and astrophysics that we have visited in previous chapters also have the effect of reinserting mind (and therefore humanity) back into nature. They challenge the dualistic assumption that mind is fundamentally alien to the cosmos. The divorce of mind from nature has been taken for granted by the scientism, materialism, and cosmic pessimism of much modern thought, but fascinating new scientific ideas are presently challenging this split.

As you will recall, special relativity, for example, suggests that the way physical reality shows itself to us is not independent of the observer's frame of reference. The world-view of classical physics had formerly allowed that our subjectivity is inseparable from so-called "secondary qualities" (those associated with the five senses), but it held that there was a realm of "primary qualities" that existed "out there" in a space and time completely untouched by human subjectivity. This realm of "objective" qualities was taken to be the *real* world, and everything else (such as beauty, value, and meaning) was seen as a mere "coating" that human subjects placed over the colorless, odorless, valueless world of primary qualities.

Special relativity, however, implies that we humans cast a long "subjective" shadow even over the primary qualities, those that we used to think were objectively the same from all frames of reference. We cannot extricate our minds from nature in such a way as to have an absolute perspective on things. We are now becoming convinced that mind is much more deeply embedded in the physical universe than we had for centuries suspected.

Likewise, quantum physics and the principle of indeterminacy apparently tie the observer intricately into the fabric of the scientifically observed world. They imply that our own mentality influences our grasp of the position or momentum of a sub-atomic particle, and that therefore the observed world cannot be sharply segregated from the human observer or instruments of observation. Some physicists (in a highly controversial thesis) even hold that the world becomes determinate only when a conscious observer intervenes (to collapse what

physicists call the "wave function" of a virtual particle). And others
have gone so far as to contend that the world is actually composed fundamentally of "mind-stuff." We do not need to embrace such ideas here
in order to point out the extent to which physics today runs counter to
past religious and scientistic ideas that stationed the human mind outside of nature.

Finally, what is especially interesting from the point of view of ecology and theology is that today some astrophysicists and cosmologists are
suggesting that the very structure of physical reality, from its earliest
moments, cannot be fully understood apart from the eventual emergence
of mind. The so-called "strong anthropic principle" discussed in
Chapter 6 maintains that the earliest physical conditions and fundamental constants at the time of cosmic origins had to have been very precisely fine-tuned if mind was ever to appear in evolution. If the force of
gravity, the rate of cosmic expansion, the ratio of electron to proton
mass, or of weak to strong nuclear forces, had been only infinitesimally
different, we (beings endowed with minds) would not be here.

If there is anything to this speculation, then mind must be a *fundamental* aspect of the universe. This, of course, would fly in the face of
the ecologically problematic dualism and cosmic pessimism that have
made mind only an accidental intrusion. And even if one does not want
to accept the stronger versions of the anthropic principle, it is still ecologically interesting that the physics of the early universe is suited (by
whatever natural means) to the emergence of life and mind. After all,
for three centuries scientific materialism has held that matter is fundamentally hostile or indifferent to life and mind, and that the physical
universe only grudgingly and by the sheerest of accidents allows life
and mind to appear and flourish for a brief season in an otherwise
mindless universe. But it is now getting much more difficult to uphold
this prejudice, especially on scientific grounds. Science now increasingly points toward the inseparability of mind and nature.

What this new cosmological thinking means *ecologically* is that we
can no longer plausibly think of the physical universe as though it were
not our home. The sense of cosmic homelessness, which underlies so
much of our ecological neglect, is no longer intellectually or theologically acceptable. If we ever learn to accept the fact that we do belong to
the natural world, something which we have not yet done in a profound
way, then we might start treating it better.

And what the new scientific ideas entail *theologically* is that we can
no longer separate concern for our own destiny from that of the whole

universe. The cosmos is *essentially* linked with our humanity. Or, better, our humanity is forever situated within the more encompassing framework of a restless universe. If we can hope realistically for some quite unimaginable restoration of our humanity beyond death, then the entire universe—including all the diversity that has emerged in evolution—has a share in it. We are grateful that the new emphasis on ecology has thus allowed us to widen the scope of our religious hope to include the whole world's salvation.

The God-religions, in fact, have often placed great emphasis on hope and promise for the world's future. This emphasis on a future fulfillment is known as "eschatology." By "eschatology" we mean here the sense that *all of reality* is shaped by God's promise. Eschatology bears the good news that a glorious future fulfillment lies in store for the whole cosmos. We think this sweeping vision of hope is fully consonant with ecological concern. Eschatological faith invites us to treasure the natural world because nature even now carries within itself the future to which we—along with the whole of creation—aspire at the deepest levels of our being. To destroy nature, then, is to cut ourselves and the cosmos off from our common future.

The reason we think religious hope corresponds so intimately with ecological concern is that it inspires us to see the natural world as the embodiment of a divine *promise*. According to the stories told by all three of the God-religions, faith in the promise first came to birth in the nomad Abraham's anticipation of fresh patches of life in the desert. A yearning for new life was quite possibly the "ecological" basis of Abrahamic faith in the future. The deepest origins of our faith are inseparable from the prospering of nature that fired the imaginations and hopes of our religious ancestors.

If at heart nature is promise, then for that very reason it demands our protection. To keep hope for the New Creation alive in our hearts we need to foster the integrity of nature here and now. For hope would surely evaporate along with the collapse of our ecosystems. Our hope for the ultimate renewal of all things can be fueled only by the present vitality and beauty of the natural world. We will end up with few hints of a final renewal of life if we continue now to defile the natural world in which we first gain any sense of life at all.

At the same time, hope in the world's future is necessary to awaken in us the aspiration to care here and now for nature's well-being. In making such a proposal, of course, we inevitably arouse the suspicion of some ecologists who fear that a preoccupation with the future will allow us to put up with too much ecological abuse in the present. Eschatology, their argument goes, causes us to dream so extravagantly of future fulfillment that we lose interest in the present. How, then, can a hope that pulls us out of the present age toward a better world move us toward an ecological concern that is effective here and now?

This is an important and difficult question, for it compels us to acknowledge that certain kinds of religious expectation are not in accord with ecological interest. Some kinds of eschatology in fact are escapist and earth-hating forms of "optimism" that despise matter and look to a completely spiritual world as the only appropriate destiny for human persons. This kind of "hope" is indeed ecologically questionable.

As we understand the central and original thrust of the God-religions, however, their eschatology is quite opposed to any escapist withdrawal from the earth. Before it got side-tracked by a dualism coming primarily from the Hellenistic world, the prophetic hope was not for a future *apart from* the natural world, but for the ultimate future *of* and *with* the created world. In any case, the current ecological situation now requires that we broaden our hope: the promise of our faith must now mean once again that the *whole* of creation is destined to be renewed by the "Coming of God."[8]

Moreover, we will hardly be motivated to care for the earth unless we are convinced that it indeed has a future. And yet, in spite of our best efforts we humans are apparently unable to bring an ideal ecological future to pass by our own powers alone. Indeed, given our recent performance, we have every reason for distrusting ourselves as curators of the earth's future. For precisely this reason we consider an eschatological faith to be ecologically indispensable. For we could easily succumb to complete despair and ethical impotence in the face of the ecological tribulation we have wrought all over the planet. The situation, as some ecologists are now depicting it, is already so grim that there is little we can do about it.

This is why it is so important today that we experience a fresh hope in nature's inherently promising constitution. A genuine religious hope in the future invites us always to see "the dearest freshness deep down things," even in a world "seared with trade; bleared, smeared with toil," one that "wears our smudge" and "shares our smell" and in which "the soil is bare now." (Gerard Manley Hopkins) It is only a persistent hope, one that does not take flight from the world, but instead continues to care for it in spite of everything we have done to it, that can energize our ecological ethics. Our kind of hope looks to the new creation of *this* world; it sees a continuity between the present age and the world's ultimate fulfillment in God. Without a hope for the future of *this* world our ecological commitments would be pointless.

Viewing our world as a promise—a promise not just for our own benefit but for that of all beings—also serves to protect nature from the compulsive modern habit of expecting it to provide complete satisfaction of all our human needs and desires. Unhappily, when the modern world lost the sense of a Transcendent Source of its creative abundance, we turned our native craving for fulfillment toward the immediate, natural environment. In the absence of the Infinite, where else could we turn but to nature? Yet nature alone, since it is finite, has not been able to supply us with all that we need. And our expectation that a single small planet could be limitless in its resourcefulness has led to our divesting it permanently of many of its non-renewable riches.

Eschatology, however, asks us to see the earth—and all of nature—as a promise rather than a paradise. The posture of hope tempers our expectations of what nature can provide, and reconciles us to its inherent limitations.

Unfortunately, the modern political world has not yet come to terms with the finitude of nature, and this is a major reason for our continuing ecological misery. The only realistic alternative, then, is to embrace the eschatological vision of nature as promise. By viewing it as promise rather than fulfillment we can overcome modernity's ecologically distressing compulsion to squeeze infinity out of that which is finite.

Moreover, the theme of promise not only allows us to tolerate nature's finitude, but also to put up with all the ambiguity and suffering we find in nature as well. Eschatology is realistic enough to acknowledge the ugliness and horror in the natural world without being forced to judge these as final. Likewise, eschatological faith reconciles us to the transience of all things in nature: we do not expect perfection from a promise, but only from its fulfillment. If we can tentatively embrace and enjoy nature as promise rather than perfection, we can put up with its defects, including its elements of severity and indifference.

In other words, a sincere hope for eventual cosmic fulfillment liberates us from an immature clinging to the natural world as though it were by itself capable of satisfying our deepest longings. In our religious perspective, only the Infinite can bring ultimate satisfaction to our limitless longing. And so, if we could once again interpret nature as promise rather than fulfillment this might allow us to treasure and delight in its beauties without bringing despair upon ourselves when we observe that the cosmos is still unfinished, or that all transient things eventually perish.

Viewed in this way the natural world is not just a proving ground to get us ready for the "next world," but a token of the future perfection toward which the entire evolution of the cosmos is, at least in our theological perspective, being persuaded.[9]

IV. Confirmation

In spite of its historical ecological ambiguity there are ways in which religion can be said to be intrinsically ecological in its basic outlook. While the contrast and contact approaches are content for the most part simply to point out the compatibility of theology with ecology or to adjust theology to the new situation, the stance of "confirmation" goes even further. We hold that *at its very core* religion already entails an ecological concern. Both within and beyond the biblical world religion consistently exhibits two features that are inherently ecological in their implications: sacramentalism and silence.

1) *Sacramentalism*. An indispensable foundation of ecological sensitivity may be found in religion's "sacramental" vision of nature. Broadly speaking, a "sacrament" is any concrete object, event, or experience through which religious faith comes in touch with the divine. All religions have something of a sacramental dimension to them in the sense that the only way they can speak about divine mystery at all is through the concrete objects of human experience. It is not surprising then that religion's sacramental materials have come especially from the natural world.

Even apart from any "historical" revelation, the God-religions, for example, agree that the divine mystery is disclosed in the beauty and diversity of nature. The luminosity of bright sunshine provides the irreplaceable experience through which we express metaphorically the illumination that comes from the divine. Likewise, the freshness of air and wind is the physiological basis of our sense of Spirit. The cleansing effect of clear running water provides a symbol for the profound experience of renewal that an encounter with the sacred can bring. And the fertility of soil and life, along with the renewal of the seasons, is indispensable to religious hope in resurrection or new birth.

Indeed, religions cannot say much about God at all apart from the richness and variety already present in nature. Nature's sacramental character gives us, then, an *intrinsically* religious reason for ecological concern. If there is cause to revise our theologies in order to come to grips with the current crisis, at the same time we need not overlook the fact that religion is essentially, and not just accidentally, already implicated with ecology. The mutual implication is so tight that if we lose the natural world, we also lose God.[10] Without being identified with nature, the divine mystery is nevertheless deeply interior to it—at least according to the sacramental vision. A more obvious religious confirmation of the need to uphold ecological integrity would be difficult to find.

That the natural world is at heart a symbolic disclosure of God gives nature a "sacral" quality which thwarts our destructive tendencies. The sacramental outlook of religion functions as a bulwark against our crass human habits, especially since the industrial revolution, of reducing the natural world to mere raw material for economic exploitation.

A sacramental ecology, therefore, encourages us to enjoy and nurture our connections to the natural world and bodily existence. Unfortunately, dualistic spirituality has distanced us from nature, suppressing our native sense of being part of the network of the earth's complex ecosystems. This same dualism has also supported patriarchal exclusivism and the oppression of women. A sacramental vision, on the other hand, sees a close link between respect for the earth and the emancipation of women.

The sacramental vision, of course, may be too challenging for most of us since it demands that we give up one of modernity's most prized ideals, that of the autonomous, isolated subject who has a "right" to possess, define, and exploit the natural world. A sacramentally inspired ecology implies that rugged individualism, whether economic or spiritual, is no longer ecologically viable. It forbids us to shape our personal identities, build our communities, or carve out our careers without taking into account the fact that each of us is part of a much wider network of created beings that is cumulatively disclosive of a divine mystery.

Likewise, sacramentalism demands that we not make any personal decisions without taking into account their potential impact on the earth-community for all future generations. A sacramental ecology, in other words, calls for a whole new kind of moral sensitivity. Our classic moral traditions have been so obsessed with questions of individual rights that they have overlooked the inter-dependent, relational nature of our existence and that of all beings. It is true, of course, that the ethical emphasis of the God-religions has been powerfully relevant on issues of social justice, but we are just now beginning to recognize that social justice is inseparable from eco-justice.

The sacramental perspective also advocates a new interpretation of what it means to be "pro-life." The pro-life ethic has been associated too narrowly with issues surrounding human sexuality. If it is to be seriously "open to life" it cannot turn away from the global population problem and the additional pressures placed on the earth's ecosystems by the sheer force of human numbers.

In summary, then, we claim that ecological concern is already implicit in the sacramental vision of the universe. A conviction that the various features of nature are inherently revelatory of the divine is indispensable to an adequate ecological vision today. A sacramental vision confirms the *intrinsic* relation between religious faith and ecological concern. And, at the same time, it implies that the integrity of nature is inseparable from the flourishing of religion.

2) *Silence*. Throughout this book we have attempted to show that the nearly universal religious posture of silence is extremely important in discussions involving science and religion. For example, on the question of cosmic purpose the most seemly approach any of us can take is to confess the inadequacy of all our ideas about it, whether scientific or religious. We are unable, either in science or theology, to get much of a hold on anything of such transcending importance.

Although religion requires a sacramental mode of referring to ultimate reality, it also obliges us to admit that in the final analysis all of our symbols, analogies, and words about the ineffable mystery in which we are hidden are themselves inadequate. In other words, sacramentalism by itself is not fully expressive of religion's intention. The most appropriate way to "express" our standing in the presence of the divine mystery is, in imitation of Job, to press our fingers to our lips, to refrain from speech, to quiet our imaginings, to fall into silence.

Our point here is that this "apophatic" posture of pure silence toward the sacred spills over into a deep respect for the autonomy of the natural world as well. Silence is fundamentally our "letting be" not only of God but also of God's world. Our contemplative reserve imitates God's own creative "letting be." In assuming the attitude of silence, religion expresses our reluctance to intrude into the mystery of God with the mundane instruments of words, images, and concepts. We allow the divine mystery to be. Likewise silence indicates our willingness to let the world of divine creation be itself.

Recognizing that nature too participates in the divine mystery, silence implies that there is a sense in which we are obliged also to leave it to itself, to allow it to be independent of all the meanings we are inclined to impose upon it. Nature cannot be fully defined in terms of human words and projects. In the modern world the will to master the world intellectually through science has been matched by the will to force nature completely into our consumerist-economic, political, military, and other technological molds of meaning. The disastrous ecological consequences of this program have lately become increasingly obvious. There is now the threat that nature will eventually become nothing more to us than raw material for economic and social "development." Nothing of its native wildness will be left over to give us a sense of the otherness of creation.

Our conviction is that the ecological crisis has something to do with modernity's loss of a genuine appreciation of the religious meaning of silence. The religiously rooted posture of contemplative silence effectively restrains the tendency to filter our sense of nature through human designs driven by a dubious craving for control. Silence implies that, along with God, God's creation is something quite other than what we might take it to be. It has its own inviolable inner reality, one that requires our standing back from it, letting it impress its wildness upon us.

Perhaps, therefore, we need to recover something like a new appreciation of Sabbath. The Jewish idea of Sabbath is an especially significant instance of the "apophatic" habit of letting things be. Sabbath means many things, of course, but at its center there is the injunction to let creation be—at least for the Sabbath's duration. While the Sabbath lasts, we allow creation to be what it was originally intended to be, and what we hope it will be again. Sabbath shares with both sacramentalism and silence a reluctance to rush in and transform nature into stuff that we can use solely for our own purposes. Sabbath, sacramentalism, and silence, we are convinced, provide us with the deepest roots of the ecological concern the world so desperately needs to recover today.

Conclusion:
Toward Conversation
in Science and Religion

What I have outlined in the preceding pages is obviously less a conversation than a prologue to conversation. My staking out four distinct positions in science and religion can be of value, then, only if it serves as a point of departure for genuine dialogue. The somewhat polemical "edge" I have given to the separate presentations in each chapter is intended only as an inducement to discussion, and not as the dead-end of lifeless hostility.

As you have followed the four trains of thought, you may have found yourself straddling the somewhat artificial fences they set up. At times, perhaps, you gave simultaneous assent to more than one of the contributions. The conflict approach may at one moment have seemed the most compelling. But at other times you may have been attracted to the lucidity of contrast, or to the cloudier experiments of contact, or even perhaps to the overtures of the confirmation approach.

In any case, it would not be surprising if at this point you still cannot identify in every respect with any of the ways we have surveyed. The boundaries between them are much more fluid than we may initially have supposed. It is possible that any one individual may be able to embrace aspects of several approaches at the same time. Indeed, as we look back after gaining some distance from them, the four ways seem to resemble less a fixed typology than differentiated phases of a single complex process.

The process of which I speak begins with conflation, the undifferentiated merging of aspects of religion with a few carelessly understood scientific ideas. Were it not for such an original confusion of religion with themes that eventually become the exclusive province of science, the red flag of conflict would possibly never be waved in the first place. Thus, even though we may consider the conflict approach to be misguided, we may nonetheless appreciate it as an important, perhaps even inevitable, stage in the larger journey toward richer understanding.

However, as the process unfolds further, the conflict approach with its stark opposing of science to religion appears too extreme, and so it often evokes the more temperate response of contrast. Contrast allows us to separate science from religion without having to envisage them as enemies. It has them playing such completely different "games" that there is no longer any possibility of either conflation or conflict. For its clarifications we may be especially grateful. Indeed, for some of us the journey from conflation, through conflict, to conversation may have to pass through the logically precise compartments established by contrast.

But many of us are not content to stay stuck in the safety of contrast. The original dream of a unity of knowledge, our irresistible longing for coherence, does not easily go away. First naively adumbrated by conflation, the passion for synthesis arises once again in our third approach (contact), beckoning us back from the brink of dualism. Having passed through conflict and contrast, the road to genuine conversation need not revert to a unity devoid of difference. Contact, therefore, seeks relationship, but only on the other side of the distinctions initiated by conflict and refined by contrast.

The fundamental unity of science and religion, however, is most explicitly anticipated in the approach that I have been calling confirmation. This fourth way suggests that science and religion, different though they may be, share a common origin in the remote and mysterious fountainhead of a simple human desire to know. Both science and religion ultimately flow out of the same "radical" eros for truth that lies at the heart of our existence. And so, it is because of their shared origin in this fundamental concern for truth that we may never allow them simply to go their separate ways.

Notes

Preface

1. Alfred North Whitehead, *Science and the Modern World* (New York: The Free Press, 1967), pp. 181-82.

Introduction

1. Gordon D. Kaufman, *In Face of Mystery: A Constructive Theology* (Cambridge, Mass.: Harvard University Press, 1993).

2. Paul Tillich, *Dynamics of Faith* (New York: Harper & Row, 1967), pp. 1-8.

1. Is Religion Opposed to Science?

1. Ian Barbour, in his important book *Religion in an Age of Science* (New York: Harper & Row, 1990), also sets forth a four fold typology, but it differs in important respects from the one I am using here. While I appreciate the clarity Barbour brings to what I am calling the "conflict" and the "contrast" positions, I do not find a sufficiently crisp logical distinction between his third and fourth types, "dialogue" and "integration." And so I would prefer to collapse much of what Barbour calls dialogue and integration into a broader third category (which I call "contact"), and then add a more distinct fourth type, "confirmation," in order to represent the growing number of theological studies that bring out the deeper ways in which religion and theology in principle under-

gird and nurture the entire scientific enterprise. Barbour also allows for this same point, but he embeds it in other facets of his own illuminating typology.

2. Karl Popper, *Conjectures and Refutations*, Second Edition (Routledge and Kegan Paul, 1965), pp. 33-39.

3. Antony Flew and Alasdair MacIntyre, eds., *New Essays in Philosophical Theology* (New York: Macmillan, 1964).

4. Bryan Appleyard, *Understanding the Present: Science and the Soul of Modern Man* (New York: Doubleday, 1993), pp. 8-9.

5. William Provine, "Evolution and the Foundation of Ethics," in Steven L. Goldman, ed., *Science, Technology and Social Progress* (Bethlehem: Lehigh University Press, 1989), p. 261.

6. See Barbour, *Religion in an Age of Science*, pp. 10-16.

7. Gerald Schroeder, *Genesis and the Big Bang: The Discovery of Harmony Between Modern Science and the Bible* (New York: Bantam Books, 1990).

8. This approach appeals to many Christian followers of the theologians Karl Barth and Rudolf Bultmann. A contrast perspective also attracts theologians influenced by the later work of the philosopher Ludwig Wittgenstein and his notion that there are many different language games, and that the criteria of meaning and truth operative in any one of these games may not be applicable to others.

9. Scientism, as we shall see later, goes hand in hand with correlative ideologies known as "scientific materialism" and "reductionism."

10. Ian Barbour, *Religion in and Age of Science*, p. 15.

11. The search for "consonance" between theology and science is advocated by Ernan McMullin, Ted Peters, and Robert Russell among others. See Ted Peters, ed., *Cosmos as Creation: Theology and Science in Consonance* (Nashville: Abingdon Press, 1989).

12. Thomas Kuhn, *The Structure of Scientific Revolutions*, 2d ed. (Chicago: University of Chicago Press, 1970).

13. See Arthur Peacocke, *Intimations of Reality* (Notre Dame: University of Notre Dame Press, 1984).

14. What I am calling "confirmation" could conceivably be included under the more generic category of "contact." However, I think there is a clear logical distinction between the two approaches. In a way that could easily be lost if we allow it simply to be absorbed into our third type, "confirmation" brings out how religion in some way nourishes science. Another reason for keeping the categories distinct is that followers of a "contact" approach may not always wish to accept some of the more radical implications of confirmation.

15. This is an approach for which one will find support especially in the writings of Bernard Lonergan, S.J. See in particular *Insight: A Study of Human Understanding* (New York: Philosophical Library, 1970).

16. See Appleyard, *Understanding the Present*.

17. See Carolyn Merchant, *The Death of Nature: Women, Ecology, and the Scientific Revolution* (San Francisco: Harper & Row, 1980).

18. Again I refer the reader to Lonergan's work, *Insight*.

19. As I stated in the Introduction, "religion" in this book refers to "theistic" belief, but, as we shall see later, the meaning of "theism" will inevitably be affected (and often considerably revised) by contact with science.

20. Michael Polanyi, *Personal Knowledge: Towards a Post-Critical Philosophy* (New York: Harper Torchbooks, 1964), pp. 299ff.

21. Schubert Ogden, *The Reality of God* (New York: Harper & Row, 1977), pp. 32ff.

22. Ibid.

23. This approach is modeled on one proposed by David Tracy, *Blessed Rage for Order* (New York: The Seabury Press, 1975), pp. 91-118.

2. Does Science Rule Out a Personal God?

1. In referring to the conflict position, unless otherwise noted, I am thinking of the scientific skeptics' version of it.

2. Steven Weinberg, *Dreams of Final Theory* (New York: Pantheon Books, 1992).

3. Daniel C. Dennett, *Consciousness Explained* (New York: Little, Brown, 1991).

4. Weinberg, pp. 245ff.

5. Albert Einstein, *Ideas and Opinions* (New York: Bonaza Books, 1954), p. 11.

6. Ibid.

7. Weinberg, pp. 241-61.

8. Ibid., p. 256.

9. See Holmes Rolston, III, *Science and Religion* (New York: Random House, 1987), pp. 35ff.

10. The expression "scientific materialism" is that of Alfred North Whitehead. See his *Science and the Modern World* (New York: The Free Press, 1967), pp. 50-55.

11. It is a similar inability or refusal to distinguish between science and scientism that underlies Bryan Appleyard's recent polemic against "science" in his book *Understanding the Present* (cited earlier). The contrast approach would find Appleyard's conflation to be no less problematic than that of the position he so viciously excoriates by naming as "science" what is really scientism.

12. Whitehead, *Science and the Modern World*, pp. 51, 58.

13. We can only hint at such connections in the framework of this book's introductory format. The task of drawing them out in a more systematic way awaits a later and different kind of volume.

14. Rolston, *Science and Religion*, p. 26.

15. Wolfhart Pannenberg, *Toward a Theology of Nature*, edited by Ted Peters (Louisville: Westminster/John Knox Press, 1993), pp. 37-40.

16. Einstein, *Ideas and Opinions*.

17. In order to ground their confidence in nature's reliability, scientists could formerly appeal to the idea that the universe is eternal and necessary. Many of them still do. However, as we shall see later on, it is getting increasingly more difficult to uphold this picture of an eternal and necessity-riddled universe, especially in view of such ideas as are found in big bang physics and chaos theory.

18. See, for example, Wolfhart Pannenberg, *Toward a Theology of Nature*, pp. 72-122.

19. Whitehead, *Science and the Modern World*, p. 18.

3. Does Evolution Rule Out God's Existence?

1. Weinberg, pp. 246-49.

2. Quoted in John C. Greene, *Darwin and the Modern World View* (New York: Mentor Books, 1963), p. 44.

3. Richard Dawkins, *The Blind Watchmaker* (New York: W.W. Norton & Co., 1986).

4. Ibid., p. 6.

5. Ibid., p. 5.

6. Ibid., p. 6.

7. See, for example, Duane Gish, *Evolution: The Challenge of the Fossil Record* (El Cajon: Creation-Life Publishers, 1985).

8. See Niles Eldredge, *Time Frames: The Rethinking of Darwinian Evolution and the Theory of Punctuated Equilibria* (London: Heinemann, 1986).

9. Not all evolutionary scientists, by any means, but a good many of them, in their dialogue with "religion," assume that most theologians are "creationists." They are usually unaware that the idea of "creation" is a highly nuanced notion in most theology. For an example of the confusion we are talking about here, see Niles Eldredge, *The Monkey Business* (New York: Washington Square Press, 1982), pp. 132-35.

10. Stephen Jay Gould, *Ever Since Darwin* (New York: W.W. Norton, 1977), pp. 12-13.

11. Stephen Jay Gould, "The Evolution of Life on the Earth," *Scientific American*, Vol. 271 (October, 1994), p. 91.

12. Hans Küng, *Does God Exist?* trans. by Edward Quinn (New York: Doubleday, 1980), p. 347.

13. For a more developed discussion of this approach see John F. Haught,

The Cosmic Adventure (New York: Paulist Press, 1984), and *The Promise of Nature* (New York: Paulist Press, 1993).

14. See L. Charles Birch, *Nature and God* (Philadelphia: Westminster Press, 1965), p. 103.

15. The recent sciences of chaos and complexity, which will be discussed later, also raise serious questions about the exclusive role of selection in evolution's creativity.

16. Gerd Theissen, *Biblical Faith: An Evolutionary Approach*, trans. by John Bowden (Philadelphia: Fortress Press, 1985). A similar proposal is given by John Bowker in his book *The Sense of God* (Oxford: Oxford University Press, 1978), p. 151.

17. For a development of these ideas see John F. Haught, *The Cosmic Adventure*.

18. These ideas are elucidated especially by what is called "process theology." See John B. Cobb, Jr. and David Ray Griffin, *Process Theology: An Introductory Exposition* (Philadelphia: Westminster Press, 1976).

19. See, for example, Ernst Benz, *Evolution and Christian Hope* (Garden City, N.Y.: Doubleday, 1966).

20. See Karl Rahner, S.J., *Hominization*, trans. by W.J. O'Hara (New York: Herder & Herder, 1965).

4. Is Life Reducible to Chemistry?

1. Francis Crick, *The Astonishing Hypothesis: The Scientific Search for the Soul* (New York: Charles Scribner's Sons, 1994), p. 3.

2. Ibid., p. 257.

3. E. F. Schumacher, *A Guide for the Perplexed* (New York: Harper Colophon Books, 1978).

4. Ken Wilber, *Eye to Eye: The Quest for a New Paradigm* (Garden City: Doubleday Anchor Books, 1983), p. 24.

5. Crick, p. 6.

6. For a purely "materialist" account of life see Jacques Monod, *Chance and Necessity*, trans. by Austryn Wainhouse (New York: Vintage Books, 1972); and, in addition to Crick's work, for an equally materialist attempt to explain "mind," see Daniel C. Dennett, *Consciousness Explained* (New York: Little, Brown, 1991).

7. See Ian Barbour, *Religion in an Age of Science* (New York: Harper & Row, 1990), p. 4. Barbour makes a similar distinction between methodological and metaphysical reductionism.

8. Crick, pp. 8-9.

9. It should be pointed out, however, that these three giants still remained theists themselves, and Newton curiously continued to dabble in occult sub-

jects to the end of his life, fashioning in the process his own peculiar brand of theology.

10. Monod, p. 123.

11. Francis H. C. Crick, *Of Molecules and Men* (Seattle: University of Washington Press, 1966), p. 10.

12. For a summary of the research see, for example, Jon Franklin, *Molecules of the Mind: The Brave New Science of Molecular Psychology* (New York: Atheneum, 1987).

13. Dennett, p. 33.

14. E. O. Wilson, *Sociobiology: The New Synthesis* (Cambridge: Harvard University Press, 1975). For a critical discussion of Wilson's genetic determinism see Robert Wright, *Three Scientists and Their Gods* (New York: Times Books, 1988), pp. 113-92.

15. See E. O. Wilson, *On Human Nature* (New York: Bantam Books, 1979), p. 200.

16. Michael Ruse and E. O. Wilson, "The Evolution of Ethics," in James E. Huchingson, ed., *Religion and the Natural Sciences* (New York: Harcourt Brace Jovanovich, 1993), p. 310.

17. Crick, *The Astonishing Hypothesis*, p. 257.

18. Schumacher, *A Guide for the Perplexed*, p. 18.

19. Following Ernest Gellner's expression, Huston Smith discusses the "epistemology of control" in his book *Beyond the Post-Modern Mind* (New York: Crossroad, 1982), pp. 62-91.

20. Cited by Schumacher, pp. 5-6.

21. See Michael Polanyi, *Personal Knowledge* (New York: Harper Torchbooks, 1964), and *The Tacit Dimension* (Garden City: Doubleday Anchor Books, 1967).

22. See the discussion in Harry Prosch, *Michael Polanyi: A Critical Exposition* (Albany: State University of New York Press, 1986), pp. 124-34.

23. This analogy is suggested by Polanyi in *The Tacit Dimension*, pp. 31-34.

24. See Michael Polanyi, *Knowing and Being*, edited by Majorie Grene (Chicago: University of Chicago Press, 1969), pp. 225-39.

25. John Polkinghorne, *The Faith of a Physicist* (Princeton: Princeton University Press, 1994), p. 163.

26. Karl Jaspers refers to this as the "axial age" in *The Origin and Goal of History* (New Haven: Yale University Press, 1953).

5. Was the Universe Created?

1. Peter W. Atkins, *Creation Revisited* (New York: W. H. Freeman, 1992).

2. Within specific galactic clusters there may be local movement of bodies toward each other, but overall the galaxies move away from each other as space expands.

3. Nevertheless, the "standard" big bang theory leaves some important scientific questions unanswered. These have been addressed by the so-called "inflationary" cosmology which posits that most of the physical conditions that define our present were not yet present in the initial conditions of the big bang, but became fixed only during an accelerated phase transition (inflation) shortly (billionths of a second) after the big bang.

4. On the other hand, such speculation may just as readily be the consequence of purely scientific attempts to interpret the equations of physics, and we may assume that in most cases there is no ideological influence at work.

5. This is the view of John R. Gribbin's *In the Beginning: After COBE and Before the Big Bang* (Boston: Little, Brown, 1993).

6. Norman J. Geisler and J. Kerby Anderson, in Huchingson, ed., *Religion and the Natural Sciences*, p. 202.

7. Douglas Lackey, "The Big Bang and the Cosmological Argument," in Huchingson, ed., p. 194 (emphasis added).

8. Stephen Hawking, *A Brief History of Time*, pp. 140-41. See also Paul Davies, *The Mind of God: The Scientific Basis for a Rational World* (New York: Simon & Schuster, 1992), p. 66.

9. Robert Jastrow, *God and the Astronomers* (New York: W.W. Norton and Co.), p. 116.

10. Quoted in Stanley L. Jaki, *Universe and Creed* (Milwaukee: Marquette University Press, 1992), p. 54.

11. In his recent book, *Wrinkles in Time*, however, Smoot refers to himself as a "skeptic" as far as religion is concerned.

12. Timothy Ferris, *Coming of Age in the Milky Way* (New York: Doubleday, 1988), p. 274.

13. Keith Ward, "God as a Principle of Cosmological Explanation," in Robert Russell, Nancey Murphy and C. J. Isham, editors (Notre Dame: Vatican Observatory and University of Notre Dame Press, 1993), pp. 248-49. The citation from Ward is not intended to imply that he himself endorses the contrast approach. In fact he seems to fit more comfortably into the "contact" position.

14. See note #6 above.

15. This is the thesis of Michael J. Buckley, *At the Origins of Atheism* (New Haven: Yale University Press, 1987); this is not to imply, however, that Buckley himself subscribes in every respect to the "contrast" approach, though it seems at times that he leans in that direction.

16. Paul Davies, *God and the New Physics* (New York: Simon & Schuster, 1983); and *The Mind of God: The Scientific Basis for a Rational World* (New York: Simon & Schuster, 1992).

17. Frank J. Tipler, *The Physics of Immortality* (New York: Doubleday, 1994). Since the main purpose of religion was always to satisfy our craving for eternal life, Tipler asks, why do we need it any longer if physics can now give us mathematical certainty that we will be raised from the dead to live forever?

Using general relativity, quantum cosmology, artificial intelligence, and a touch of Teilhard de Chardin, he assures us that nature requires that intelligent life will survive forever. To those who reply that the sun will eventually incinerate the earth and its biosphere, Tipler argues that "life" in the form of artificial intelligence will inevitably have ventured far beyond our galaxy long before our planet disappears. We will have launched tiny self-replicating forms of information-processing that will eventually spread intelligent "life" to safer regions of the universe. In the end, this intelligent life (which Tipler consistently defines in terms of informational capacity) will "take control" of the entire cosmos.

But suppose we live in a "closed" universe, that is, one destined for a final gravitational collapse at immense temperatures. Won't the "big crunch" destroy life completely? Not at all, Tipler replies. Chaos theory now allows that the universe will not collapse at the same rate everywhere. So there will forever be some variation in temperature among different patches of the cosmos, and this differential will provide sufficient energy potential for indefinitely prolonged information-processing.

Billions of years from now there will finally emerge an "Omega Point" comprised of such extraordinary calculational competence that it will be able to bring us all back from the dead. It will do this through an "emulation," i.e. a perfect computational simulation, of the patterns that now give us our identity. Because each of us is ultimately reducible to bits of data, we can realistically expect that the informationally precocious Omega-Point will process us back from the dead and into eternal life.

How can this happen? Tipler answers that we are now imprinting sets of retrievable information about ourselves, however faintly, on a "light cone" that will extend indefinitely into the future of the cosmos. Omega-Point will be able to read this data and print us out in the flesh once again. Thus, Omega-Point, a notion Tipler adapts from Teilhard, is very much like what theology calls "God," for he "exists necessarily," "loves us," and seeks to save us from absolute perishing.

Tipler proclaims all of this while insisting that he is an atheist, a materialist, and a reductionist. His thoughts about Omega-God follow, he says, not from the flimsy reports of religion, but from pure physics. We don't need, therefore, to participate any longer in the superfluous religious acts of prayer and worship. The existence of "God" and the certainty of eternal life will be brought home to us clearly enough if we just follow the equations of physics. (This note is adapted from the author's review of Tipler's book in *America*, Vol. 172, No. 1 (January, 1995), 24-25.

18. Jaki, *Universe and Creed*, p. 27.

19. Ibid.

20. Hawking, *A Brief History of Time*, p. 174.

21. Paul Tillich, *Systematic Theology*, Vol. I (Chicago: University of Chicago Press, 1951), p. 113.

22. Teilhard de Chardin, *The Prayer of the Universe*, (New York: Harper & Row, 1968), pp. 120-21.

23. See, however, the discussion by C. J. Isham and J. C. Polkinghorne, "The Debate over the Block Universe," in Russell, et al, ed., *Quantum Cosmology and the Laws of Nature*, pp. 135-44.

24. This point will be considerably amplified in Chapter 7 with its discussion of the new sciences of complexity and chaos. See Michael Foster, "The Christian Doctrine of Creation and the Rise of Modern Natural Science," *Mind* (1934), 446-68.

6. Do We Belong Here?

1. Some physicists even conjecture (perhaps wildly) that the universe becomes determinate only when it intersects with observers.

2. See the discussion by Rolston, pp. 67-70.

3. This idea is said to have come from the physicist Leon Lederman.

4. For example, Alan Guth's inflationary cosmological hypothesis, which seems to settle many of the difficulties with standard big bang theory, is widely accepted even though, unlike relativity theory, there is no way to test it. See Alan Guth, "Inflationary Universe," *Encyclopedia of Cosmology*, edited by Norriss S. Hetherington (New York: Garland Publishing, Inc., 1993), pp. 301-22.

5. See especially John D. Barrow and Frank J. Tipler, *The Anthropic Cosmological Principle* (New York: Oxford University Press, 1986).

6. Heinz Pagels, *Perfect Symmetry* (New York: Bantam Books, 1986), pp. 377-78.

7. Perhaps, however, the inflationary hypothesis that came out of the early 1980's eliminates the need to pack so much into the initial cosmic conditions. Many of the remarkable coincidences that the SAP attributes to initial conditions could have come about by physical necessity during an "inflationary epoch" only small fractions of a second after the big bang. See, for example, George Smoot, *Wrinkles in Time* (New York: William Morrow & Co., Inc., 1993), pp. 190-91.

8. John Gribbin, *In the Beginning: After COBE and Before the Big Bang* (Boston: Little, Brown, 1993).

9. Smoot, *Wrinkles in Time*, p. 191.

10. See the similar point made by Nicholas Lash, "Observation, Revelation, and the Posterity of Noah," in *Physics, Philosophy and Theology*, edited by Robert J. Russell, et al (Notre Dame: University of Notre Dame Press, 1988), p. 211.

11. Gribbin, *In the Beginning*, pp. 249-53.

12. This approach is especially characteristic of some forms of "existentialist" theology, particularly those associated with Rudolf Bultmann and his followers.

13. Moreover, in the final chapter of this book we shall point out that the SAP's connecting our existence so closely to the physical cosmos may have some bearing on the issue of ecology also.

14. *The Quickening Universe* (New York: St. Martin's Press, 1987), p. xvii.

15. See Freeman Dyson, *Infinite in All Directions* (New York: Harper & Row, 1988), p. 298.

16. For development of this Whiteheadian theme see the author's earlier book, *The Cosmic Adventure* (New York: Paulist Press, 1984).

7. Why Is There Complexity in Nature?

1. Two of the best introductions to "chaos theory" are James Gleick, *Chaos: The Making of a New Science* (New York: Viking, 1987) and Stephen H. Kellert, *In the Wake of Chaos* (Chicago: University of Chicago Press, 1993). The new science of "complexity" is summarized in Roger Lewin, *Complexity: Life at the Edge of Chaos* (New York: Macmillan, 1992) and M. Mitchell Waldrop, *Complexity: The Emerging Science at the Edge of Order and Chaos* (New York: Simon & Schuster, 1992).

2. James. P. Crutchfield, J. Doyne Farmer, Norman H. Packard and Robert S. Shaw, "Chaos," *Scientific American* (December, 1986), pp. 38-49, cited by Arthur Peacocke, *Theology for a Scientific Age* (Cambridge: Basil Blackwell, 1990), p. 42.

3. See the books by Waldrop and Lewin for numerous interviews with scientists who are now framing their questions in these interesting ways.

4. For examples of this line of thought see Lewin, pp. 167-68.

5. See Alfred North Whitehead, *Science and the Modern World* (New York: The Free Press, 1967), p. 94.

6. See John T. Houghton, "A Note on Chaotic Dynamics," *Science and Christian Belief*, Vol. 1, p. 50. However, John Polkinghorne has expressed some doubts about the significance of such quantum effects in the macro world: *Reason and Reality* (SPCK/ Trinity Press International, 1991), pp. 89-92.

7. The now classic example of such skepticism is Jacques Monod's book *Chance and Necessity*, cited earlier.

8. These ideas, once again, have been articulated most fully and explicitly in process theology, but they are quite compatible with other forms of religious reflection as well.

9. John Polkinghorne, *The Faith of a Physicist* (Princeton: Princeton University Press, 1994), pp. 25-26, 75-87.

10. Stephen Jay Gould, *Ever Since Darwin* (New York: W. W. Norton & Company, 1977), p. 12. Recently, Gould has been acknowledging that natural

factors other than selection, such as physical catastrophes, are also a factor in evolution, but even so his position remains firm that purely materialist principles are enough to account for evolution's creativity. See, for example, "The Evolution of Life on the Earth," *Scientific American*, Vol. 271 (October, 1994), p. 91.

11. Stuart Kauffman, *The Origins of Order* (New York: Oxford University Press, 1993), pp. 15-26.

12. See Moltmann, *God in Creation*, pp. 86-93.

8. Does the Universe Have a Purpose?

1. James Jeans, *The Mysterious Universe*, Revised Edition (New York: Macmillan, 1948), pp. 15-16. (First published in 1930.)

2. E. D. Klemke, "Living Without Appeal," in E. D. Klemke, ed., *The Meaning of Life* (New York: Oxford University Press, 1981), pp. 169-72.

3. Gould, *Ever Since Darwin*, p. 13.

4. Ernst Mayr, "Evolution," *Scientific American*, Vol. 134 (September, 1978), p. 50.

5. Steven Weinberg, *The First Three Minutes* (New York: Basic Books, 1977), p. 144.

6. Alan Lightman and Roberta Brawer, *Origins: The Lives and Worlds of Modern Cosmologists* (Cambridge: Harvard University Press, 1990), p. 340.

7. Ibid. p. 358.

8. Ibid. p. 377.

9. "Evolution and the Foundation of Ethics," in Steven L. Goldman, ed., *Science, Technology and Social Progress* (Bethlehem, Pa.: Lehigh University Press, 1989), p. 261.

10. Job 38:1-4, *New American Bible*.

9. Is Religion Responsible for the Ecological Crisis?

1. Convened by then Senator Albert Gore, Carl Sagan and a number of religious leaders in Washington, D. C., May, 1992.

2. See Russell Train, *Vital Speeches of the Day* (1990), pp. 664-65.

3. Ibid.

4. John Passmore, *Man's Responsibility for Nature* (New York: Scribner, 1974), p. 184.

5. Lynn White, "The Historical Roots of Our Ecological Crisis," *Science*, Vol. 155, pp. 1203-1207.

6. William James, *Pragmatism* (Cleveland: Meridian Books, 1964), p. 76.

7. See the earlier discussion of Stephen Hawking's idea that the universe has a finite past, but possibly no clear beginning. Such a scenario would still

not affect our conviction that the cosmos has a fundamentally narrative character.

8. See Jürgen Moltmann, *God in Creation*, trans. by Margaret Kohl (San Francisco: Harper & Row, 1985).

9. For a development of these ideas see John F. Haught, *The Promise of Nature* (New York: Paulist Press, 1993), pp. 101-42.

10. Thomas Berry, *The Dream of the Earth* (San Francisco: Sierra Club Books, 1988), p. 11.

Index

Science and Religion